UNKNOWN MONGOLIA

A Record of travel and Exploration in
North-West Mongolia and Dzungaria

UNKNOWN MONGOLIA
A Record of travel and Exploration in North-West Mongolia and Dzungaria

BY

DOUGLAS CARRUTHERS
GOLD MEDALLIST OF THE ROYAL GEOGRAPHICAL SOCIETY

WITH THREE CHAPTERS ON SPORT
BY

J. H. MILLER, F.Z.S.

AND A FOREWORD BY
THE RIGHT HON. EARL CURZON OF KEDLESTON
G.C.S.I. ETC.

WITH 168 ILLUSTRATIONS, PANORAMAS
AND DIAGRAMS, AND 6 MAPS

VOL. II.

SECOND EDITION

Published by

Gyan Publishing House
5, Ansari Road
Daryaganj, New Delhi-110002
Phone: 011-47034999, 9811692060
E-mail: books@gyanbooks.com

Distribution Network
gyanbooks.com
India, USA, Canada, UK, Australia, France

© **Publisher**

ISBN : 978-81-212-4634-7 (Set)
ISBN : 978-81-212-3001-8 (PB)
First Published, 1914

2nd Impression 2020

Printed at: Gyan Press, Delhi.

UNKNOWN MONGOLIA

A Record of Travel and Exploration in North-West Mongolia and Dzungaria

BY

DOUGLAS CARRUTHERS

GOLD MEDALLIST OF THE ROYAL GEOGRAPHICAL SOCIETY

WITH THREE CHAPTERS ON SPORT

BY

J. H. MILLER, F.Z.S.

AND A FOREWORD BY

THE RIGHT HON. EARL CURZON OF KEDLESTON,
G.C.S.I., Etc.

*WITH 168 ILLUSTRATIONS, PANORAMAS
AND DIAGRAMS, AND 6 MAPS*

VOL. II.

SECOND EDITION

LONDON

HUTCHINSON & CO.

PATERNOSTER ROW

1914

MONGOLIAN WILD SHEEP.

Ovis ammon.

By J. G. MILLAIS.

CONTENTS

VOL. II

CHAPTER XI

LIST OF ILLUSTRATIONS

VOL. II

MAPS

DIAGRAMS

INDEX TO IMPORTANT SUBJECTS IN THE ILLUSTRATIONS

UNKNOWN MONGOLIA

CHAPTER XI

SPORT ON THE PLATEAUX OF MONGOLIA

By J. H. Miller

THE north-west corner of Mongolia has many beauties in summer. Its round-headed bluffs of dark shale, slashed with snow-drifts, rise from rolling downlands covered with a luxurious growth of short, yellow-green grass, brightened by brilliant patches of gentians, crocuses, edelweiss, and other Alpine flowers. Its innocent-looking, but treacherous, bogs give birth to sparkling streams, which form the numerous rivers that flow through barren foot-hills on to still more arid plains, and terminate in large saline lakes. Groups of the dome-shaped tents of the nomads are scattered over the plateaux, and, wherever grass is plentiful, along the edge of both river and lake ; countless flocks and herds, the only wealth of their wandering owners, dot this matchless pasture-land, and from a cloudless sky a brilliant sun beats down upon plain and plateau.

In winter this land of extremes presents a very different picture ; everything is then locked in the grip of the frost fiend ; snow lies everywhere, except on the exposed tops which the pitiless wind blows clear, causing it to form deep drifts on the leeward side. All animal life is either hibernating, or seeking the protection of the lower foot-hills. The camps of the hardy herdsmen are now clustered in sheltered hollows ; their owners' time is largely spent in waging war against the wolf-packs, which nightly harry their sheep-folds, and in interminable tea-drinking, smoking, and chatting round a meagre " tezek " (dung-fed) fire.

What appeals most strongly, however, to the sport and nature loving Briton is that, among the higher plateaux of the Little Altai,—the range which forms a part of the Russo-Chinese frontier,—roams one of the finest beasts in nature, the father of all sheep, the *Ovis ammon*. An adult ram of this gigantic sheep stands over 50 in. at the shoulder, and carries horns that exceed 60 in. in length and 20 in. in girth, and, with the dry skull, weigh 45 lb. No other beast, for its size, carries such a weight of horn. There are few species of big game that appeal more to the heart of the hunter and lover of the wild regions of the earth, than an old ram in his upland solitudes. Apart from the magnificent horns he carries, his unrivalled wariness tests the resources of the hunter to the utmost. Luck plays a very small part in sheep-hunting ; skill, patience, and perseverance are required to a high degree.

Every hunter has his own ideas as to what species of big game makes the finest trophy, and forms the most worthy quarry. It may be the giant moose of Alaska in his primeval forests, or the shaggy markhor on his beetling crags, or the graceful koodoo on the plains of Africa. But, in me, the elusive wild-sheep always produces the greatest thrill.

The existence of the *Ovis ammon* was first made

known to Europe by William Rubruck, who, in his account of a journey to Mongolia in the middle of the thirteenth century, mentioned seeing a " kind of wild animal which is called 'arcoli,' which has quite the body of a sheep, and horns bent like a ram's, but of such a size that I could hardly lift two horns with one hand; and they make of these horns big cups." The first European hunter to shoot this great wild-sheep was Major Cumberland, who, on information received from that remarkable traveller, Mr. Ney Elias, journeyed to the Altai and procured several specimens. That was in 1895, and since then not more than one hunter a year, on an average, has visited this region ; so that a really large " ammon " head still remains one of the rarest and most prized of trophies.

It was late August when we reached Achit Nor, one of the numerous lakes which dot the Mongolian plateau. Every few days a severe snow or hail storm swept over us, which, together with the frequent " honking " of wild geese overhead, warned us that winter was not far distant, and that, if we wished to hunt the ammon and get across the passes of the Great Altai before they were closed, we must not delay. Achit Nor, at this season, presented a remarkable spectacle with its teeming thousands of wild-fowl. Undoubtedly great numbers breed there in the large area of marsh and reeds at its northern end. The greater portion, however, were merely using it as a resting-place on their long flight southwards from their summer haunts in Siberia. There were swans, two kinds of geese, and many varieties of duck, gulls, divers, and waders, including both green and golden plovers.

Every morning and evening large numbers of duck

and geese " flighted " out on to the boggy grass-land. Owing to the laws of Buddhism, which prohibit the unnecessary taking of life, and, no doubt, partly through laziness, the natives on no account molest these wild-fowl. The birds therefore show a marked indifference to the presence of man, allowing a horseman to ride within 50 yards of them, or less, without doing more than raise their heads. But, as we soon discovered, an attempt to approach them on foot was courting failure, for they would not allow us within 200 yards. The reason for this is that a Mongol hardly ever walks. Even to go from one yurt to another, a distance of perhaps not more than a few hundred yards, he will always mount a horse, which is kept ready saddled and tied to his yurt for the purpose.

We devised a scheme at length, by which we were able to secure several fine fat geese with a rook-rifle. One would ride and lead the other's horse, taking a line which would bring us within 50 yards of the flock. Then the second, who had been walking concealed behind the led horse, would fall to the ground behind some slight cover, and get a steady shot, while the eyes of the birds were on the retreating horses and man.

In this district we came across an encampment of Russians and Tartars. They had been travelling about during the summer, trading with the natives, and had collected large quantities of wool, hides, and marmot-skins, in exchange for cloth, tobacco, cooking utensils, etc., and sometimes for money. They were working for one of the large merchants at Biisk. The profits must have been very great. Take the marmot-skins, for instance. They are purchased in thousands at an absurdly low price (10 to 20 kopeks each), and sent

TYPICAL SHEEP-GROUND IN NORTH-WEST MONGOLIA.

322]

to Europe, where they are dyed and sold as imitation sable. The wool is purchased from the natives for 3 to 4 roubles per poud (36 lb.) or the equivalent in kine, and sold later for double that amount. The trade is largely in the hands of the Chinese, who sell to the Russian merchants, which minimizes the profits of the latter. However, Russia has already inserted " the thin end of the wedge " in Mongolia, and with the new state of affairs the entire trade of this vast country will fall into the hands of Russia.

Properly administered, there is no reason why this ideal grazing country should not become one of the leading stock-rearing countries of the world. If a branch line to Kobdo, from the proposed Kiakhta-Kalgan railway, is built, the whole of North-west Mongolia will be brought within rail-communication of the European market, and this land of great possibilities will have received the stimulus it requires. There is every likelihood of this line some day being continued through to Tomsk, via the thriving town of Biisk, engineers having pronounced the Altai highlands to present no serious engineering difficulties.

Having changed our mixed caravan of oxen and horses for eight camels, on August 28th we started again for the frontier post of Suok, hoping there to get hold of some hunters. A march of six hours took us out of the Achit plain, well up into the foot-hills of the Altai. Marching up a dry water-course, we were struck by the arid nature of the hills. Above the valley bottom, where there was a little scrub and coarse grass, the hillsides were entirely devoid of growth, with the exception of the ubiquitous " burtsa "—a small bush, which when dry makes excellent fuel. On the following

morning three hours' march took us out of this inhospitable nullah on to a broad, grassy upland, where
the three small Chagan Nor lakes sparkled in the sun,
and where herds of horses and camels gave life to the
scene. On this upland we came across numbers of
derelict ammon horns, showing that we had reached
their winter range. A day's march due west on to
the higher ground, and we should no doubt have seen
them in the flesh, but we had decided to go farther
along the hills towards Suok, where we had hopes of
obtaining hunters before starting up towards the main
divide.

The word "suok" is Turkish for cold, and you may be
pretty certain that, if a nomad of Central Asia indicates
a place by such a name, it is no place for a European
in winter. Though marked large on some maps, it is
merely a small Chinese frontier post on the main Kobdo-
Biisk route. When we were there it consisted of no
more than half a dozen yurts, occupied by a small
official and a few disreputable soldiers. They had no
uniform but a blue "jumper," which had a glaring
red "disc" on the breast, covered with Chinese
characters ; and their arms embraced every description
of antique gas-pipe. The head-man was most kind
and obliging. We drank tea with him in his stuffy
little yurt, overheated with a Russian stove, while he
looked at our passports. Their size and colour impressed him, but I doubt very much if he could read
them, though he pretended to do so. Chinese etiquette
demands that a call should be returned immediately.
The snow was being driven before a biting north-easter
at the time, and I fancy that he did not particularly
enjoy his quarter of an hour in a flapping, draughty tent.

On informing him that we intended to spend a few days hunting in the neighbourhood, he advised us to visit the chief of the Altai Uriankhai, living in the Chagan-gol Valley, two marches farther on, who would be able to provide us with horses and hunters. He said that there were none in the vicinity of Suok.

The storm raged all through the next day, preventing us from moving. The wind howled through the tents, driving the snow under the flaps, and us into our blankets, where we spent the day reading and trying to keep warm.

September 1st broke still and clear, but three inches of snow covered the ground, and this produced a terrible glare in the powerful sunlight. A short march over undulating foot-hills brought us to the broad river-bed of the Uigur, as the upper Suok River is called. We were now close under the western end of the lofty, rounded Bain-Khairkhan mass which fills up the area between the Chagan-gol and Suok Rivers. The evening was spent in rifle-practice, much to the interest of some inhabitants, who thought it a frightful waste of ammunition, but thoroughly appreciated the empty cases. The range and accuracy of our weapons were a revelation to them.

The next march was done very rapidly ; we changed horses half-way at a small encampment, named Belota. After crossing the low, western end of the Bain-Khairkhan ridge, we suddenly came upon the Chagan-gol Valley. At this point it is broad and sandy, with several small lakes linked by a sluggish stream. The sides of the valley are composed of old moraines, through which the stream has cut its way. Away to the south in the direction of Dolto Nor, the head of the Kobdo River, the lofty, jagged peaks of the Great Altai rose up and formed a marked contrast to the featureless country, through which we had been marching for the last few days.

We pitched our camp close to a cluster of yurts. In exchange for a few safety-pins and a yard or two of scarlet ribbon, we got as much milk and fuel as we could want. On the following morning we saw an imposing-looking cavalcade approaching : it turned out to be the chief of the Altai Uriankhai and his retainers. He was a cheery old soul, and plied us with questions incessantly. How far was it to London ? How many horses, cattle, and sheep had we ? What did we pay for our wives in England, and how many did we each have ? To all these and many more questions Makandaroff found suitable replies, which, if not truthful, certainly did not belittle us in any way. As the success or failure of our ' sheep '-hunt depended on getting on the right side of the old fellow, we presented him with an old telescope which had been brought from England for such a purpose. His pleasure was almost pathetic, and, when it was focussed on to some horses a mile away, he giggled with childish delight. From that moment our success, as far as he was concerned, was assured. We were promised horses and men for the following day.

As usual, we had the greatest difficulty in convincing the men that it was only the old rams we wished to shoot, on account of their horns. This was more than they could grasp. What use could we make of " koshgor " horns ? Perhaps we made them into medicine, as the Chinese did with the maral horns. But if it was the horns we wanted, why didn't we pick

A MONGOL TYPE.

up those which were lying about on the ground ? We could collect a hundred in a day, and an old koshgor running wild over the hills was so hard to get near. At last, after much chatter, a grizzled old veteran pushed his way to the front. He understood what we wanted. Some years before he had been, he said, a caravan-man to two white koshgor-hunters [1] like ourselves. He was a marmot-hunter by profession, and had plied his trade for some thirty years. Though he had never bothered much about the " rams," it being much easier to get within shot of females with his old muzzle-loader, yet he knew where they were, and guaranteed to take us to a place where we should see large numbers every day. The nearest way to reach the best place which he knew of was to retrace our steps as far as Belota and strike up west from there.

While Carruthers and Price spent the day after wild-fowl, I took a man with me and climbed on to the plateau-like top of the Bain-Khairkhan ridge, which protrudes eastwards from the main divide between the Suok and Chagan-gol Rivers, in a solid round-headed block rising 8,000 or 9,000 ft.

It was delightful on this invigorating autumn day, with the sun shining down from a clear still sky, to move from one ridge to another, spying the ground ahead from each vantage-point, whilst lying comfortably on the short, springy turf. Some wild life was almost continually in view. We saw marmots, snow-cock, a wolf, a small herd of ewes and young, and five young rams that day. I decided to try and shoot one of the rams for meat, but it was terribly difficult stalking country, and, in spite of the most snake-like wriggling,

[1] Probably Prince Demidoff and Mr. St. George Littledale.

300 yards was as near as I could get. The shot resulted
in a broken front leg. We pursued it for many miles,
but to try and catch up with an ammon, which has no
more serious wound than this, is pretty hopeless work,
and eventually we lost the tracks on a shale slope, and
reluctantly had to give it up.

On the way back to camp we almost rode on to the
top of six gazelle feeding in a hollow among the hills.
My man advised a drive, as the surest way of getting a
shot. From this and subsequent experiences, I have
come to the conclusion that gazelle are one of the few
beasts that can be successfully driven. They are foolish
and inquisitive animals, and can be moved in almost
any direction by men who understand their habits.
Making a wide detour, I took up my position on a narrow
neck connecting the small depression with a much
larger one. The Mongol, leading the two horses, then
began to move slowly towards my position. Instead of
at once clearing out of the neighbourhood, the gazelle
began to move slowly towards me. They would trot
for a short distance and then wheel round for a look
at the man, making a very pretty picture as they bounced
about on all four feet at once, whisking their tails, and
extending the white hair of their rumps as a danger-
signal. When they came within rather less than 100
yards of me, I knocked one over, and, at once getting
into a sitting position, doubled up two more, just like
shot rabbits, as they streamed past at about sixty yards.
For running shots like this, a ·256 Mannlicher, with a
Lyman aperture sight, is, to my mind, the ideal weapon.
As trophies they were of no account, being only yearling
bucks; but their meat was a welcome change from the
everlasting mutton. The gazelle, with the exception

of the roe-deer, is the finest of all the Central Asian game, from an edible point of view.

Next day we started off for our hunting-ground under the guidance of the old marmot-hunter. We had only six light horseloads of baggage with us, the bulk of the heavy stuff being left with the old chief to be picked up on our return. A severe blizzard came on before we had gone far, necessitating an early camp ; in the teeth of the storm the horses made very slow progress.

This is typical of the weather we experienced in the Altai during the end of August and the beginning of September. There would be a few glorious days, then a sudden drop in the temperature and a blizzard of Arctic severity, followed by another fine spell. We spent a chilly night of it with the thermometer at 18° Fahr., and a howling wind tugging at the tent-ropes. The morning broke clear, revealing a land of whiteness, and the dark tail of the storm, disappearing to the southeast. Another long day's march due west, up and down over the low outer hills, brought us to where the Uigur stream divides into several heads. Our camp was pitched in a sheltered position, with abundance of tezek, close to two small tarns which were full of grayling.

We were now on our hunting-ground, and what hunter is there who has not experienced that " first night on a new ground " feeling ? As he lies in his blankets, pondering over the possibilities of the morrow, hope, doubt, success and failure, all chase through his mind. Old red-letter days and days of blank disaster are raked up and gone over in detail. At length he falls into a troubled sleep, with visions of colossal

" heads " which will not allow themselves to be approached. But in the morning the necessity for action clears away all this, and he starts out full of confidence.

To hunt any of the big sheep of Central Asia successfully, it is of the utmost importance to make a really early start from camp. As Makandaroff put it in his very picturesque language, " What time hunt *mouton nécessaire* rise early. *Mouton* be very good *général.*"

Wild-sheep generally spend several hours during the middle of the day, especially during the hot summer months, in lying down in one of those unapproachable positions which the hunter learns to know only too well. A very favourite site is on a shale-slope, which harmonizes perfectly with their own colour, near the crest of some commanding, round-topped hill, though not actually on the top, for that would advertise their position to their enemies. The wind, curling over the crest to them, secures them on their only blind side, for few beasts possess a more highly developed sense of smell. In every other direction their restless gaze wanders incessantly over a vast expanse of smooth rolling grass and shale, across which, as a rule, it is quite useless for a human being to attempt to approach them. If sheep have been driven into rougher and more broken ground, as is often the case in the Tian Shan, where it is impossible for them to take up a position commanding an extensive view, they have the almost uncanny knack of selecting a resting-place where, owing to the formation of the ground, the wind converges upon them in all directions. For this reason the horse-shoe-shaped head of a valley is much favoured by them. It is principally persecution, from time immemorial, by their most dreaded enemies, the wolves,

CAMP ON THE MONGOLIAN PLATAEU IN AUGUST.

[30]

that has made them the wonderful tacticians they are. But the hunter has not always to contend against such insurmountable difficulties. In the early morning, and again in the evening, they leave their impregnable position to graze. The rolling nature of the ground which they then have to pass over gives the hunter his opportunity. Whilst some succulent feed holds them in a fold of the ground, a close approach is often possible. On several occasions I have got within fifty yards or less of a herd.

I do not intend to go into details here about the equipment for a hunting-trip to the Altai. I shall confine myself to suggesting one or two labour-saving methods.[1]

When sheep-hunting it is, to my mind, of the greatest importance to be equipped for a night out. It often happens that, in following a wounded beast, one gets benighted many miles from camp, or perhaps one does not find game till the evening, when it is too late, or the ground is unsuitable for a stalk that day. In either case it is a waste of time and labour to ride, perhaps ten miles, back to camp and return again in the morning. What I consider the best equipment for a night's bivouac is either a *tente d'abri*, or a light ground-sheet, in case of bad weather, a small cooking-pot, in which one can pack one's provisions, such as bread, tea, sugar, cold mutton, salt, bovril, and chocolate, according to individual tastes ; a large mug and a spoon. A small flarer, or spirit-lamp, should be carried, as there is never any wood on sheep-ground, and tezek may not be handy, or may be sodden by a storm. These

---

[1] Major Swayne, in his book *Through the Highlands of Siberia*, goes deeply into the question of equipment.

things can easily be carried on the hunter's horse, leaving plenty of room on one's own for coats, blankets, etc.[1] By this means, the disturbing feeling of having to hurry can be done away with.

It is always worth while to take two men out with you, so that the second man can be left in charge of the horses while you and your hunter stalk the sheep. In this way the horses can be brought up by signal, and much time and unnecessary fatigue saved. I can, however, only recommend this provided that your "second horseman" is used to the ways of the European hunter, or is above the average in intelligence. Otherwise he may prove a source of great danger and annoyance. More than once has a stalk been ruined by the second man, who, having got tired of waiting, and wanting to see what was happening, has ridden boldly on to a skyline, and frightened the game. And the reverse of this can try one's temper pretty severely, especially after an unsuccessful stalk. It is exasperating to signal for the horses to be brought up and have no reply, and be compelled to trudge back to where they have been left, only to find one's "second horseman" fast asleep.

I seemed to have been asleep only an hour or two, when Mac woke me up by pulling the tent-flaps back and saying that the horses were being saddled and it was time to be moving off. At five on a September morning, 8,000 ft. up, with 15° of frost in the air, one does not feel one's best, and it is advisable to get over the discomfort of crawling out of the warm blankets

---

[1] I strongly recommend a pair of leather saddle-bags, also a Cossack saddle, which can be purchased in nearly any Russian town, and is quite the best for hunting or caravan work.

and pulling on frozen boots as quickly as possible. Luckily, no other dressing is necessary, with the exception of donning a heavy overcoat. After gulping down the usual unsatisfactory early meal and seeing that the saddle-bags were stocked with provisions, cartridges, etc., I mounted a shaggy little Mongol pony, and, followed by the old hunter and another " local," made for some high ground to the north. At the same time the two other parties moved off in different directions. We looked like cavalry patrols starting out to reconnoitre an enemy's position.

A piercing cold wind seemed to cut right through me, in spite of a sheepskin coat and Canadian mits, as we crunched our way up a half-frozen stream-bed in the cold grey morning light, that made me look with longing eyes towards the small patches of sun which were just tinting the highest points. The indifference with which the Mongols and Kirghiz treat both the heat of summer (and in the thin atmosphere of the plateau the sun has terrific power) and the frightful cold of winter is almost incredible. It is not an uncommon sight to see young children turned naked outside the yurts, in all weathers, to get hardened ! This Spartan treatment leads to the " survival of the fittest," and has produced a people whom it would be hard to beat for indifference to climatic extremes.

On reaching the head of the valley, the old man indicated an outcrop of rock as being a suitable place from which to start spying. Leaving the " second horseman " behind, we crept forward to this vantage-point. A large stretch of country lay before us. We were on the edge of a considerable plateau composed of undulating grass-land, with outcrops of rock here and there, and patches of shale on the tops of the low ridges. The whole land, with the exception of the steep slopes facing south, was thinly covered with snow, while the numerous small tarns and boggy hollows were frozen over.

To my mind, one of the chief joys of sheep-hunting is the opportunity one has of using the glasses and telescope. Owing to the openness of the country, and clear atmosphere, vast stretches can be spied from any elevated position, and game of some kind is constantly in view. I had been lying there for half an hour or so, revelling in the warmth of the newly risen sun, and carefully quartering the country ahead with the glasses, when suddenly they revealed some brown smudges just below the crest of the ridge, a good two miles away. Changing the Zeiss glasses for the telescope, I was able to make them out to be eleven " rams," lying down. However, they were against a background of such protective colouring, and the distance was so great, that it was impossible to say if they were really big ones or not. The old man, after looking through the telescope, which I had wedged between two rocks, pronounced them to be " kara " (black), and therefore " bolshoi koshgor " (big rams). I did not, however, attach much importance to his decision, as all natives will try and persuade one that game is " big " in order to encourage one to shoot some for meat.

As we watched, they exhibited one of those sudden panics that I have often noticed among " sheep " and ibex ; these frights are caused by a sudden change in the wind, which leaves them open to attack in some direction. After rushing madly downhill for a short distance, away from that now dangerous skyline, they

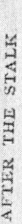

AFTER THE STALK

334]

seemed to recover from their fright, and, after gazing up wind for a few minutes, one by one, they began to paw the ground and lie down again.

A lengthy discussion now took place as to our next move ; it was carried on in a mixture of Russian and Turki. The old fellow had picked up a few words of the former from wool-merchants and traders, and of the latter most Altai Mongols have a smattering, from contact with their neighbours, the Kirghiz. Having decided on our line of approach, we retreated to the horses, and, by taking advantage of the folds of the ground, were able to ride over the greater portion of the intervening distance.

On reaching the rounded end of the hill on which the " rams " were lying, though still half a mile down-wind from them, we again left the horses and proceeded on foot, our objective being the crest of the ridge almost above the herd. Constantly trying the wind, which was very light, with particles of wool from the old hunter's coat, we reached our new vantage-point. Choosing a cluster of rocks, I slowly raised my head inch by inch above the crest till I was able to get the glasses on to the herd, and then my heart gave great throbs of excitement as, for the first time, I realized that before me were as fine a lot of heads as any hunter had ever looked upon. As the old Mongol scanned them his wrinkled face slowly broadened into a grin. Turning to me with an " I told you so ! " look, he said, " Bolshoi koshgor," at the same time clasping his thigh with both hands to indicate the girth of the horns. They were now about 400 yards below, and slightly to our left, on a gently sloping hillside. At first sight it looked as if a closer approach were out of

II—2

the question, and I was making up my mind for a long wait, when a more careful scrutiny revealed a narrow, shallow trench that ran from the crest down the otherwise smooth hillside. Giving the hunter strict injunctions to stay where he was, and not to move till I fired, I slung the telescope over my shoulder, and, dragging my rifle after me, began to worm my way down the trench. It was an anxious and painful crawl, or rather wriggle, the cover being none too good, and the stones unusually sharp.

At last, with bleeding hands and aching frame, a point was reached which I judged to be as far as it was prudent to go, so, making a small screen of stones before me, I peered through them. What a sight it was that riveted my gaze! I was actually within shot of eleven old ammon rams, the smallest of which had horns certainly not less than 50 in. in length, and the largest a good 60 in. Wedging the telescope between the stones, I looked them all over thoroughly, but, among so many beauties, it was some time before I could decide which carried "the head of heads." It is probably harder to judge the size of the horns of sheep than any other species of game ; in profile it is impossible to estimate their size at all accurately. In hurried shots this often leads to your shooting at some small five-year-old beast, whose horns bend out sharply from the head, and therefore catch your eye first, when there may be several really fine heads in the herd, whose " nip in " escapes you in the hurry of the moment. .

However, on this occasion I had ample time, and eventually decided in favour of an old fellow whose horns seemed of great thickness, " nipped in " close to the head, and terminating in a slight downward bend. I was still about 250 yards from them, rather too far to make certain of a lying shot, so I decided to wait till they got up to feed. It was now 8.30, well past their usual feeding-time. I take it, that the reason the old rams become so irregular in their habits at this season is that, having spent all the summer grazing on the finest grass, they become so fat and lazy towards autumn that they only feed for a very short time, and at irregular intervals during the day.

For a good hour I lay there with the snow-water slowly working its way through my clothes, in the constant dread that the wind would shift, and the old man would get tired and show himself (always a great danger with these people), or that some other cause would rob me of this chance of a life-time. At a moment like this one's feelings are much too acute for enjoyment, but I shall always treasure the recollection of that hour, spent in such close proximity to those hoary old patriarchs, as among the finest of my hunting experiences. They seemed to be in no hurry to move, they were evidently enjoying to the full the warmth of the sun. Every now and then one would get up, nibble at a tuft of grass, and then, after pawing the ground, lie down again. Some were lying with their necks stretched out along the ground, as if resting themselves from the terrible weight nature has imposed upon them. Others were sitting up, and chewing the cud, keenly on the look-out. The ram I had chosen was lying broadside on to me, so that I was only able to see his horns well when he now and then turned his head for a look in my direction.

My patience was almost exhausted, when one by one

they got up and began to feed. My ram was the third to rise, and, as he stretched himself broad-side on, I let drive with my ·318, the answering thud telling me all I wanted to know. In a second they were pounding downhill, never even stopping for the usual backward look ; another shot as they disappeared only succeeded in knocking up the snow under the belly of the last. Running down, I at once found an enormous blood-spoor, and knew that, with any luck, the big one was mine. The old hunter looked very crestfallen as he came up, thinking that I had made a mess of the whole thing, but, on seeing the blood, his spirits at once revived, and, by placing his head on one side and closing his eyes, he wished me to understand that we should very soon find the ram lying dead.

On the arrival of the horses, we mounted and followed along the clearly marked trail at a good pace. We had covered some four miles of undulating country, and the blood-trail was getting less and less, when suddenly, as we rode too carelessly over the top of the rise, up jumped the ram from among the rocks as if nothing was the matter, giving me no time to dismount and shoot. After going a short way, he slowed down to a walk. I now had another look at him, and could see that I had hit him rather too far back in the ribs ; it shows the extraordinary vitality of these beasts, that, in spite of a terrible wound and enormous loss of blood, he could travel about four miles, and still keep on his legs.

We now sat and watched him as he made his way down a long slope, across a stream, and up the farther hillside. But here the slope was too much for him, and he soon lay down again. Dark clouds now began

A 61-IN. OVIS AMMON.

to roll up from the north-west, and I realized that, if that head was to be mine, matters must be brought to a speedy conclusion. Another long detour brought us above him again, and, after another uncomfortable downhill slither, the tops of his horns appeared not fifty yards off. The recognition was mutual ; but, before he could do more than jump to his feet, a copper-capped bullet pierced his shoulder and he went sliding down the steep face of the hill. He carried a marvellous head, even finer than I had hoped. The horns were 61½ in. in length, 20½ in girth at the base, and had a spread of 37½ in. He stood 53 in. at the shoulder, and his age was estimated at fifteen years.

In autumn coat the coloration of an old ammon ram is very striking. The nose is white, forehead and cheeks grey-brown, neck and upper part of the body dark chocolate, freely sprinkled with white hairs, which slightly predominate on the shoulders and along the back ; this gives them a very grizzled appearance. The belly and rump-patch are white, legs grey-mottled above and white below the knees. In full winter coat an ammon ram is of a dirty-white colour on the body and neck, and pure white on the nose, legs, and rump. The ammon differs from nearly all other large Central Asian sheep in that he does not grow a long neck-ruff. In summer the coat is exceedingly short, but in winter it lengthens all over the body and neck to about two inches.

The two men were delighted with our success, and chatted incessantly as they plied their knives—not, I fear, because I had got what I wanted, but with thoughts of the meat orgy that was to follow. While keeping an eye on them, to see that they cut a good long head-skin, I tackled the cold mutton and bread in my saddle-bag. It was then nine hours since we had left camp, but, in the excitement of the chase, hunger had been forgotten.

In spite of a flurry of snow and an icy wind, we were a cheery trio as we returned to camp. In the intervals of much snuff-taking, the old hunter kept up a flow of talk in his mixture of Mongolian and Russian ; the fact that I only understood an occasional word did not bother him in the least.

Carruthers and Price had both seen a good many sheep, but nothing of any size; so next day, while they started off early, I saw to the cleaning of the head, and then moved our camp some five miles farther up the valley.

Our men now began to give trouble ; though they had been with us only three days, they said they wanted to return. Their excuses were various, the chief one being that their presence was needed to protect their families and flocks from the wolves. This is one of the chief difficulties one has to contend with in Central Asia ; the natives are so independent, and, in the out-of-the-way parts, care so little for money, that we frequently had the greatest difficulty in persuading them to accompany us. As long as you are merely travelling straight through the country, everything goes smoothly ; one chief hands you on to the next, and you are treated magnificently; but directly you wish to stop or to go off the main tracks, there is difficulty. The only thing to do, on entering a new country in which you intend to hunt, is to go straight to the head-man of the district, even if it be some distance out of your way ; make friends with him by giving him a good present, such as a cheap pair of field-glasses, or an automatic pistol, and request him politely but firmly, to supply you with men for as long as you wish to remain in his district. On this occasion I had all the men up and pointed out, through Makandaroff, that if there was any more grumbling, we would report the matter to the authorities at Suok, and have them severely beaten. This quieted them for the time, but they continued to work in a very half-hearted manner.

Carruthers did not get back to camp till a late hour that night. As it began to grow dark we became a little anxious, for to spend the night out without food or fire, and with 20 degrees of frost, would be anything but a cheerful experience. As large a fire as possible was kept going with the limited supply of dry horse-dung at our disposal, and every half-hour both barrels of the 12-bore were fired off. At about nine o'clock horses were heard approaching, and Carruthers and his men rode into camp. It appeared that a band of " rams " had only been found late in the afternoon, and that by the time he had got within shot it was getting dark. He brought in one head, and had hopes of re-trieving, on the following day, two more beasts that he had hit, it being too late to follow them up at the time.

It was one of those glorious, crisp, still mornings, which one associates with the plateaux of Central Asia in their most pleasant moods, as we sallied out on the following day, and I felt thoroughly in tune with the inspiring scene around me. As the old man and I rode along over the springy turf, the shrill whistle of the marmots resounded on every hand. By the autumn these jolly animals have amassed such quantities of fat, preparatory to their winter sleep, that they present a most comical appearance. Their short legs are almost invisible, and, as they make for their holes, they look just like large muffs rolling down the hillside. Though these animals, along with the snowcock, add greatly to the picturesqueness of the scene, they are no friends of the hunter. On several occasions, whilst after sheep or ibex, my stalk has been spoilt either by the whistle of a marmot, whose quickness of eyesight is almost unequalled, or by the weird cries of a covey of snowcock as they sailed out over the valley.

During the morning we came across a marmot-hunter, a wild-looking figure clad in tattered sheep-skins, and armed with an ancient long-barrelled muzzle-loader, with the usual forked rest. During the summer these hunters wander about the hills, carrying nothing in the way of food except a goat-skin sack of " kummis " and a small bag of salt, tied to their saddles. They rely almost entirely on marmot-flesh for their meat, only occasionally killing a wild-sheep, when an easy opportunity presents itself.

There are two methods of hunting the marmot adopted by these people ; one is merely to make a low breastwork of sods within 30 yards or so of a well-used burrow, and lie patiently behind it till a beast appears ; the other requires slightly greater skill and energy. On locating the marmot outside his hole the hunter advances boldly towards it at a rapid walk, carrying his gun in his right hand, and incessantly waving a bunch of white sheeps'-wool attached to a stick, or a fox's brush, in his left. This unusual sight so excites the curiosity of the marmot that he will often sit bolt-upright at the entrance to his hole, and allow the hunter to approach close enough for a hurried shot.

A THREE DAYS' BAG.

3421

We covered an enormous stretch of country that day, and saw large numbers of sheep ; they were mostly females, but one herd of thirteen rams contained two or three beauties. However, the first day's success was not destined to be repeated. They had evidently been disturbed, and had taken up such an unapproachable position, both with regard to wind and the openness of the country, that, though we tried every artifice, they eventually got our wind, and made tracks for the higher ground. We came across a great quantity of derelict horns that day ; in one small valley below a cliff I counted fifty in about half a mile ; it is in places like this that most of the horns are met with, the reason being that the driven snow lies deep in such places in winter. At that season packs of wolves are continually harrying the sheep ; a herd, in its mad rush for safety, gets caught in a drift ; the females and young rams, unencumbered with 40 lb. weight of horn, make good their escape, while the old rams get stuck fast and are killed. This accounts for the predominance of fair-sized horns lying about in certain localities.

On reaching camp, I saw that Carruthers' hunter had found and brought in the two heads shot the day before, one of them being a beauty of 55 in. Carruthers himself, soon afterwards, returned with another fair head of 50 in.—a pretty good two days' work. A council was held that night, at which we decided that, as we still had such enormous distances to travel before reaching our winter quarters at Kulja, we could not afford any more time for hunting the sheep. It was very disappointing to have to turn our backs on the old rams just when we had got into the cream of the shooting, but, considering the short time we had been hunting, we had done fairly well.

However, we were destined to spend one more day in the Uigur Valley, as on the following morning Carruthers developed a severe chill, necessitating a day in bed. Price went out hunting, and I contented myself with taking photographs and measuring derelict heads. Not far from camp I came upon a remarkably fine wapiti head with both horns attached to the skull; though it was very much dried up and bleached, it measured 50 in. in length, 47½ in. in spread, and 10 in. in girth above the burr, with twelve well-developed points. I was told by hunters that the snow lies to such a depth in winter in the forests on the Russian side, and the wapiti are so hard put to it for food, that they come right up on to the sheep ground, where large areas are blown clear of snow.

A knowledge of the present distribution of *Ovis ammon typica*, as far as it is known, may be of use to future travellers, especially to those who contemplate pioneering on new hunting-grounds. Undoubtedly, in by-gone ages, the distribution of these sheep was considerably wider than it is at the present day. At the period of Central Asian history when the whole land was one great battle-field, and every able-bodied man was drafted into the ranks of the vast hordes which swept backwards and forwards under the banners of Jenghis and other conquerors, people could have had little time for hunting, and, in all probability, lived in compact communities for safety's sake; this allowed the sheep to roam undisturbed over large areas to-day overrun by the nomads.

In more recent times the introduction of firearms

into the country has undoubtedly helped to thin out the game; but, with the exception of the wapiti, this is only a minor cause for their steady decrease, both in number and distribution; the primary cause is undoubtedly the rapid increase of the population on the Chinese-Russian frontier. Not only is the birth-rate among the Kirghiz increasing, but yearly large numbers are driven over to the Chinese side by the advancing Russian settlers. This necessitates the opening up of new grazing-grounds year by year, so that the game is slowly but surely being driven into higher and more inaccessible regions. The contraction of their grazing-grounds is the chief cause of the steady decrease in the numbers of the wild-sheep of Central Asia.

The southern slope of the Tannu-ola Range, at the point where we crossed it, was the first place where we came upon signs of sheep, in the shape of a few old horn-cores and fragments of horn. But they were of great age, and I can safely say that, at the present time, no sheep reach as far east as this. The western slope of the Kundelun group was the first place where we came upon fresh horns, it being the limit of their winter range in this direction. The natives say that there are sheep at the head-waters of the Kemchik; the distant view we got of the country in that direction certainly looked most promising, both the altitude and formation being suitable; this would be the most northerly limit of the ammon. To any one desirous of exploring new ground, the frontier range between the head-waters of the Kemchik, in the neighbourhood of Lake Kendikti, and the Chagan-bugazi Pass, is quite one of the most likely regions.

Between the Chagan-bugazi and Ulan-daba is the

region which sportsmen have most visited, and, without doubt, it is the nucleus of the ammon ground. The higher pastures of this broad mass of ideal sheep-country lie above the summer range of the Mongols, and rams are still undoubtedly plentiful there. The Bain-Khair-khan, in the days of Demidoff and Littledale, must have abounded in rams, but to-day the natives graze their flocks over the greater part of it, and the chances of shooting a good head there are remote. There is ample proof that the range of *Ovis ammon typica* extends along the whole length of the Great or Mongolian Altai, to the eastern extremity of the range.

Though more than one Russian explorer mentions having met with sheep in the Eastern Altai, it is to Sir Francis Younghusband that we are indebted for by far the most interesting information on this subject. In his remarkable journey of 1887 across the Gobi, from Pekin to Hami, he struck the Great Altai at its most easterly extremity in longitude 100° East. He estimated the height of the range, even at its terminal portion, as 9,000 ft. above sea-level, and the natives reported grassy plateaux in the centre. These two combinations sound suitable for ammon. Though Sir Francis did not visit these high plateaux, where the sheep would have been at that season (July), yet on the outlying southern foot-hills horns were found lying on the ground which, from their great girth of 19 in. and general shape, undoubtedly belonged to *Ovis ammon typica*.

When we were in the desert north-east of Guchen, the Baitik Bogdo Range, a southern and somewhat isolated appendage of the Altai, was visible to the north. The Kirei Kirghiz, when asked what game was

LOADING UP THE AMMON HEADS.

to be found there, informed us that there were plenty
of "arkar." It would appear, therefore, that if sheep
inhabit such outlying hills as the Baitik Bogdo, and
those that Sir Francis Younghusband visited farther
east, in all probability there are some magnificent
hunting-grounds among the high plateaux of the Eastern
Altai.

The eastern extremities of the Altai and Tian Shan
ranges are only divided by a narrow strip of desert
a hundred miles in breadth ; yet it is of such an absolutely barren nature as to completely prevent the range
of the *Ovis ammon typica* of the Altai overlapping
that of the *Ovis ammon karelini* of the Tian Shan.
Sir Francis Younghusband describes this gap as being
" the most desolate country I have ever seen." Directly
the lower slopes of the Tian Shan were reached, this
traveller came upon horns decidedly different to those
on the Altai side ; they were thinner at the base and
more angular than those found farther north. A magnificent pair which he picked up there, and which are
still in his possession, measure 62 in. in length and
16 in. in girth. Our own experiences of the Karlik
Tagh sheep bear out his observations ; we saw considerable numbers of horns in these mountains, either
lying on the ground or in possession of their owners,
all of which were similar in thickness and twist to those
we saw later on the Borotala. In their winter dress
these sheep (*Ovis ammon karelini*) grow a pure white
throat-ruff, 3 in. in length, a characteristic which the
Ovis ammon typica of the Altai does not possess.

The following night we encamped at Belota, and the
next day, while Carruthers took the caravan over to
the Chagan-gol, Price and I, with one man, hunted our

way thence over the Bain-Khairkhan, this being our last chance of seeing sheep.

Right on the top, at an altitude of about 9,000 ft., we saw an enormous herd of gazelle ; there must have been nearly two hundred of them. They were principally females and young, with a few small bucks. These gazelle (*G. gutturosa*) are found all over North-western Mongolia, north of the Great Altai, and south of the Tannu-ola ranges ; the most north-westerly limit of their ranges is the steppe round the Russian frontier post of Kosh-Agatch ; from there they extend right across Northern Mongolia as far as the eastern extremity of the plateau. In winter they are to be found in the sheltered valleys among the foot-hills or out on the open plains round the lakes ; but in summer they ascend right up into the mountains. In this respect they differ from *G. subgutturosa,* of which we saw a great deal later, in Dzungaria. This latter species, though occasionally found in the summer, when the grass of the plains is burnt up, in low hills at an altitude of 6,000 ft., never, like the former, reaches the elevated boggy plateaux that one associates with wild-sheep.

The general colour of *G. gutturosa* is light fawn ; the limbs, cheeks, under-parts, sides, and rump are white ; there are no dark face-markings, as in most gazelle, though the top of the muzzle is slightly darker than the fawn of the back. The tail is short, with a brown tip ; it is in the shortness and colour of the tail that it differs most markedly from *G. subgutturosa ;* for in the latter it is considerably longer and black. Its horns also differ from those of the *G. subgutturosa* in being rather thinner and shorter, and more closely and boldly ringed ; instead of diverging directly from the skull they are parallel at the bases, diverging sharply above, with the tips gently bending inwards again.

The almost complete absence of dark face-markings and the shortness and light colour of the tail are the marked characteristics of the three species of gazelle that are peculiar to the Chinese Empire. These are *G. picticaudata* of Tibet, *G. prjevalskii* of the Ordos, Ala Shan and Kansu, and *G. gutturosa* of North Mongolia. I do not include *G. subgutturosa*, with its comparatively long black tail, as, although it inhabits Dzungaria and Chinese Turkestan, it is not peculiar to China, Russian Turkestan and Western Asia being the centres of its distribution. In comparing the horns of the three Chinese gazelle, I find that they have common characteristics which differ from those of other Asiatic species. The above description of the horns of *G. gutturosa* stands also for the other two varieties, with the exception of the backward bend, which is decidedly more pronounced in *picticaudata*, and slightly more in *prjevalskii*. There is also a slight difference in the formation of the rings. For the first two-thirds of their length they diverge very slightly, the terminal portion bending out, and then in, sharply. Those of the Dzungarian gazelle diverge considerably from their base upwards with a decided backward bend, the terminal portion forming a less pronounced hook.

Later on, we observed a few female ibex and arkar. This range is evidently a favourite breeding-ground, but I doubt if there are any big rams there at the present day ; at any rate, we saw none.

After a long day in the saddle, just at dusk, we dropped down into the Chagan-gol Valley, and found our camp pitched some five miles below the camp of the

Mongol chieftain, which we had left seven days before. A long march over an uninhabited country, with no living thing to break the monotony except a few gazelle and an occasional wheeling vulture, took us out of the Chagan-gol Valley and onwards towards the Great Altai Mountains, whose snow-capped ridges now appeared to rise no great distance ahead of us. We here left the Mongols and entered the land of the Turk, for at this point begins the territory of the Kirei, or Keraites, a Turki race, the descendants of the people whose name once resounded far and wide across the whole of Asia— as the followers of that romantic, yet elusive person, " Prester John."

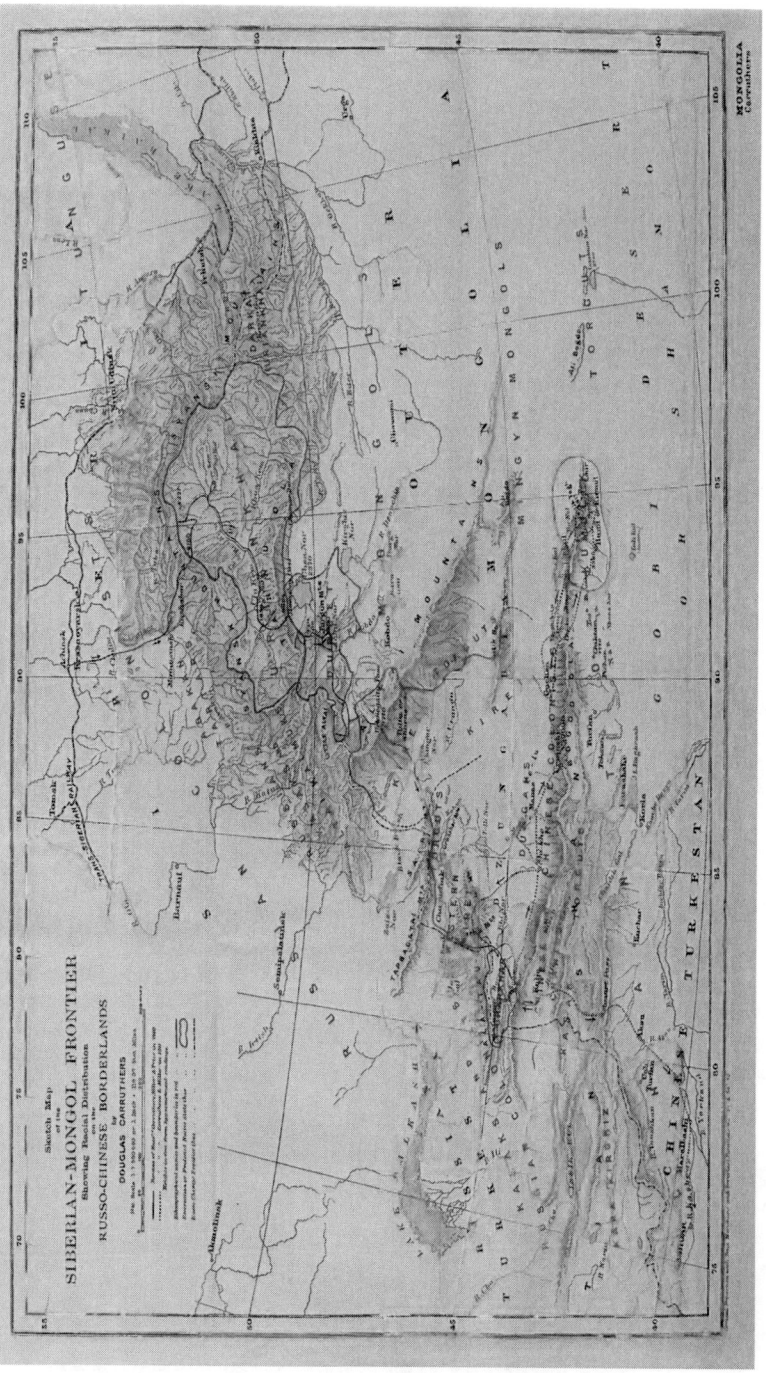

Sketch Map
of the
SIBERIAN-MONGOL FRONTIER
Showing Racial Distribution
on the
RUSSO-CHINESE BORDERLANDS
by
DOUGLAS CARRUTHERS

MONGOLIA
Carruthers

CHAPTER XII

THE KIREI OF THE ALTAI, THE CHILDREN OF PRESTER JOHN

" The name of ' Prester John' has an attractive interest both for those who love the romances of the nursery, and for those who study the more sober facts of medieval history. To both it is a puzzle and a paradox, and has given rise to much discussion. That a Christian king and priest reigned in an isolated far-off land over a Christian people, environed by pagans and barbarians, was a belief of most medieval writers. Some of them fixed his residence in Abyssinia, others in India, others again on the borders of China. The legend gradually grew more definite as the various envoys to the Mongol Khans returned and brought news of their having been in contact with the Christian people, and opinion became settled that the Prester John of history was the King of the nation of the Keraits, a disciple of the Nestorians."—SIR H. H. HOWORTH.

THE Kirei [1] represent a section of the Kirghiz family, and one of the purest branches of the great Turkish race. In fact, if we endeavour to trace back the history of the Kirghiz, we find that they came into existence, —from an unknown origin, as it were,—in the Kemchik valleys of the Yenisei basin, at a period when it would be almost impossible to draw distinctions between the

---

[1] There are various forms of spelling, such as Kirai, Kerrit, Kerait, and in the earliest writings it takes the form of Crit.

Mongol and the Turkish races; we can look on the Altai ranges and the Kemchik pastures as being the birthplace of a section of the Turkish race, and on the Kirei as being the truest examples of the original Turks.

The migrations of the Kirghiz before the sixth century A.D. are as little known to us as are the movements of other nomad peoples of those days. Their history is mysteriously wrapped up in that of the Uigurs, and we know little of them definitely until they rose to some power in the sixth century, contemporaneously with that of the Uigur Empire. Previous to that the Kirei are supposed to have occupied the country to the east of Lake Baikal, at the sources of the Amur ; out of this region they were pushed,—by invading hordes of Khitans,—southwards towards the Hoang Ho, to which region they are assigned by most writers. I imagine, however, that a large section of the tribe always remained north of the Gobi, probably in the Altai, or at the sources of the Kemchik and Abakan, where to this day Kirghiz people are living, and amongst whom there is a tribe called Kirei. Subsequently the Kirei formed a part of the Naiman kingdom, which included a powerful confederation of Turkish tribes who overcame the Uigurs, and ruled over the region between the Kerulun and the Altai, making Karakorum their capital. On the break-up of the Naiman confederacy, the Kirei took their place as the ruling power, their chief centre being on the banks of the Black Irtish and on the ranges of the Great Altai. This period of their greatness extended over both the eleventh and the twelfth centuries. Eventually they were incorporated in the Empire of Jenghis Khan, and, no doubt, owing to their

A KIREI FALCONER.

fighting qualities, formed valuable contingents to the Mongol armies as they moved westwards.

After this the nomadic Turkish tribes, as represented by the Kirghiz and Kasaks, became more or less independent, until recently when Russia and China compelled them to accept the jurisdiction of their respective Governments,—the Kirghiz, with their kinsmen the Kasaks,[1] being now scattered over wide areas of Central Asia from the Altai Mountains to the Sea of Aral. Of all the different tribes of Kirghiz, however, the Kirei hold first place in point of historical interest. Long ago they claimed attention as being an isolated Christian tribe in the middle of pagan Asia, the subjects of the mysterious Prester John,—a Christian monarch who was not only credited with vast wealth and power, but was ruler of a kingdom of great size. No other tribe has created such excitement in the West nor has been endowed with such a wonderful reputation as that of the Kirei at the end of the eleventh century. It is this particular period of their history that excites our interest, and makes this account of them, at the present day, of unusual value. We saw them in the very heart of their own territory, we crossed and re-crossed their country, and met with them both in their mountain-pastures and on the sand-dunes of the low-lying plains ; we kept constantly before us the records of their past, and this intensified and doubled the curiosity which their encampments would in any case have elicited.

I will briefly recount the romance of the Kirei—as subjects of Prester John—and then state what appear

[1] The true Kirghiz, also called Buruts, Kara-Kirghiz or mountain-Kirghiz, inhabit as a rule the highland region, such as the Pamirs, parts of the Tian Shan, and the Altai. The Kasaks, who are an offshoot from the original stem, hold the lowlands and plains.

to be the facts, so far as we know them, of the history of these people. The story of the Kirei, their connexion with Nestorian Christianity, and their supposed but wholly mythical power and wealth, is typical of the days when Asia was so little known to Europe that any stories originating from thence quickly grew into fabulous tales of amazement and wonder. A report, for instance, filtered through to Europe in the early part of the eleventh century—that is to say, at the time when Asia first began to occupy a place in the minds of Western people—of the conversion to Christianity of a powerful Eastern potentate and his subjects. The accounts, however, were so extravagant in their embellishment of the might of this great Khan, yet, at the same time, so poor in detail, that it was difficult to decide who he was and where his kingdom was situated.

During the eleventh, twelfth, and thirteenth centuries, the solution of the problem of the elusive Prester John occupied the close attention of all writers and travellers; endless traditions and fables collected around the name of this semi-mythical, kingly pontiff, until it became quite impossible to separate truth from fiction, though men continued their attempts to discover the whereabouts of his fabulous kingdom, as if it were an El Dorado. Many letters, supposed to have been written by the Khan, passed between him and the Pope, the Emperor of Constantinople, and the King of France; all of these proclaimed not only his greatness, power, and wealth, but also the extent of his dominions, exaggerating his importance to such an extent that, although these fables were believed at the time, they, in the end, defeated their own object, and received no credence.

The following are extracts from one of the letters accredited to Prester John which so greatly stimulated the imagination of the Western mind in the twelfth century:

"Know and believe that I am the Priest John, the servant of God, and that I surpass in riches, in power, and in virtue all the kings of the earth. Sixty-two kings are tributary to me. . . . We believe that we have no equal, either for the quantity of our riches or the number of our subjects. When we issue forth to make war on our enemies we have borne before us, upon thirteen cars, thirteen large and precious crosses, ornamented with gold and jewels. Each cross is followed by ten thousand horsemen and a hundred thousand foot-soldiers, without counting the men of war charged to conduct the baggage and the provisions of the army. . . . If you can count the sands of the sea, and the stars of heaven, you may number my domains, and reckon my power."

The writer of this document adds that the variety of fauna found within the dominion of the Kirei includes the elephant, dromedary, camel, and salamander; that there are immense forests filled with serpents, and an arid sea of sand, and their land is the home of cyclopes, centaurs, pigmies, giants, and cannibals! Every conceivable exaggeration grew up around this Eastern potentate and his dominion; in fact, Prester John and his country became a byword for fantasy, magnificence, and prosperity.

Foolish as these accounts seem to us now, yet they contain much truth. There is no doubt that Prester John was a real person, and whether there existed more than one Eastern monarch or African potentate who could claim to be the original Prester John is of little consequence, as the question can never be decided ; but, taking the accumulated evidence into careful consideration, the Khans of the Kirei in the eleventh and twelfth centuries seem to accord very closely with the accounts of this priestly king.

It appears certain that early in the eleventh century a great wave of Nestorian Christianity spread itself across Asia, and, amongst other conversions which are known to have taken place, was that of the Khan of the Kirei and of many of his subjects. On this point all medieval writers agree. No doubt the missionaries, eager to show the magnitude of their conversions and the importance of their converts, wrote these very exaggerated accounts *in the name* of the Khan ; they were doubtless products of their own imagination, and, although attributed to the Khan, it is probable that he was unaware of their contents. The Nestorians were a great political power throughout Inner Asia in those days, and the conversion of so powerful a tribe as the Kirei would carry great weight ; it is noteworthy that the date of their conversion marked an increase in their power and prestige, this being the starting-point of those conquests and invasions which brought their name into prominence, and which spread their reputation far and wide.

The Kirei supremacy continued until the Tartar tribe, of which Jenghis Khan was chief, became their rivals, and finally their conquerors. Thus the Kirei disappeared off the field of Central Asian politics, and the Mongols became the leading race. The subsequent history of the two races shows clearly the manner in which the Mongols rose to power, became Buddhists,

A KIREI MAIDEN.

and finally fell into the condition in which they remain at the present day. The Christian Kirei also lost their power, but they became Mohammedans, and have now reached a state of superiority and a degree of prosperity far in advance of that of the Mongols.

At the present day the range of the Kirei includes their old home on the banks of the Upper or Black Irtish, and the greater part of the western Altai pastures, but the territory on the east of the Altai, which must once have been theirs, is now in the hands of the Mongol Khans. The territorial boundaries of the Mongol chiefs are inviolable, and the Kirei are hampered in their desire to advance in this direction by the Chinese authorities who uphold the Mongols' rights.

The main resort of the tribe is along the western flanks of the Altai, being the area drained by the tributaries of the Black Irtish. Only in one part,—in the neighbourhood of the lakes Dolto Nor and Dain Kul, at the sources of the Kobdo River,—do the Kirei possess pasturages on the eastern side of the watershed of the Altai Range. Here they own a fine country, consisting not only of summer pastures, forests and lakes, but also numerous sheltered valleys. This portion of their territory is monopolized by the chief and his section of the tribe. Towards the west the range of the Kirei extends into the Dzungarian plains, as far as the lakes Ulungur and Zaisan—on the Russian frontier. Farther westwards still, along the marches of Russian and Chinese territory, there exists a Western branch of Kirei, separated from the Altai Kirei, and serving under a different chief. To the southwards their boundaries are less clearly defined. They occupy the well-protected and low-lying valley of the Upper Irtish as their winter quarters, and the greater part of the Urungu Valley falls within their territory ; beyond this, uninhabited steppes and areas of sand-dunes allow them free progress as far as the Bogdo-ola Mountains, the southern border-range of Dzungaria.

We visited the Kirei in many of these localities. Our experiences in connexion with the section of the tribe owning the pastures of the Upper Kobdo Valley proved to us that they spent the summer in the highlands around Dain Kul and Dolto Nor, and wintered in the valley of the Upper Kobdo, at the rather high altitude of 6,000 ft. The inhabitants of the Dzungarian flanks of the Altai descended to the valley of the Upper or Black Irtish for the winter. In this latter locality we found them in the course of our journey across Dzungaria. The Kirei were indeed fortunate in the possession of such a well-favoured winter resort. Great belts of tall reeds sheltered them from the winds, groves of poplar and willow supplied ample firewood, and plenty of grass was to be found for their animals. There should also be good pasture for sheep, judging by the immense flocks we came across in that country. The encampments were pitched in snug quarters amongst the reeds and the poplars, so well protected as to be almost hidden from view; their existence was quickly discovered, however, by the presence of many golden-eagles tethered to the higher branches of the poplar trees. Inner Asia is the home of falconry, and the natives not only use hawks and falcons, but even train the great golden-eagles for the purpose of hunting such large quarry as gazelle, foxes, and even wolves. All these Kirei seemed prosperous in themselves and rich in flocks.

KIREI IN WINTER QUARTERS.

The Western branch of the Kirei are distributed along the Russo-Chinese frontier of Dzungaria, and range into the territory belonging to both nations ; the Tarbagatai, Sair, Barlik, and Maili ranges forming their headquarters. Some are Russian subjects, others are Chinese, but all move freely, regardless of the delimitations of the political frontiers. The chief of the Western branch, Mahmot Beg by name, is a cousin of Jenghis Khan, chief of the Altai Kirei, and resides in the Maili Mountains.

The southern section of the Kirei spend their time between the valley of the Urungu River and the small group of mountains, called Baitik Bogdo, which lie in the plains to the south. These hills, we were told, are favourable for summer grazing, and well watered, but in winter migration is necessary, the nomads then trekking either northwards to the Urungu Valley, or southwards to the sand-dune area lying near the foot-hills of the Bogdo-ola Range. During our journeys in the month of February in Southern Dzungaria, we visited encampments of the Kirei in the belt of sand-dunes which extends to within ten miles of the town of Guchen. There we found they had made a remarkable use of a region which, being waterless, was an impossible dwelling-place for nomads, except at this particular season when snow covered the ground and served as a water-supply. Their movements being dependent upon the snowfall, they begin to migrate southwards in November and to go north again during the month of March. By these means the Kirei are enabled to pasture their flocks over the sand-belt covered with dwarf scrub and grass, and bordered, along its northern edge, with forests of saxaul. Their encampments presented a curious appearance, hidden away in a hollow of the dunes, or sheltered amongst the giant saxaul bushes. The yurts were closely grouped and the flocks, which consisted chiefly of sheep and goats, were well guarded from the attacks of wolves ; they had a few camels, but their horses they had left behind them in the Baitik Mountains.

This particular section of the Kirei, who really belong to the Altai district, are exhibiting a tendency to extend their boundaries farther to the southwards. Whether they had been pushed out by increase in the population, or for what special reason they had come to this country, we were unable to ascertain. From all appearances, they were discontented with their lot, wishing either to return to the main Altai or to make a permanent home on the Bogdo-ola. The desire to move elsewhere was, no doubt, caused by the relative poverty of their territory, as compared with that of the rest of the tribe. The Baitik Mountains cover, at the best, only a small area ; they support, besides the Kirei, a small sedentary population of Torgut Mongols, and, being of no great altitude, any appearance of desiccation would quickly make itself felt by these people. Moreover, the existence, within view, of the untenanted range of the Bogdo-ola must be very tantalizing to them ; for this reason the Kirei yearly renew their endeavours to establish themselves on those inviting pastures. Every winter a certain number succeed in reaching the foot-hills, where they spend a few months peacefully, without let or hindrance ; but in the spring they must pack up and trek northwards, otherwise the Chinese soldiery is sent out to harry them.

The Kirei of the Altai are under the jurisdiction of the Amban of Sharasume, to whom they pay a nominal tax, as well as the tribute paid to their own chief. Those of the tribe who migrate in winter to the Bogdo-ola Mountains in Southern Dzungaria, are taxed by the officials of Guchen for the use of their winter pasturage. We came across a few of the latter, who complained to us of ill-treatment at the hands of the Chinese; but they themselves were in fault, having considerably overstayed the time allotted to them. We found others who had avoided interference by claiming that they were Russian subjects.

This digression, in relation to the early history and to the present-day distribution of the Kirei, is necessary on account of our having, at this juncture, arrived at the frontiers of their country.

We will now resume the thread of the narrative and return to the spot where we first came in contact with these people. On leaving the hunting-grounds of the Uigur plateau a break occurred in the usual routine of our journey. Survey work was stopped by the speed at which we were forced to travel, and excused by the comparatively well-known nature of the country through which we were now passing. Winter was fast approaching, as shown by the fact that, in the month of September, our camps were repeatedly under snow ; we therefore hastened to cross the Great Altai Range, which lay between us and the warm lowlands of Dzungaria. Pressing forward across the plateaux that lie in the extreme north-western corner of Mongolia, we found ourselves, in mid-September, approaching the lower foot-hills of the Altai Mountains. This country was a fine one, good for the shepherd, and pleasant to traverse. Rivers of clearest water ran across the downlands, and frequent larch groves gave the region a less bleak aspect than was the case with much of the country over which we had been travelling.

On September 14th we camped close to an upper tributary of the Kobdo River, amongst Mongols, unmistakable by their untidiness and dirt ; on the following day, without any change of scenery, climate, or political division, we found ourselves amongst a new people—the Kirei. This may not seem of importance to the general reader, but in reality it represented an ethnographical change of great and unusual interest. We had *in a day* passed out of the Buddhist-Shammanist world into the Mohammedan world—from the Mongol to the Turk. In fact, we now entered, at a distance of 3,000 miles from Mecca, the farthest outpost of Islam in Asia.

I well remember, while riding along with our Mongol horsemen, accosting the first follower of the Prophet whom we met in the course of our journey, and remarking on the natural politeness with which he invited us to his yurt. Within, a fine old gentleman —a perfect Turkish type—rose to greet us. With a word of welcome, which in other Mussulman countries could only have been extended to co-religionists, he bade us be seated. His dwelling was a yurt of the ordinary construction, yet very different in appearance to that of the Mongol yurts. Here we not only felt at home, but greatly appreciated the cleanliness of our surroundings and the true hospitality and exquisite manners of our host.

These well-made yurts, covered with white felt, were in direct contrast to the black, torn, and ragged tents of the Mongols. The interior spoke of prosperity, and showed a distinct appreciation of comfort. Clean carpets

CAMP BESIDE THE UPPER KOBDO RIVER.

of felt covered the floor, and many household belongings stood around the sides—gaudily-coloured boxes, a bed, quilts and cushions, saddlery and a falcon ; while the right-hand side of the tent displayed a profusion of cooking-pots, kettles, kummis-bags, and other signs of a commissariat, such as would arouse the envy of any Mongol housewife. No little Buddhist altar adorned the head of the yurt, no lazy priest lounged on the seat of honour, while, in place of poorly clad and disreputable-looking inhabitants, we were delighted to see rosy-cheeked children, and plump, healthy-looking women, clad in becoming costumes of black and white. The men, too, were of remarkably fine build as compared with the Mongols. There was almost an appearance of opulence in these Kirghiz encampments ; in comparison with the Mongols and Uriankhai, these Kirei tribesmen might be described as "gentlemen-rovers," rich in flocks and herds, well-housed, owning a fine country, and with sufficient leisure at their disposal to indulge in horse-racing and in falconry.

The comparison between the low Mongol soldiery who accompanied us and these lordly Kirei was instructive. All spoke of a higher standard of life, and a superior moral code ; we realized at once the immense social gap which lay between these two people. The special type of our Mohammedan host was well preserved ; he was obviously Mussulman, and through him we realized the far-reaching influence of religion and the power it possesses of engraving itself upon the character of a people. Here is no decadent form of Islam, it is one and the same faith as followed by the nomads of Arabia or North Africa. The world-wide uniformity of this belief has created an absolute unity of type.

All pointed to the fact that the Mohammedan faith formed the basis on which stood the superiority of the Kirghiz over the Mongols, and convinced us that their well-being and progressiveness emanated from the same cause. Independence, cleanliness, and abstinence were the traits which stood out most strongly, and were those in the most direct contrast to the character of the Mongols. A greater contrast still is shown in the wide difference which exists in the social conditions of these two nomad peoples. Whereas the Mongols are serfs living under the control of their rulers and of their priests, the Kirghiz are a free, self-governing people, forming a powerful democracy where all men are more or less equal.

The power of Islam is chiefly noticeable here, in that these two people were originally of the same Shammanistic faith. Yet Islam alone possessed the power of up-rooting the " Black Art." The influence both of Christianity and Buddhism on the Shamman tribes has been mentioned in Chapter VII. Neither of these religions has proved a success; Islam, on the other hand, has had such an effect on the Turki tribes that their ancient belief in Shammanism is now only discernible in certain rites and customs. The " Baksa," or " wonder-doctor " of the Kirghiz, for instance, represents the Shamman priest under a new cloak; but he is now suppressed by the Mullahs, and has no longer any religious power.

We came across, even in this extremely remote corner of the Mohammedan world, several men who had made the pilgrimage to Mecca, and later on, in the course of our travels, we made the acquaintance of Mahmot Beg, chief of the Western Kirei, who had made the pilgrimage in person, together with his wife. It is of interest to note the route taken by pilgrims from the Altai to Mecca. A road-and-water journey of 800 miles leads them northwards to the Siberian railway, the railway carries them to Odessa on the Black Sea—the meeting-place of all pilgrims from Central Asia—and from there they take ship to Jedda. The return journey is generally made by the new railway from Medina to Damascus, whence they reach the coast at Beirut.

So great is the force of religion amongst the followers of the Prophet that, although they owe allegiance either to the Emperor of China or to the Tsar of Russia, they look neither to Pekin nor to St. Petersburg, for they consider Stamboul to be their religious and political capital. On many occasions we met Moslem missionaries from Constantinople " on tour " amongst the outlying encampments of nomads in Central Asia. Railways and telegraphs have brought even these far-removed colonies into closer communication with the Protector of their faith, and with the centre of their belief; greater ease of transport is likely to advance still further the cause of Islam in Asia.

Our sudden introduction into the Moslem world made us realize the fact of the remarkable force and progress of Islam in Central Asia. Along the frontier between Islam and Buddhism, there is to be noticed a steady pressing forward of the Mohammedan, a determination to gain possession of the best pasturages, and a strong desire to move *eastwards* and to move *higher up*. In many places the movement merely results in the colonization of vacant lands, in other

places it means competition with the resident population, while in others it results in the actual pushing
back of the rightful owners. If it were not for the zeal
shown by the Chinese in protecting the Mongol rights of
ownership, many localities would be rapidly overrun
by the Mohammedan-Turki tribes. All the regions not
exclusively reserved for Mongols are becoming, year by
year, more thickly populated by newcomers of Moslem
faith.

As a rule, this movement appears to be from Russian
into Chinese territory, the Chinese being quite unable
to check the immigration. The Chinese do not want
these immigrants flooding their country, because they
get nothing out of them, for the newcomers still
remain Russian subjects, and are a constant source
of trouble to the authorities on this account. It is
equally certain that the movement into Chinese territory is caused by no love of Chinese rule. Whatever
M. Vambéry says about "an approach between Moslems
and Buddhists," and a growing tendency for Mohammedans to side with Celestials against a common foe
in the person of the European, his theories find no proof
in these localities. The Turki Moslems prefer to be
under Russian rather than Chinese rule, and, I believe,
would side with the *West* against the *East*, in the same
way as the Buddhist Mongols have recently thrown in
their lot with Russia against China.

Whether, or not, the immigration is being directly
caused by the continual influx of Russian colonists into
Russian Central Asia, it is hard to say; so far as one
can judge, this element probably plays a definite part
in producing a movement of the nomadic tribes from
the plains into the mountains,—which latter happen

KIREI WOMEN GOING TO A WEDDING.

MISTRESSES OF THE YURTS.

to lie along the Russo-Chinese frontier, and chiefly on the Chinese side of it. In such localities as the Tian Shan this is undoubtedly the case, for the Kasaks of the Russian territory,—finding their lands too cramped and too crowded, through rapid increase in their population and by reason of the influx of Russian colonists, —are now moving into Chinese territory, where there is more space in which to settle.

There are other localities where this Russian influence is entirely absent, and yet we find the same movement of the Mohammedan nomad tribes ; this fact is therefore undoubtedly due to an increase in the population, or to a demand for better pastures, owing to desiccation. This latter reason would account for the universal desire to move into *higher* country.

With the Kirei, for instance, in spite of the ample lands and the best pasture in the Altai ranges, an attempt is being made by those members of the tribe who inhabit the most southern portion of their territory—namely, the Baitik Mountains and the Dzungarian plains—to acquire the rights to pasture their flocks still farther south, in the Bogdo-ola ranges. As a fact, the Kirei are endeavouring to extend their borders towards the well-pastured and unoccupied ranges of the Eastern Tian Shan, but are hindered in their project by the determination of the Chinese authorities to keep those regions for themselves.

Thus we see that the nomadic Moslem tribes of this part of Inner Asia exhibit signs of progress and increase which the Buddhist tribes do not show.

At this season—mid-September—the Kirei were on their autumn migrations, and as we rode along the banks of the Upper Kobdo River we accosted small bands of

II—4

nomads moving down to their winter quarters. They had come from the high pastures on the flanks of the Great Altai, and from the lands surrounding the lakes, which lie embosomed in the grassy uplands at an altitude of about 7,000 ft. At this season they sought the sheltered valleys of a lower altitude, where protection from cold and a lesser snowfall made the severity of winter more endurable. The valley presented a lively scene, with the continual movement of family parties with their household belongings, flocks and herds ; as well as small caravans of camels carrying wool, hides, and felt—the products of the by-gone season—slouching past on their way to Kobdo, the trade centre of the Mongolian Altai.

The Kobdo River was here a fast-flowing stream, fifty yards in breadth, with banks pleasantly dotted with groups of giant larch-trees and willow-scrub. We discovered here the temporary camp of the chief of the tribe, with a considerable following of retainers; so we pitched our tents near by in order to interview him, and to ask for means of transport through his country. The chief, we discovered, was on a visit to Chuguchak, a town lying on the Russo-Chinese frontier in the Dzungarian plain, at a distance of about 400 miles from his home. His eldest son, however, did the honours in his stead, and the factotum of the princely family looked after our needs.

Jenghis Khan-Kam, paramount chief of the Kirei, claims descent from the great Mongol emperor of that name. This claim is curious, for, although Jenghis overthrew the Kirei confederacy, it is extremely doubtful that he set up a Mongol ruler over a Turki tribe. The present chief is certainly of pure Turkish descent.

To claim Jenghis Khan as his ancestor suits his vanity, as in a similar way many Bokharan nobles claim descent from Alexander the Great ; the truth being that they probably gave their women-folk in marriage to the great Emperor or to his generals. The suffix " Kam," the title given to us by his own people, is of immense interest. The earliest mention of the King of the Kirei, by Rubruck, describes him as Coir-Cham : " Cham being his title, the word having the meaning of Soothsayer, which is applied to their princes because they govern the people by means of divination." [1] The same term is employed at the present day to denote the Shamman priests.

The personal get-up of these nomads was extravagant and showy. The men were generally dressed in gay colours, not in the dingy black of the Kara-Kirghiz of the Pamirs or the Western Tian Shan ; but the women always "sported,"—if they could afford it,—the "Kara-chapan," or black quilted-coat, as well as the high-piled head-gear of white material. In some details their dress differed from that of all other Kirghiz tribes, the chief difference being the boots of tanned leather, with high heels of a rich dark green colour ; it was the fashion also for all Kirei of rank to wear the soft plumes of the Eagle Owl as a crest to their fur-lined caps.

The yurts of the chief were exceptionally large, and the white felt covering was gaily embroidered with red and blue designs. Hospitality was shown us by means of a liberal supply of kummis and sheep, and promises of everything we wanted ; but, when it came to the actual supply of transport, we were faced by very different methods to those to which we had been accustomed.

[1] *The Journey of Friar Rubruck*, p. 100 (Hakluyt Society edition).

With this difficulty of procuring transport we gained our first experience of the independence of the Kirghiz. We were bluffed at each renewed demand for transport, by such absurd statements as, "the passes are closed," "we have no horses," "the Mongols had better take you on farther." Two whole days were thus spent in haggling with the wealthy owners of innumerable herds of horses, all of whom did their best to evade their duty to us as strangers travelling through their country, before we enforced our demands. I allude to this in order to draw attention to the different points of view that existed between the Mongol and the Kirghiz: the former considered himself our vassal, the latter considered himself our equal.

We were now forced to provision both ourselves and our caravan for the crossing of an uninhabited area, which included also the passage of the Great Altai. Since the Kirei had now deserted the highlands, this meant a journey of five days' duration before reaching the settlements on the lower foot-hills of the Dzungarian side of the range. We therefore purchased sheep, for food, and, with the Kirei men and horses in place of the Mongols, we recommenced our travels.

On September 17th we visited Dolto Nor, the lowest of the group of lakes which form the sources of the Kobdo River, the main caravan being led up to Dain Kul, by the direct route to the Urkhogaitu Pass over the Altai Range. The country surrounding these lakes forms the main summer resort of the Khan of the Kirei and his section of the tribe. Situated at an altitude of 7,000 ft. immediately below the forest-belt on the mountains which rise directly to the south-west, this plateau supplies excellent summer pastures for innumerable

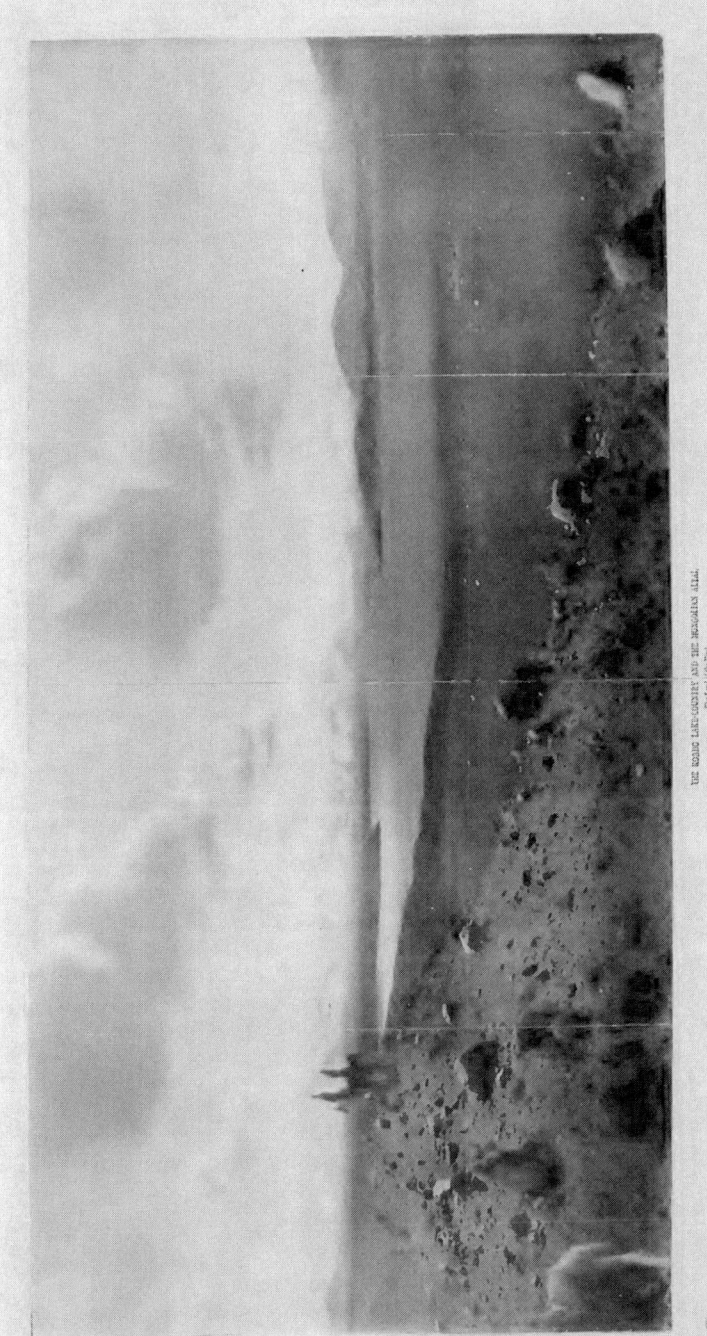

THE NIGER LAKE-COUNTRY AND THE MOUNTAINS BEYOND

The Land of the Black

flocks and herds. The country is peculiar, for it is
formed entirely of miniature hills and dales—remnants of
old moraines. At this season it presented a somewhat
melancholy appearance; there was no pasture, and the
lakes were lifeless, showing barren shores of black stones
with neither reeds nor rushes to enliven the dead brown
of the landscape. But the islands dotting the lakes
were partially covered with forest, and in spring or
early summer the view would be entrancing.

Beyond the lakes, rose suddenly in a long even ridge,
the walls of the main chain of the Altai. We noticed a
considerable belt of larch forest, with the snow extending
as far down as the top of the tree-limit, which must here
have been about 8,000 ft. No peaks of any special
beauty or height rose above the even and slightly indented
ridge; on the whole, this panorama of the Altai was
disappointing, and we considered the range misnamed
" Great." The actual height of this range,—which
we will rename the " Mongolian Altai," in distinction
from the Russian Altai,—seems to average, according
to Prof. Sapoznikoff, about 10,000 ft. There is only
one summit which reaches an altitude of 13,120 ft.
in the entire length of 700 miles,—between the Russian
frontier and where the ranges sink away into desert.
At the point, however, where the Mongolian Altai breaks
away from the Russian Altai there is a group of five high
peaks, one of which reaches an altitude of 14,760 ft.
With the exception of these summits the " Great " Altai
is in reality a rather inconspicuous and narrow range.

Altitude, however, is not everything; the Altai
in September under fresh snow presented a feature of
remarkable beauty, its unbroken wall—for there is
only one feasible pass over many hundreds of miles—

giving us a deep impression of its importance as a boundary between Mongolia and the region lying beyond ; between the cold, bleak plateaux and the hot lowlands ; between a land which is exclusively Mongol and a land where many races strive together for mastery, and, most significant of all, between the spheres of the great faiths—Buddhism and Islam.

On leaving the Dolto Nor we rode over undulating moraines, and finally across a small plain, as hard and as smooth as a billiard-table, which had been utilized by our sporting friends, the Kirei, as a race-course. The annual race-meeting is held in July, when severe tests of the capacity and staying powers of horses and riders take place, as instanced by races run over a course of 20 miles ! A line of posts and rails to which the nomads tied their horses was the only sign of it being used as a race-course. Towards the edge of the plain the lake of Dain Kul was to be seen, tucked away under hills covered with golden-tinted larch forest ; and here it was that we made our last camp in Mongolia. On the morrow a long day's journey took us over the watershed of the Altai. The route was in every way an easy one; in fact, the crossing of the range can be accomplished without much difficulty by laden camels, and we ourselves rode on horseback over the pass, without even dismounting. There was not much snow, and what little there was lay both on the south side and on the north, shale and rock being the feature of the pass. Later we realized that the southern flanks of the Altai receive the greater precipitation, the forest and pasture being larger and finer on the south, and the outlying spurs being more covered with snow than the northern side of the ridge. It was at an altitude of 9,711 ft. that we crossed the watershed and camped on a snow-patch below, near which juniper and birch-scrub gave us fuel.[1]

The crossing of the Urkhogaitu Pass led us down to the head-waters of the Kran River, which finds its way eventually into the Irtish, and so on to the Ob River and the Arctic Ocean. In the course of two days' journey our caravan descended from the cold, rocky crest of the Altai, over grassy hills and through pleasantly forested valleys, to the lowest altitude we had experienced for many months. From the nomads'-land of breezy plateaux and wind-swept pastures we descended to forests, steep-sided valleys, and rushing rivers, and, still lower down, to irrigated lands, fields of ripe corn—already half harvested—and to settled conditions of life.

The scenery in the Kran Valley was gorgeous during the pageant of autumn: the larch trees were golden, and the birches and poplars had turned cinnamon-yellow and wine-red. We now had before us a new phase in our journey, namely, across a country apart from, and possessing little in common with, the rest of Central Asia. On reaching the mouth of the mountain-locked portion of the Kran Valley, our eyes suddenly gained a view of endless plains which lay spread out before us. Dropping, by an easy descent, to the foot of the range, we passed on towards this new land which stretched in featureless expanse to a far horizon, and, arriving at Sharasume, halted there in order to arrange our future movements.

[1] The Urkhogaitu, or Urmogaitu, is the only pass used as a trade-route between Northern Mongolia and Dzungaria. It is only open, however, for a short season. At the beginning of June, Major George Pereira had considerable difficulty in crossing it, but reported several caravans as having accomplished the passage at the end of that month. By the middle of October the pass is again closed.

CHAPTER XIII

DZUNGARIA—THE LAND OF UNREST

BEFORE embarking upon our voyage over the ocean-like steppes of Dzungaria, it may be well to give a brief survey of the country ahead of us, to record its history and to describe its physical features. An apology ought to be made for using the name Dzungaria,[1] as it suggests that the local inhabitants are Dzungars, whereas Dzungars no longer exist; the name remains, for no other title can be found for this odd corner of Inner Asia. Dzungaria does not belong to Chinese Turkestan—from which it is separated by a giant wall of mountains; it is not Mongolian—for the Altai Mountains form a boundary between the two countries; and, although it merges into the Gobi Desert on the east and into Southern Siberia on the west, it has nothing in common with either of those regions.

"Dzungaria" originated from the name of a small branch of a Mongol tribe, and when that branch became powerful and built up an empire, the name was extended to the whole confederation of tribes which that empire embraced. The original territory of the Dzungars was of much greater dimensions than the area to which their name is now applied; but the site

[1] The situation of Dzungaria in respect to China Proper justifies its meaning, namely, "on the left hand."

of the present-day Dzungaria always formed the centre of the Dzungar dominions.

Racially and historically the name is now a thing of the past; but, although the race has died out, to this day "Dzungaria" remains as a definite expression for an important geographical division of Asia.

I have called her the Land of Unrest, for Dzungaria has been for all time a debatable land, the common battle-ground of rival races and conflicting creeds,—a veritable cock-pit of Inner Asia. This strange land is situated midway between China and Siberia, on the boundaries of two great Empires, yet sufficiently far away from the centre of each to have avoided—until quite recently—being caught up in the net of empire. She is not rich enough to tempt a permanent colonization by either people, she is too far away for either to hold securely. Yet, lying on the high road to everywhere in Asia, every one passes this way; but only *passes*, for nothing seems to remain permanently in Dzungaria. The geographical features of the region have been fatal to permanence. She has been a thoroughfare for migrating peoples, the abiding-place of none; her conquerors have been destroyers—not constructors.

Situated, moreover, on the threshold of the Moslem and Buddhist worlds, in a region which has been the camping-ground of all the wild tribes which have, at different periods, overrun Asia, Dzungaria has inevitably been the prey of each recurring wave of migration which has broken across its boundless steppes. She has been the scene of wars and massacres,—the victim of the wildest vicissitudes, on a scale such as only Asia can produce. She was invaded by the Huns and overrun by the Mongols long before the Dzungars, suddenly rising to eminence, first set up a kingdom. While they, too, after overrunning wide areas of Asia, suddenly collapsed and left nothing but a name. When the Chinese invaded Dzungaria they killed off her population to a man—of six hundred thousand inhabitants not one remained. In order to repopulate this newly acquired territory, the Dungans (Chinese Mohammedans) were transported from Western China ; but the colonists became more powerful than their masters, and Dzungaria was once again the scene of massacres, for Islam rose against Cathay, and the Dungans killed the Celestials by hundreds of thousands. Small wonder, then, that Dzungaria has remained unsettled and uncivilized, that she has produced neither cities nor large cultivated areas, and that, although for the moment her throbbing deserts are at rest, her atmosphere is still one of uncertainty and alarm.

Although the name Dzungaria originally denoted a tribal area, it happened also to include a region remarkably well defined by natural boundaries; thus "Dzungaria" now represents a purely topographical division, standing apart and distinct from the surrounding regions. The Dzungaria of to-day embraces the whole of the inter-Altai-Tian Shan region, and is bordered by Mongolia on the east and Southern Siberia on the west. The land, as a whole, is lowland as compared with the rest of Mongolia, and forms part of the Siberian plains rather than of the Central Asian tableland. Yet, on the other hand, Dzungaria has the character of an inclined plain with a long and gentle ascent from the plains of Siberia to the plateau of Mongolia. The average altitude of the floor of this plain is about 1,500 ft. above sea-level ; in the west the level drops to 700 ft., and in the east, where it merges into the Gobi Desert, rises to 2,500 ft. Of a total area of 147,000 square miles, about two-thirds consists of plain, the remaining portion being composed of mountain-ranges, situated like a wall around the central basin, and forming in themselves a natural frontier against Mongolia, Siberia, Chinese and Russian Turkestan.

The plains of Dzungaria are of a complex character. For the most part they are composed of hard, dry steppe covered with a scanty growth of saxaul and tamarisk; but this is varied by large areas of saline desert and sand-dunes. The rivers descending into the plain from the border-ranges,—with the exception of the Manas River, —do not run far before sinking below the surface, thereby forbidding the employment of irrigation methods and causing the interior to remain arid and unproductive. In consequence, a certain portion of this region can never be of economic value, while the remainder, which is either reached by water or can be brought within its reach, presents itself as a suitable country for future expansion, although it is not yet utilized to any great extent. Nomad life, however, is not entirely absent from these regions, for even the sand-dunes supply a little pasture, and this is used by the shepherds in winter. In summer the inner deserts are destitute of human life, and even the explorer will find them most tedious to traverse, owing to their soft, salt-encrusted surface, the lack of water, and the great heat. No one but a "Mongol, a misanthrope, or a madman" would venture into Central Dzungaria in midsummer.

The border-ranges are the life of Dzungaria; they supply the pasture for the nomads, and the water for the agriculturists; they,—together with the warm zone of country lying at the foot of the mountains, between them and the deserts,—compose the whole of inhabited Dzungaria. In comparison with the deserts, the surrounding highlands are paradises of wealth and beauty. Well-named, indeed, is the southern border-range—the Tian Shan—or Heavenly Mountains. This giant range, together with its continuation—the Bogdo-ola and the Karlik Tagh—runs the whole length of Southern Dzungaria. A continuous line of ice-peaks and untrodden snow-fields lift themselves in exultation above the dusty plain, and send down their melting waters to supply the colonists with all they need to turn their lands to good account. The southern wall of Dzungaria is almost unbroken. In a length of eight hundred miles there are only two passes suitable for wheeled traffic ; one, leading over into Chinese Turkestan,—the Dabachin, situated to the south of Urumchi at the junction of the Tian Shan and Bogdo-ola, and the other, a nameless pass between Tou-shui and Ta-shih-tu which leads over the plateau between the Bogdo-ola and Barkul ranges. One other pass alone—the Talki—permits free intercourse between Dzungaria and the Ili Valley.

The second range of importance, which affects the welfare of Dzungaria, is the Altai. For a distance of four hundred miles these mountains form a frontier between Dzungaria and Mongolia, and supply not only immense pastures for nomads, but facilities for agriculture, and rivers which form a water-way to Siberia. The Mongolian Altai is the north-eastern border-range ; it abuts on the Russian frontier on the one hand, and stretches out into the Gobi Desert on the other.

On the north and west a string of ranges, orographically disconnected, but geologically the same, form a

TYPICAL SCENERY IN THE BORDER-RANGES OF DZUNGARIA.

In the Tian Shan Mountains.

378]

barrier between Dzungaria and Siberia; the barrier is, however, sufficiently broken to permit of easy communication between the two countries. The Tarbagatai, the Sair, the Urkashar, and Barlik groups, together with the Ala-tau, form this northern frontier. They are further described in another chapter.

"Mountains," says Rickmers, in his description of the physical features of the "Duab of Turkestan," "have been called the skeleton of the land, being guiding-lines to the eye; but we can extend the analogy to the backbone, which is also the nerve-centre, and as such the ruling influence in the development and vitality of a continent. The solution of Asiatic problems lies in the mountains."

The chief peculiarity of Dzungaria is its character as a mountain-locked basin, the position of its encircling ranges, in respect to the Siberian plains and the prevailing moisture-laden winds, making Dzungaria subject to phenomenal climatic conditions. The ranges surrounding Dzungaria are peculiarly situated in comparison with other mountainous regions of Inner Asia, for *all* these ranges, whether in the north, south, or west, appear to exercise a *positive*, and not a *negative*, influence (as is the case with so many of the ranges in Central Asia) on the country lying between them.

The Tian Shan, for instance, receives a heavy rainfall on its northern flank, which produces pine-forests and pastures, while the southern side of the watershed is a veritable abomination of desolation. This chain of mountains supplies Southern Dzungaria with refreshing summer rains, but at the same time minimizes the precipitation on its southern flank in Chinese Turkestan. We ourselves, whilst wandering in the desert zone at a distance of fifty miles from the foot of the mountains, experienced, at the end of May, heavy rain-storms. It rained continuously for twenty hours on one occasion, making the country almost impossible for travelling, the rain-storms creeping up from the west, and breaking across the plains to the north, as frequently as they did on the ranges to the south.

Curiously enough, the north-western border-range—the Altai—has reversed climatic conditions, the slopes facing south-west, and *not* those facing north-east, having the greater precipitation. Prof. Sapoznikoff,—the most recent as well as the most trustworthy writer on the Mongolian Altai,—says that, if the volumes of water flowing off the two sides of the range be compared, it is found that the flow of water from the south-west is by far the greater, this proving to be an exception to the rule generally accepted in regard to mountain-ranges in Inner Asia, where the north side has usually the greater precipitation. This contradiction is explained by the fact that the spurs on the south-western slopes are longer and higher than those on the north-east, and on this account become the better condensers of the moisture. The currents of air from the west and north-west encounter these outlying spurs and are relieved of their moisture; thus the precipitation on the farther side of the range is greatly minimized. The result is that the forests and pastures of the Dzungarian slopes of the Altai make very favourable conditions for a nomadic life, while the river-valleys grant facilities for future colonization.

The northern border-ranges of Dzungaria are, in like manner, clothed with forests and grass, the lower portions of the southern flanks alone being covered with desert flora.

It is this special factor in the climatic conditions of

Dzungaria that causes the locality to be such a well-favoured one, for of its total area only one-tenth is unproductive.   The course of desiccation, now in progress in Chinese Turkestan, does not extend to Dzungaria ; no sand-buried cities or dying forests are to be found ; and, as far as we could judge, the rivers extend as far out into the plain as they have done during a very long period.

The hydrography of Dzungaria is also peculiar.   The entire drainage from the encircling mountain-ranges is caught by self-contained lake-basins, with the exception of a portion of the Altai which drains, by way of the Irtish River, into the Arctic Ocean.   Much water drains from the surrounding ranges into the plain, but, on reaching it, the majority disappears below the surface, to reappear again at the level of the lakes.   The main rivers of Dzungaria, namely, the Borotala, the Emil, the Manas, and the Urungu, succeed in passing the belt of gravel and reach their destinations *above* ground, carving out for themselves deep ravines in the soft clay of the plains.

Between the highlands and the plain lies a zone of country neither mountain nor desert, free from extremes of climate, and rendered suitable for man's use by its admirable position.   This zone is to be found in characteristic form along the northern foot-hills of the Tian Shan, where rivers from the snow-clad ranges to the south pour down their waters through innumerable valleys on to the plain, thus supplying material for the carrying out of irrigation schemes.   The area of land rendered productive by these means is very considerable, and by systematic irrigation a still greater area could be brought into use.   The Manas River, for instance, wastes itself by evaporation in the Telli Nor, while pregnant lands on either bank lie dry and unutilized.

Much water disappears also in the zone of piedmont-gravel, but reapproaches the surface at about twenty miles from the foot of the mountains (at an altitude of from 1,500 to 2,000 ft.) in sufficient quantity to enable the land to support forests of stunted poplars and jungles of reeds and scrub. The productive belt is very narrow, but here and there tongues of vegetation stretch out across the plain, and denote the courses of the various rivers, which supply the necessary underground moisture.

This zone has been occupied, from time immemorial, by one of the earliest races of Central Asian agriculturists—the Uigurs—and at the present day it forms a colony for Chinese, Dungan, and Turki cultivators. Here have been built the large towns, including the government capital, and the centres of internal trade between Siberia, Mongolia, Turkestan, and China Proper. A boom in land speculation is taking place, which may greatly increase now that the former dumping-ground for colonists—Mongolia—has become a forbidden land to the Chinese; Dzungaria alone, of lands *within* the Empire, remains untenanted.

From these physical features and climatic conditions results the history of Dzungaria.

Dzungaria, before taking its name as the land of the Dzungars, was a no-man's-land, claimed at different periods by such ephemeral empire-builders as the Kara-Kitai, the Uigurs, the Naimans, and the Mongols; yet, it was never entirely under the sway of any of these peoples. The earliest traditions about this region centre around either the southern portion,—the site of the present capital, Urumchi,—which has always been a favoured locality, or the Emil Valley on the northern border, which, on account of its situation on the high-road between Eastern and Western Asia, has for ages formed the camping-ground of " princely-shepherds " and nomad-kings. These two localities contain all the principal historical associations of Dzungaria.

Landmarks in the history of Dzungaria are difficult to discern at so great a distance ; in fact, they are entirely lost to view if we look back beyond the ninth century A.D. Before that date all Inner Asia was the play-ground or battle-field of numerous unsettled, roaming bands of nomads, about whom we know very little. During the first three dynasties of China (until 249 B.C.) her western borders were not in relation with the Empire. At the commencement of the Hun Dynasty the spirit of conquest resulted in the incorporation of Kansu as a province, but no notice appears to have been taken of the far western regions, such as Turkestan and Dzungaria, nor is there any mention of them in the Imperial Annals, before the reign of Chien-lung in the eighteenth century.

Between the second century B.C. and the fifth century A.D. one particular tribe—the Huns—caused great changes and upheavals in Inner Asia. Emerging from the depths of Manchuria, they harried the marches of China and wandered across into Dzungaria on their way to Europe. This great human flood, however, left no trace behind it, and we have to wait until the ninth century A.D. before we find any part of Dzungaria actually occupying a position of importance. At that period the Uigurs, being driven out by pestilence, famine, and Kirghiz invaders from their home in Mongolia, migrated to Southern Dzungaria, and set up their second kingdom on the slopes of the Tian Shan mountains, with their capital at Bishbalik—the site of the present Urumchi.

The Uigur Kingdom embraced but a small portion

II—5

of Dzungaria—namely, the southern borders, at the foot of the Tian Shan—a district which corresponds precisely to the present-day colonies of Chinese and Dungans. This district was, in fact, the only portion offering facilities to an agricultural people, Dzungaria being divided into two zones, the northern portion for nomads and the southern for agriculturists. The remainder of the Uigur Kingdom was composed of the rich oases of Chinese Turkestan, on the southern side of the Tian Shan.

At this particular period Turki nomadic tribes, such as the Naimans, held the northern portion of Dzungaria, and the Kirei were resident in the Altai.

This state of affairs continued until the early part of the twelfth century, when another immigration of strangers occurred. In 1123 (according to Sir Henry Howorth) a prince of the Kitan, or Liao Dynasty, emigrated from China with a small band of followers. Gathering, on his way through Shensi, a considerable number of Turki adventurers, he travelled across the confines of China to the " land of Kirghises," and settled in Northern Dzungaria, where he built a town on the banks of the " Imil " (Emil). The result was the origin of the kingdom of the Kara-Kitai, who extended their power until they embraced not only all Dzungaria, but also Chinese and Russian Turkestan. The Kara-Kitai became the suzerains of the Uigurs and all the smaller nomadic peoples, until the Mongol avalanche was set in motion and eventually destroyed them.

Early in the thirteenth century the Mongols arose, and, sweeping all Inner Asia, entirely altered the map of racial-distribution. The Mongols were destroyers, not organizers, in consequence of which all permanent con-

MONGOL COIFFURE.
A woman of the Khalka tribe.

ditions in Dzungaria disappeared; but, since Northern Dzungaria formed the high-road between the extremities of the Mongol Empire, it played an important part, and the encampment of some great chieftain was always to be found in the Emil Valley. After the death of Jenghis Khan, Dzungaria fell to the lot of his third son, Oktai, or Ogodai, who also held Mongolia Propei ; it seems, however, to have been a bone of contention between Oktai and his brother Chagatai, who ruled over the Middle Kingdom of Turkestan and Afghanistan, and was generally in a state of unrest. Later, in 1254, the Emil district of Northern Dzungaria formed the headquarters of Kuyuk Khan, grandson of Jenghis.

As the power of the Mongols decreased, China regained her influence, and constant fighting took place along the Chinese-Mongol borders, until, in the middle of the fifteenth century, she finally threw off the Mongol yoke. Then Mongolia and Dzungaria lapsed into intrigues and quarrels between themselves, and nothing of note is recorded until the end of the seventeenth century, when movements of great importance again took place in Dzungaria.

A section of the Western Mongols, named after their leader, Eliutei, or Eleuth,[1] had been slowly gaining power in these regions, until in 1690, under their Khan Galdan, they conquered Samarkand, Bokhara, and Yarkand—

[1] The Eleuths are generally styled Kalmuks, a name which has stood for all branches of Western Mongol tribes, but has in itself no specific meaning. " Kalmuk " is not a Mongol word, but it seems to have been in use amongst the Turks for a very long period. Some writers claim that the word means "remnant," *i.e.* the broken branches of the great Mongol people who were left, as it were, as the Mongol flood receded from the west ; while others suggest that " Kalmuk " is only a corruption of " Kalpak," *i.e.* " fur cap," a name in use among Mohammedan Turks for all Mongol tribes.

the great cities of Turkestan. On the death of Galdan, his nephew Rabdan, who was chief of a small branch of the Eleuths named Songares or Dzungars, succeeded to the possessions of his uncle. He established a firm hold over all his subjects, and gave the name of his own tribe to his entire kingdom ; hence the origin of the name Dzungaria. Here arose, for the first time, a power whose headquarters were in this hitherto nameless portion of Inner Asia.

Rabdan must have been a man of remarkable ability. He is said to have hindered the Russian advance into Turkestan, and to have reduced the kingdom of Hami. He warred with China and invaded Tibet, where he contented himself with looting the monasteries. Eventually the Chinese drove the Dzungars out of Tibet, and retook Hami on behalf of its Khan,—who remained vassal to them,—while the Dzungars were pushed back into their own Dzungaria.

Then followed a short period when the Chinese stood aside and allowed anarchy to prevail amongst the tribes on the far western confines of her dominion. Rabdan, Khan of the Dzungar Empire, died, and his son continued a similar course of war and quarrel. All authority was lost on account of continual intrigue and assassination, many of the inhabitants fled from the country, including the Torguts, who migrated *en masse* into Russian territory, and the Empire gradually fell to pieces. Finally the leadership passed to an adventurer, Amursana, who played his cards first for the Dzungars, and then for the Chinese, and created such disturbance that, at last, when the Chinese appeared again on the scene, they annihilated the Dzungars and annexed their country. Of a population of 600,000 souls not a

Dzungar was left alive, and this country became once more an unhappy and depopulated land.

This date, 1750, marks the beginning of the period of Chinese ascendancy in the far western portion of her Empire, under the great ⸱Emperor Chien-lung, whose great ambition was to restore Chinese prestige in Central Asia. Dzungaria being depopulated, Chien-lung imported, as colonists into the country, Solons and Sibos, loyal fighting races on whom the Chinese could depend ; these people were given land in the Ili Valley; while Dungans (Chinese Mohammedans) settled in considerable numbers along the northern foot-hills of the Tian Shan. Chinese colonists began to recognize in Southern Dzungaria and the Ili Valley a new colony where life was easier than in the crowded home provinces ; while criminals and outlaws found that in this direction they could best escape the long arm of the law. Gradually Dzungaria began to assume a respectable and almost settled appearance. Towns of importance grew up, and even the Torguts, after their none too pleasant experiences in Russian territory, were invited to return and were offered lands in which to dwell.

All went well until disturbances and unrest amongst the Chinese Mohammedans, in the provinces of Kansu and Shensi, sent a wave of dissatisfied insurgents across to Dzungaria. In 1864 the Mohammedans rose against their rulers, the Dungan colonists captured the capital—Urumchi, and killed 130,000 Chinese ; the Ili Valley was also devastated, five out of its six towns were destroyed, and Dzungaria became once more the scene of bloodshed and war. For seventeen years disorder continued, and it was not until 1878 that the Chinese succeeded in crushing the revolt. In 1881 these outlying regions—Turkestan and Dzungaria—which had for ever been " a thorn in the flesh " of the Chinese, and had been lost and won several times, were incorporated into a province and named Sin-Kiang—the New Dominion. With characteristic persistency the tenacious Chinese have once again built up their fabric of government, greater towns supersede the former ones, colonists continue to pour into the country, trade grows, and, although ruined towns and villages still disfigure the landscape, there is not only every likelihood of progress in the future, but less chance of retrogression.

Such is the kaleidoscopic story of Dzungaria. Small wonder is it that ethnological confusion reigns at present in the ancient land of the Dzungars. The migratory hordes and conquering armies passing backwards and forwards, have left a flotsam and jetsam which now forms its population ; within this area reside remnants of every race which has used it as a camping-ground or attempted to make it a home. There are Mongols, Kalmuks, Kirghiz, Turki descendants of the ancient Uigurs, Chinese, Dungans, and Russians.

The tribal distribution is to-day much the same as it was formerly, in that Northern Dzungaria is still the nomads' land, while its southern borders are the home of the agricultural and settled section of the population. In enumerating the various races inhabiting Dzungaria at the present day, I shall deal with them under the separate headings of Nomadic Residents and Sedentary Residents, *i.e.* agriculturists, merchants, and officials,— including in this category occasional visitors. Roughly speaking, the Chinese form the merchant and official class, besides being the market gardeners ; the Moham-

NOMADS OF THE PLAINS.
Khalka Mongols.

medan Dungans and Chantos are the grain-growers ; while the Mongols and Kirghiz are the ranchers.

All Dzungaria outside the cultivated zone lying under the northern spurs of the Tian Shan is, practically speaking, a land in which the tribes live under nomadic conditions. Its physical features have been dealt with in another part of this chapter, and we can now supplement this by a description of the various peoples who wander over it. Mingled with the nomadic population is a small population of cultivators ; the lower Borotala in the west, for instance, holds out possibilities for agriculture, as also do the Emil Valley in the north, the Irtish in the east, and the lower Manas River,—flowing through the very heart of the central steppes,—all these may some day become centres of large sedentary communities. The nomadic tribes consist of the Turkish Kirei and Kasaks, as well as the Torguts and Charkhars of Mongol origin.

The distribution of the main section of the Kirei has been given in Chapter XII ; the very important mountain district surrounding the Emil Valley, on the northern frontier of Dzungaria, is inhabited by a western branch of these people. The Tarbagatai, Urkashar, Barlik, and Maili mountain-ranges are all used by them, the Kosho, or Kun Valley, between the Chagan-oba and Maili Mountains forming the centre of their range.

Kirghiz tribes, not belonging to the Kirei family, are to be found in certain localities in Tian Shan,—the southern border-range of Dzungaria,—as far east as Urumchi ; but, for the most part, Mongol—or, more truly, Kalmuk—tribes of Torguts hold the eastern portion of this range.

The Torguts of Dzungaria are divided into two

sections : those of the Kobuk Valley in the north, where
they live, in small reservations, under their hereditary
Khan ; and those of the Tian Shan, who have their
headquarters on the Yulduz plateau, but extend in small
communities along the whole Dzungarian side of the
range. The story of the Torguts is typical of the history
of Inner Asia, being that of a people buffeted about
by changing circumstances and generally " on the
move." All that now remains of the Torgut tribe in
Dzungaria, is merely the remnant of the once numerous
and important section of the Mongol people, who were
driven out during the stormy period of Dzungarian
ascendancy towards the end of the seventeenth century. The whole tribe then wandered westwards
across Southern Siberia, attempted to fight the Russians,
and finally promised them allegiance in return for
territory allotted to them on the banks of the Volga.
The exiles, however, did not rest securely in their new
home ; they were harassed by the other nomad tribes
of the region, who were jealous of their possessions,
and they eventually fell out with their Russian masters.

In 1770, within eighty years of their migration from
the east, they started off once more on a movement
which has been compared to the Exodus of the Israel-
ites from Egypt, and described as " the most extraordinary emigration of modern times." The entire
tribe, with the exception of a few thousand families,[1]

---

[1] Accounts vary as to the number of Torguts resident on the Volga
and of those who attempted the journey back to Dzungaria. The Torguts
estimated themselves at 50,000 tents; but, as this did not include lamas,
and as they naturally minimized their total on account of the levies
demanded of them, the number was probably nearly 65,000 to 70,000
families. It is said that 15,000 families remained on the Volga. Russian
accounts put the number of those who left the Volga at 40,000 families,
while the Chinese claim that 50,000 arrived back in Dzungaria.

under their leader Ubashi Khan, attempted to escape from the arms of Russia and to return to their old home, the desire being increased by an invitation from the Emperor Chien-lung, who, after depopulating Dzungaria, wished to find desirable colonists and promised the Torguts a home in their native land. The migration of a people, including men, women, children, flocks and herds ; the transport of all household belongings ; the actual journey, undertaken—as it was—in mid-winter, over bleak and barren steppes, for a distance of three thousand miles from the Volga to Dzungaria, form adequate material for a romance. Harassed by enemies, decimated by disease, starving, fighting for their lives and their belongings, unable to retreat, forced to advance or to die, the Torguts marched by slow and painful stages back to their own land. After running the gauntlet of Russian Cossacks and Kirghiz plunderers for eight months, the remnant arrived on the confines of China, and were given lands in the Kobuk district [1] of Northern Dzungaria, the Yulduz plateau, and the Kunguz and Tekes Valleys in Tian Shan. There exists also a small section of Torguts resident in the southern slopes of the Altai at the sources of the Urungu River, and on the Baitik Mountains, which latter region they share with the Kirei.

In Western Dzungaria is another reservation for a Mongol tribe, namely, the Borotala Valley. In this abundantly watered and well-protected region on the

[1] My reasons for considering the Kobuk Torguts a portion of the tribe who migrated to the Volga and back again, are gathered from the accounts given by Tsh'ovenn-iven, first Tao-tai of Southern Dzungaria, who relates that " in the thirty-sixth year of Kien-loung (Chien-lung) the Torguts, having at their head their chief, Tortsi-bek, settled themselves at seven days' march distant from and to the east of the town of Tarbagatai, in a place called Kiabek sali " (Kobuk sali, or Kobuk Valley).

south side of the Ala-tau Range dwell a section of the Charkhars, the story of whose introduction to this land compares with the strange wanderings of the Torguts, in that the migration of Charkhars was compulsory and not voluntary. We, in these days of sedentary life, narrow conventionalities, and, in most cases, carefully delineated frontiers, can scarcely realize the magnitude of those men-movements which took place in the old days. In former times a conqueror thought nothing of shifting a whole nation across a continent, or of colonizing the lands he had laid waste by importing bands of captives. The world is now so cramped and crowded, that carefully surveyed and jealously guarded frontiers forbid such excursions as those made by the Torguts, the Eleuths, and the Charkhars. A nation, or even a tribe, would find considerable obstacles in its way if it started to overrun Asia.

The Charkhars were once a ruling tribe in Southern Mongolia, outside the Great Wall. Owing, however, to their formidable numbers and warlike nature, the Chinese greatly feared them, and, when opportunity occurred, they took the chance of breaking their power and transporting them in bulk to the furthermost corner of the Empire. The Borotala Valley was given them as a reservation on which no other tribes might encroach, and, if I mistake not, they are better off there than if they had been left in Southern Mongolia, for those "lands of high grass" have since been overrun by Chinese colonists, to the detriment of the few nomads who remained.

The Charkhars abound in large encampments along the banks of the Borotala, and even a few Chanto and Chinese farmers have found a footing for themselves

A CHARKHAR OF RANK.

by renting land at an exorbitant price from the chiefs, who were said to extort from them 50 per cent. of their produce. The upper portion of the valley belongs to the " Kho-ching " section of the Charkhars, who were the original settlers, while the " Chi-ning " occupy the lower portion and the district of Sairam Nor.

We noted the superior type of the Charkhars, in comparison with the Torguts. They were *almost* clean-looking, possessed some fine yurts, and appeared to be well-to-do. We were again struck by the paradoxical condition of a people having the appearance of being at a standstill in a magnificent and pregnant land. There is land to waste in the Borotala ; it would hold a far denser nomadic population, not to mention an agricultural one ; the Chinese protection of the Mongol rights of ownership alone hinder the Kasaks and the Chantos from overrunning it. Yet, in spite of every advantage, the Charkhars do not appear to increase.

From this it will be seen that the nomadic population is chiefly concentrated on the border-ranges of Dzungaria. In the far east—on the slopes of the Altai—are the Torguts, in the north-east—the Kirei, on the northern border-ranges—the Torguts and Western Kirei, in the west—the Charkhars, while on the southern side is a sprinkling of Torguts and Kirghiz. The central plains, except along the course of the Manas River, are practically uninhabited.

There now remains to be described the zone of country between the spurs of the Tian Shan and the deserts ; the area where much water from the snow-clad mountains makes irrigation-methods practicable, sedentary life an advantage, and, consequently, the building of towns a necessity. The inhabitants of this district consist of the resident-sedentary class, for the most part new-comers, and include colonists, merchants, and the official element. The vast proportion of the settlers are Dungans and Chinese, who take up small holdings and lead an easy and profitable existence. There are also a few Chantos from Chinese Turkestan, but these latter fare badly when they come in contact with the crafty Celestials. The Dungan population is considerable, especially in the well-favoured Manas district. They all came originally from the provinces of Kansu and Shensi, but beyond this fact the origin of the Dungan, or " Turgani," is very vague ; it has, indeed, been called " the most obscure problem in Asiatic history." [1] The Dungans are strict Mohammedans, in that they rigorously observe the two dogmas, of abstinence from the eating of swine's flesh and from the use of spirits ; neither do they touch opium. They are, in consequence, a healthier, hardier, bolder, and braver race than the Chinese, and of even greater activity and astuteness.

The Dungan is a wonderful fellow, although rather insolent and unmanageable. He is even superior to the wily Chinese when it becomes a question of business sagacity. The Chinese formula for the comparative capabilities of the Christian, the Jew, the Dungan, and the Celestial is as follows : One Jew can cheat ten Christians ; one Chinaman is the equal of ten Jews ; but one Dungan can get the better of ten Chinese !

The Chinese Mohammedan has caused trouble in the past. He has been overcome by superiority of numbers, but he has forgotten nothing, and only waits until his chance occurs again. If there were no likeli-

[1] See Appendix A.

hood of interference on the part of Russia, the Dungans would revolt again on the least provocation.

The Chinese element is chiefly official and commercial, and, in consequence, makes up the resident population of the towns. In Dzungaria there are altogether five towns of greater and two of lesser importance. Of the first mentioned there are: Urumchi, the capital, where resides a Futai—the governor of Dzungaria and Chinese Turkestan, a Grand Treasurer, a Tartar General, and a considerable garrison; Chuguchak—on the northern frontier—of economic and strategical importance, but not at present utilized to any great extent; Manas, the agricultural centre—the granary of Dzungaria; Guchen, the terminus of the trans-Gobi trade-route, and Barkul, of no particular note. Of lesser size are Shi-kho, at the junction of the Chuguchak and Ili roadways, and Sharasume, the new military post in the Altai. These towns form the temporary homes of the Chinese rulers, the military element, and the traders.

Here the Celestials live, completely oblivious of the fact that they are, in reality, exiled, among entirely foreign surroundings. They show here that extraordinary adaptability to their surroundings which marks them all the world over, whether in the Port of London, in San Francisco, Australia, or South Africa.

Besides the Chinese, Chanto merchants do a very considerable trade in local produce, and are the agents for Russian goods, which find a ready market. In Urumchi alone the Turki population numbers a quarter of the whole.

Over this nondescript population rules—or rather ruled—the Emperor of China through the agency of the

Viceroy of Kansu and Shensi, who deputes a Governor to look after the affairs of Dzungaria.

Dzungaria gave me the impression of a vast land awaiting development, but cursed by the blight of unrest, continual insurrection and rebellion. Without a strong government these potentially wealthy lands must long remain vacant. Dzungaria represents the neutral zone between vast China and vaster Russia. Will the Dragon arouse herself, and send her surplus millions to make this land a garden, or will Dzungaria be swept up by a greater Russian Empire?

CHAPTER XIV

FROM THE ALTAI TO THE ILI VALLEY

On September 20th, 1910, we reached Sharasume, a small military post which the Chinese have built comparatively recently in the Kran Valley, with the intention of guarding this, the only, route connecting Dzungaria with Northern Mongolia. We found Sharasume to consist of several " Yamens "—residences of Chinese officials—a mud fort for the garrison, and a group of houses and stores belonging to Chinese, Tartars, and Chantos.[1] This post represented the headquarters of the Chinese Amban of the Altai, who was immediately under the Emperor in Pekin, and reported directly to him. Quite recently the garrison had been strengthened, and there had been an increase of military activities, in order to re-establish the prestige of the Celestial Empire. When on the spot we were at a loss to discover the exact reason for this innovation, but recent affairs in Mongolia have proved to us that it was merely an attempt to bluff the

[1] The name of Chanto will constantly recur throughout the following chapters, and needs some explanation. It is the Chinese generic name for all Mohammedan-Turki sedentary people, meaning literally " wound round their heads," or turban-wearers. It corresponds to the Russian term " Sart," as applied to the sedentary population of Russian Central Asia. All the inhabitants of Chinese Turkestan are Chantos, but they have no such broad title for themselves,—as a people they have no name, —describing themselves only according to the towns to which they belong, viz. Kashgarlik, Turfanlik, Kumulik.

Mongol chieftains. In this out-of-the-way frontier post, at a distance of 1,500 miles from Pekin, the Chinese kept up as great state as if they were at home. But the prestige of the Empire they represented became a negligible quantity when we reviewed the poorly clad, slouching band of ruffians who, armed with old German rifles and *pikes*, formed the garrison.

Sharasume had, however, the makings of an important settlement; it was not only the centre of a large nomadic population, thus holding out good prospects for trade, but the Kran Valley—although undeveloped—possessed all that was necessary for the creation of a large agricultural district. Even now there is a considerable area under cultivation, though supplying only sufficient for local consumption. The Chinese and Chantos possessed promising market-gardens, in which they grew vegetables and melons; whilst wheat, millet, and a few oats were cultivated in irrigated fields by the semi-nomadic Kirei and Torgut Mongols. This led to the interesting discovery that in the Kran and Upper Irtish Valleys signs were not lacking of the nomads becoming more or less sedentary, in that, they were cultivating the land, and even building occasional isolated farm-houses. The population of the Kran Valley must be considerable, but, being a migratory one—the cultivators of the land near Sharasume moving down to the steppes after the harvest is over—it is difficult to estimate. The settlement itself had a population of about 2,000.

In the bazaars we found all we needed in the form of stores, such as rice, flour, eggs, tea, and sugar; we even bought apples which had come from Urumchi in Southern Dzungaria, and dried apricots imported from Turfan in Chinese Turkestan. The traders were chiefly Chantos from the large oases of Southern Dzungaria, all of whom had originally come from the towns of the Tarim basin. Sharasume is an isolated settlement. Its nearest neighbour is Kobdo, at a distance of a hundred and sixty miles, but from Kobdo it is separated by the main chain of the Altai; Chuguchak in Northern Dzungaria is about two hundred and forty miles distant, while Urumchi and other towns of Southern Dzungaria are over two hundred and sixty miles away. Over these wide stretches of country there are neither towns nor villages.

We now began to formulate plans for our intended exploration in Dzungaria. Before us lay the fact that the fast approaching winter would hinder all scientific work, the birds were already migrating to warmer regions, the mammals were hibernating; and a country under such conditions of snow and intense cold would render impossible the carrying on of survey-work.

Travelling, however, was comparatively easy, and the itinerary drawn up gave us time to traverse Dzungaria and to bring us closely in touch with its winter aspect before the coming spring allowed us once more to start detailed work.

Leaving Sharasume on September 24th, we were faced by a forty days' journey along the northern frontiers of Dzungaria, to Kulja in the Ili Valley, where we had our winter quarters for a couple of months during the reconstruction of our caravan and outfit. There, Price left us for a journey through Russian Turkestan and the Caucasus on his way to England, while early in January Miller and I started again, and followed the trade-route which runs the whole length of Southern Dzungaria. During March and April we explored and mapped in detail the extreme eastern portion of the Tian Shan

II—6

mountain-system—the Karlik Tagh. In summer we again traversed Dzungaria in its central portion, visiting the Western Kirei in their home on the Barlik and Maili ranges and the Charkhar Mongols in the Borotala Valley, thus completing our investigation of the varied inhabitants of Dzungaria. On July 23rd we returned to Kulja, having thoroughly carried out our programme.

Our objective on setting out from Sharasume was the Chinese frontier town of Chuguchak, two hundred and fifty miles distant, which we hoped to reach in eighteen days, with the help of twelve Bactrian camels hired through the medium of the officials at Sharasume. Our request for transport met with immediate response, but we were given to understand that there was a fixed rate of hire for such transport. This little incident brought home to us that we were now travelling under new conditions, and that Mongolia, with its tax of " free transport for travellers " was a thing of the past. Dzungaria forms a portion of a vast western appanage of China, only recently incorporated into a province, and named Sin-Kiang—a term which means, literally, the New Dominion ; it includes Chinese Turkestan, the Ili Valley, and Dzungaria, and exists under the same administration as does any province of China Proper. Thus, Dzungaria is subject to China, and differs from Mongolia, which is—or rather was—under the protection of the Manchu rulers.

Our route led us across the valleys of the lower Kran and of the Black Irtish, a short distance to the east of the point where the two valleys joined ; we found this region to be one of vast reed-beds, lagoons, and sand-hills, with belts of poplar and willow-trees bordering the river-courses. The altitude was not more than 1,500 ft.

THE BARKUL MOUNTAINS, A PORTION OF THE SOUTHERN BORDER-RANGE OF DZUNGARIA.

THE EXPEDITION CROSSING DZUNGARIA.

(133)

above sea-level, and the pleasant warmth of the air felt like the heat of midsummer to us—fresh from the bitter winds and exposure of the Mongolian plateau. Small wonder is it that these low-lying valleys are favoured so greatly as winter quarters by both Kirghiz and Mongol shepherds; it arouses in us no surprise that it was here Jenghis Khan made his principal " rendezvous," and here that he massed his troops before starting westwards on his conquering marches.

The upper Irtish Valley is fairly well populated by Torgut Mongols and Kirei Kirghiz ; there are possibilities for cultivation and openings for trade ; it is also probable that in the near future the Irtish River may be used for the purposes of transport.   In the summer the Siberian Irtish is navigated as far up as Lake Zaisan—a short distance away on the Russian side of the frontier ; recently, however, it has been discovered that no reason exists why the river should not be used for navigation right up the junction of the Kran and the Irtish, at a point not far below where we crossed the latter river.   Should this be carried out it would be a considerable aid to the wool-merchants, who buy up the produce of the flocks belonging to the Kirei and the Torguts, as it would bring the Russian markets into much closer communication with them.[1]

We crossed the Kran with ease by means of a shallow ford, but found the Irtish just north of the Ulungur Lake a deep-flowing, sluggish stream of a hundred yards in

[1] A name which looms large on even quite recent maps is Bulon-tokhoi, a town situated at the southern end of Lake Ulungur.   Forty years ago Russian travellers described the town as a fine centre for commercial purposes, and as consisting of two quarters containing 160 houses of Chinese and 150 of Mongols.   Now, however, Bulon-tokhoi has disappeared, and its trade has shifted to the better situated centre of Tulta or Sharasume.

width, and we were obliged to search carefully before we could find a place suitable for crossing without harm to our baggage. The water was clear and blue, margined by sand-banks, which showed that in time of flood the river would be at least a hundred and fifty yards wide.

Beyond the Irtish extended a barren hill-country leading over the Naryn Kara and the Kara-adir to the Kobuk Valley, another centre of nomadic life. These isolated localities, inhabited, probably, by people of different races, are typical of Dzungaria ; to-day we may be with the Turki-Kirei, to-morrow with a Mongol colony ; while a week's journey over uninhabited steppes may separate these from a Chinese town or a Dungan settlement. The unusual variety of races inhabiting Dzungaria gives an interest to a country which might otherwise, from lack of character, be monotonous and tedious to traverse.

This stage in our journey led us past Lake Ulungur, which stores a large volume of water descending from the slopes of the Altai, and apparently absorbs the same, having no visible outlet. We caught glimpses of this lake from the Naryn Kara range, and noted its character, as being that of a typical desert-lake : barren, yellow, desert hills surrounded it ; no margin of green bordered its shores, the only vegetation being a fringe of dead reeds. A Russian explorer, Miroshnishenko, took some trouble in 1873 to prove that the Lake Ulungur must drain into the Irtish, which flows past only four miles away. There is, however, no visible communication between the two, though a Kirghiz legend speaks of a subterranean passage connecting the lake with the river. By measuring the volume of the Irtish some way *above* the lake, and again below

Miroshnishenko found the flow of the river to increase 89,000 cubic ft. of water per minute, in spite of the fact that the Irtish receives no tributaries throughout this section of its course. The most recent scientific explorer in these regions, Prof. Sapoznikoff, refutes this opinion, basing his arguments on the following grounds. Firstly, the water of the lake is at a *lower* level than that of the Irtish ; secondly, the water is strongly saline (2 gr. to the litre), a peculiarity of enclosed basins ; and thirdly, neither the lake nor the river flowing into it contain certain fish, peculiar to the Irtish. My own opinion is that the Ulungur does not now connect with the Irtish, although it may have done so at an earlier period ; even then, it was not by the nearest route, on the eastern side—where the Irtish and the lake are only a few miles apart—but by way of the low-lying depression on the west.

We camped for a night in this plain, called Mukutai, and noted that, although the ground was very saline, good grass grew, and there was a very large encampment of Kirei making use of it for pasture. The whole of this depression showed signs of being under water at certain seasons ; it is dead level, and the Ulungur Lake spreads itself into it for some way in the form of lagoons and shallows having no definite boundary. A small rise of water in the lake would bring a great area of the Mukutai plain under water. We camped about ten miles from the margin of the lake ; on the other side of us, at about twenty miles' distance, there was a small stream which drained direct towards the Irtish River, and, were it not for lack of water, would undoubtedly reach it. Thus it seems that, if at one period the water of the Lake Ulungur stood at a higher level, it must certainly have flowed out through this hollow, and joined the Irtish some eighty miles farther to the north-west.

Travelling westwards as rapidly as our well-laden camels permitted, we arrived, three days after leaving our camp near Ulungur, at the Kobuk Valley. The Sair Mountains, rising on the north to an altitude of 12,000 ft., supplied ample water, which irrigated the Kobuk pastures before running to waste in the deserts to the south. Here we found a large community of Torgut Mongols inhabiting a locality which, since the earliest days of recorded history, has been a desirable camping-ground. The story of the Torguts of the Kobuk steppe, and of their migration from the far west has been given in a previous chapter, and their past condition, there described, is decidedly more interesting than their present. Exceptional dirt and disease—even for Mongol degenerates—made these people most objectionable to deal with; it is probable that at no very distant date, the fast-increasing Kirghiz or Kasak tribes will encroach on their territory to the lasting detriment of the Torguts.

There was an air of settled life amongst the people of the Kobuk, for the yurts clustered in closely packed groups round the Buddhist temple and the residence of their Chief. We observed attempts being made to cultivate the soil, and the yurts frequently possessed a " kraal "—or enclosure—close by, in which they kept their flocks and a supply of hay for the winter's use. The temple and its precincts, together with the abode of the Chief, composed a block of buildings. The Chief, who held the title of Wang, was the hereditary ruler of the tribe, and, although the possessor of a house built

MAKANDAROFF AND HIS PETS.

CAMP BREAKFAST.

404]

in a quaint mixture of Russian and Chinese styles, he preferred to use his yurt. The Wang entertained us in the house, which was furnished chiefly with large mirrors and numerous clocks, besides a gramophone and a photograph of himself!

The Kobuk being half-way between Sharasume and Chuguchak, we changed our camels for fresh ones supplied by the Wang, and made tracks westwards. Camel transport is slow work under the best conditions, and is exceptionally tedious when all ambition is centred on advancing as quickly as possible and reaching one's destination. The actual distances covered by either camels or horses in a day's march does not really differ to any great extent. Camels move more steadily and slowly, keeping up continuously from dawn to dusk; horses, on the other hand, trek faster but for a shorter time. We used to break camp every morning at 7, start the caravan by 9 or 10, and travel till about 4.30 p.m., thus averaging fifteen to eighteen miles a day. We covered the distance between the Altai and the town of Chuguchak in two stages of nine and eight days each, changing camels half-way. The cost of the eleven camels and the six riding-horses came to about £22 for the whole journey. We ourselves rode on horseback. Our caravan had quite an imposing appearance, consisting, as it did, of a string of eleven baggage-camels, half a dozen natives—and our own party of four—all on horseback; added to which were nineteen of our caravan-horses from far-distant Siberia. These were driven along unladen, as we intended to sell them on reaching a likely market.

Travelling by the longest stages allowed by the rapidly shortening days, we left the Kobuk steppe and crossed a pass of 6,300 ft., called Kergen Tash, lying between the Urkashar Range and the Sair Mountains. This route led us into Russian territory for ten or twelve miles, before it turned back and recrossed the frontier at the Bai Musa Pass, which was an open gap, of 4,300 ft. in altitude, between the Tarbagatai Range on the north and the Kojur spur of the Urkashar on the south. As a means of communication between the Chuguchak district and that of Zaisan, this track, being suitable for wheeled traffic, is of some importance. Even this short return to Russian territory showed us definite traces of Russian progression. We observed a picket of frontier guards at the Bai Musa Pass, and in the distance —northwards—a large new settlement, where there was said to be a garrison of Cossacks and a go-ahead colony of emigrants from Semipalatinsk.

The Emil Valley—which we passed through on our way to Chuguchak—is of much historical interest. This valley, situated on the main road between Eastern and Western Asia, providing, as it does, the one easy means of access from the east to the west, is now, and always must have been, of great strategical value. It was mentioned by Carpini, one of the earliest Western writers, who travelled through the country on his way to visit the court of Kuyuk Khan—grandson of Jenghis Khan—in Northern Mongolia. It must have been in those days a district of real importance, for Carpini wrote that the Mongols " had built anew, as it were, a city called Omyl, in which the Emperor had erected a house." Evidently the old city was destroyed when Jenghis first sacked the Empire of the Kara-Kitai —of which this district was a part. The Emil district formed the seat of Kalmuk ascendancy at the end of the seventeenth century, and it was here the Dzungars fixed their capital during the short-lived period of their empire. China now holds the upper half of the Emil Valley, but Russia, holding the lower portion, exercises her control over this gateway between east and west. The district is, without doubt, a rich one; it is low-lying, well watered, and bordered on north and south by sheltering mountain-ranges. On entering we found the country positively swarming with Kasaks, who were moving with their flocks into their winter quarters in the sheltered valleys of the Kojur and Urkashar ranges. As far as the eye could see, were herds of horses and flocks of sheep, numbering tens of thousands, ; here and there were scattered villages of yurts and isolated mud-houses—the farms of the sedentary Kasaks and Chanto cultivators; such a confusion of nomadic and settled conditions of life we had never before witnessed. Should a future colonization of the nomads' plain take place on a large scale much trouble is obviously in store for them. Even now the herds of the nomads were wandering over the fields of the farmers; but, as the harvest was over and the grain being threshed, the confusion was of no consequence.

A further sign of the approach of winter—confirmed a week later by the first fall of snow—was a remarkable migration of sand-grouse, which we watched on October 10th and 11th, as we moved across the Emil steppes. With a strong west wind behind them, large packs and small parties of sand-grouse were to be seen hurrying towards the south-east. During the two days' trek the birds continued to pass over us, the large packs flying high, but small flocks of half-dozens flying quite low and all moving with the directness of flight and the great speed peculiar to the sand-grouse family. The majority consisted of the common Central Asian variety, Pallas'; but there were also many large Black-bellied Sand-grouse amongst them. This was probably the great autumn migration of all the birds of the Sergiopol and Semipalatinsk steppes to their winter quarters, in the plain of Dzungaria.

On October 11th we camped outside the high walls of Chuguchak. Although we had been travelling for nearly five months, this was the first town of any description we had entered since leaving the Siberian town of Minnusinsk, which showed the true character of the Siberian-Chinese frontier,—a sparsely populated nomads'-land, not requiring much administration. Chuguchak was a typical Chinese town, as seen throughout China Proper, with high walls, great gateways, and yamens. There we found ourselves once more in touch with civilization, for the Russian element brought into the town an atmosphere of the West, and progress was represented by the post-office and telegraph-lines; we could here telegraph, if we wished, to Pekin or Europe, and did, actually, receive letters from Europe.

The population of Chuguchak is estimated at 9,000, this figure including both Chinese and Russians, as well as a very mixed community of traders who were called Chantos if they were Chinese subjects, or Sarts if they belonged to Russian Turkestan. There existed also a small colony of true Russians and a few Tartars. Business was at high pressure; the streets were full and the bazaars were crowded, the buyers being chiefly Kirghiz and Kasaks from the surrounding steppe purchasing their winter supplies. An appearance of progress prevailed, as well as a somewhat blatant show of

IN CHUGUCHAK.

408]

military strength on the part of the Chinese, which must have greatly amused our Russian friends. The morning air resounded with bugle-calls and the continual firing of salutes; but it is doubtful whether this suggestion of power impressed even the natives.

Chuguchak is the chief outlet to Siberia for all Dzungaria. Its future may be full of possibilities. Here lies the only open road between Western China and Russian Asia; for all other tracks,—with the sole exception of a peculiar deep-cut trench, the Dzungarian Gate, which lies to the west of Chuguchak,—must pass the mountain barrier. By way of an easily graded pass of 5,945 ft. above sea-level, situated about eighty miles to the south of the town, one can travel without hindrance from the Siberian plains to the Dzungarian deserts and on to China, Mongolia, or the Gates of Pekin.

Although eager to pursue our journey to Kulja, and with no desire to stay more than a day in Chuguchak, we found ourselves delayed for *fifteen* days in the most aggravating manner before being able to start again. The nearness of a Russian post-road and its methods of quick transport made us think of reaching Kulja through Russian territory; telegrams requesting permission to do so were even despatched to the Governor-General at Tashkent, but when the reply came that the permit would have to be obtained in St. Petersburg, former experience made us aware that, under the circumstances, it would be far quicker to *walk* to Kulja.

Two other routes were open to us: the road which runs southwards, joins the Pei-lu, or northern high-road in Southern Dzungaria, and thence turns westwards to the Ili Valley; or a horse-track running in a direct

line over mountain, hill, and hollow by way of the
Barlik Mountains, the Dzungarian Gate, and the Lower
Borotala to Sairam Nor and the Ili Valley.

The former of these routes was a well-used trade-route,
divided into regular stages, by which means the journey
could be accomplished in twenty days. The country to
be passed through was uninteresting, had often been
traversed before, and the thought of spending twenty
days in carts did not in the least attract us. We decided
accordingly to take the most direct but most arduous
of the routes, and began to arrange our transport. The
finding of this delayed us still further, owing to its being
the busiest season for caravans. Eventually we procured thirteen camels from a Chanto owner, at the rate
of 36s. per camel for the journey of eighteen to twenty
days ; the Chinese authorities supplied us with two
" jigits," or out-riders, who would escort us from one
frontier guard-house, or " karaul," to another ; and
finally, on October 27th, we set off in very bad weather,
over the Emil plain, at that time half under water and
most unsuitable for camel transport.[1]

The route we followed was practically the frontier
line of the two Empires ; we managed to reach a Chinese
guard-house each day, and were informed of the existence
of corresponding Russian posts to our west. On one
occasion we actually visited a small post which served as
a quarantine station for all cattle and flocks going from
China into Russian territory ; apart from this we saw
nothing to indicate that we were anywhere near the
frontier. As we rode along the foot-hills of the Barlik

---

[1] We had the first touch of winter during the third week in October,
when snow fell, which later turned to rain. The temperature varied,
during the period between the 13th and 27th, from 80° to 12° Fahr.

group [1] we beheld, spread out to the west, a wonderful expanse of steppes and of lakes, shimmering as in a mirage, giving strange contrasts of blue and of yellow, and stretching in endless succession as far as the eye could reach towards the distant plains of Northern Turkestan. On the east the Barlik ranges rose to an altitude of 9,500 ft., and, far away in the dim distance, the loftier snows of the Ala-tau lifted themselves into the blue; but, separating us from them, was a break in the mountain-wall,—a deep-cut depression dividing the Siberian plains from the Dzungarian deserts, and lying between the ramparts of the Ala-tau on the west and those of the Barlik on the east.

We had frequently heard of the terrors, dangers, and winds of the Dzungarian Gate. We had read the records of such early travellers as Carpini and Rubruck, both of whom mentioned that " there blows nearly continuously such a wind through this valley, that persons cross it with great danger, lest the wind should carry them into the sea." We therefore approached this remarkable geological phenomenon both with interest and a certain amount of anxiety, for the weather was unusually unsettled, snow-clouds were threatening us, and we were unwilling our caravan should be " blown away into the sea."

Even at a distance, with the Dzungarian Gate lying before us—unseen, we instinctively became aware of its presence; for when we came within sight of Ala Kul, whilst crossing the open foot-hills of the Barlik Range

[1] The Barlik proper overlooks the Dzungarian Gate on the east. We found the natives using Barlik for the whole mountain-group to the east. I use the term, therefore, to include the Chagan-oba, the Dzusau, and the Maili ranges.

some twenty miles from the lake-shore and some 2,000 ft.
above it, we were in absolute stillness ; and yet, strangely
enough, the waters of Ala Kul were tossed into waves—
the white crests being clearly seen with a glass, while
even with the naked eye breakers could be distinguished
dashing on to the southern shore of an island in the
middle of the lake. Although we were becalmed, there
was evidently a gale blowing through the " Gate,"
and as we approached nearer we became at every step
more keenly alive to the action of this wind-trough.
At night we heard a distant roar as the imprisoned
winds of the Dzungarian deserts escaped through this
narrow defile. The only night we camped on the
very shore of the straits, the wind increased to such
a violence that our tents, though well protected in a
valley, were by the morning all blown away, for the
wind swept in great gusts over the hills, and the
back eddies tore them down ; the noise was terrific,
and sleep out of the question. This wind came from
the south, but threatening storm-clouds to the north
made us far more uneasy.

Fortunately we succeeded in crossing the depression
in a nine hours' trek without mishap, a strong head-wind
being the only cause for annoyance. Had there been
rain or snow falling, travelling would have been impossible, but the wind was luckily from the south and
comparatively warm, the temperature at night only
just touching freezing-point. Only just in time did we
escape from this home of the winds, for the day after
crossing the valley,—when travelling southwards along
its western flanks,—the wind swung round to the north
and swept cruelly through the gap, bringing with it hail
and frozen snow. Had we then been journeying north-

wards the making of any headway would have been out
of the question, for neither man nor beast could have
faced the elements; travelling as we were—*with* the
wind—we endured the cold and congratulated ourselves
on our fortunate escape. A bleak, inhospitable landscape now surrounded us, mountains, clad in fresh snow,
showed up here and there through breaks in the blurred
atmosphere, and great cloud-banks swept through the
" straits," as if rushing through some gigantic funnel.
We enjoyed no rest until we were safely ensconced in
the broken and wind-worn granite range lying to the
north-west of Ebi Nor.

The natives relate the usual traditions as to the
origin of the winds in this locality. In the myths
of Central Asia a "hole in the mountain," or "an
iron gate in a lake" is the usual explanation of the
origin of winds. In the case of which I am writing
the island called Ala-tyube—a small extinct volcano in
Ala Kul—is made responsible for the furious winds which
sweep through the depression ; the wind is called " ebe,"
or " yube " by the Kirghiz, and in special cases, when
it reaches its maximum velocity, the term " buran " is
applied. From autumn to spring the prevailing wind
is from the south-east.[1] I think, however, that the

[1] I found considerable difficulty in getting reliable information as
to the prevailing winds of this district. A Russian who had lived at a
frontier post in the Dzungarian Gate said that the strongest burans always
came from the south-east, while the rain-winds came from the north-west.
He said that " the air was always moving," but that autumn and spring
were especially marked as the windy seasons. Chinese soldiers in the
guard-houses on the high-road which passes the south end of Ebi Nor
where there is a belt of sand-dunes, claimed that, when the sand moved,
it always came from the north-west, or the direction of the Dzungarian Gate.
Their statement was proved by the fact that their guard-houses in the
sand-belt were banked up by high sand-dunes on the north-west. The
burans, they said, also came from the direction of the Gate. In contra-

wind which causes havoc amongst the nomads, and kills off men and flocks when caught unprotected, is this north wind when it attains the velocity of what is called a " buran."

We experienced one buran only during our journey across Asia, and it took place in this very locality during the following summer. On June 20th a buran struck us from the north when camped on the south side of the main ridge of the Dzusau portion of the Barlik group, which stood up like a wall close above our camp, and gave us protection from that quarter. In Central Asia the highest gale is inconsiderable in comparison with a buran. A vast difference lies between the two : a buran blows steadily, without lulls, and with a force against which it is useless to contend.

Miller describes how this buran caught him, when on a hunting expedition :—"On the second day away an ever-increasing wind began to blow from the north-west, though the sky was cloudless. By the evening it had blown up into such a gale that we had the greatest difficulty in reaching the yurts for which we were making. It was all our horses could do to move against the force of the wind, which frequently shifted us in our saddles. By night-time the yurt in which we had taken shelter began to suffer. The huge pieces of felt which covered the roof worked loose, and were whisked away, causing the frame-work to rattle down upon us. It was only the

diction of this, I noticed that all the sand-dunes at the south end of Ebi Nor were formed by winds which must have blown from the east-north-east. Ebi Nor, by its very name, is "wind-lake," and it would be hard to give an impression of the sight its frozen waters presented in midwinter. We saw it in January, from the crest of a sand-dune on its southern edge. Its southern shores were a jumble of great blocks of ice piled up in fantastic shapes, and the actual surface of the ice was as if its waves had been instantaneously frozen solid in stormy weather.

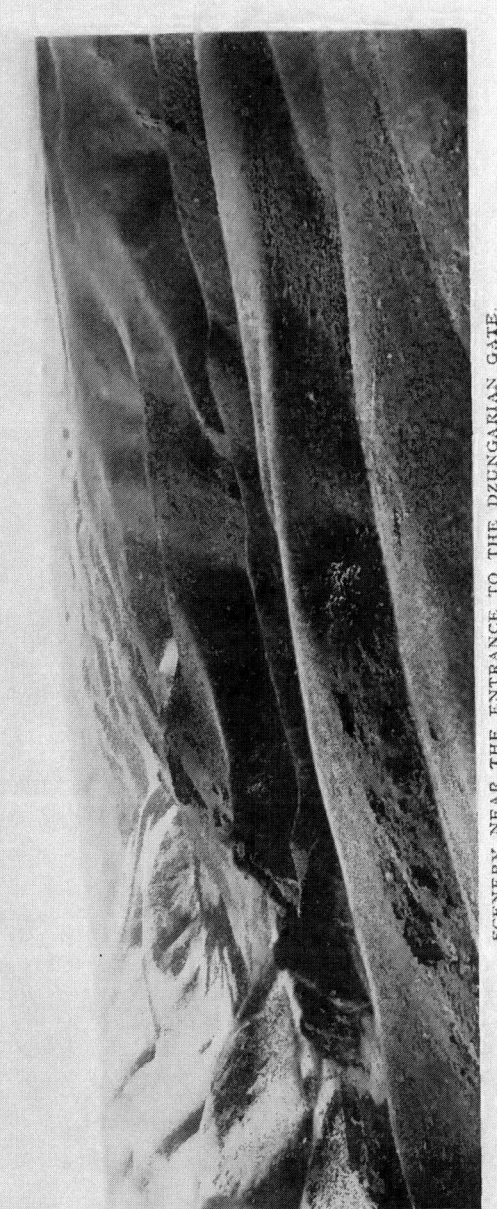

SCENERY NEAR THE ENTRANCE TO THE DZUNGARIAN GATE.

414]

heavy pile of household belongings heaped against the wall that kept it standing, and afforded us shelter. The morning light revealed the havoc which had been wrought. Some of the yurts had been blown over intact, and lay on their sides like discarded bee-hives, while others had been completely demolished, and this in spite of the fact that a yurt, owing to its shape and construction, is of all tents the most perfectly adapted to withstand wind. Our own flimsy tents had, of course, been demolished at an early hour, and an uncomfortable night was spent in holding on to various belongings."

But that was in summer, and under the leeward side of a mountain-range. I leave the reader to imagine what the buran would have been in the trough of the Dzungarian Gate, carrying possibly frozen snow, or sand, and in the winter, when the atmosphere with no wind is scarcely endurable, and when the temperature runs down to −20° and −30° Fahrenheit. Stories are told of shepherds and their flocks being killed off after a few hours' exposure to the winter burans, it being the chief concern of the nomads of the district to find shelter from these terrific wind-storms.

The Dzungarian Gate is a defile about six miles wide at its narrowest point, and forty-six miles long, connecting Southern Siberia with Dzungaria. It forms a natural pathway from the plateau of Mongolia to the great plain of North-western Asia, and is the one and only gateway in the mountain-wall which stretches from Manchuria to Afghanistan, over a distance of three thousand miles. On the west, the Ala-tau drops suddenly from peaks above snow-line to the level of the floor of the depression, 700 ft. above the level of the ocean,—the lowest altitude in the inland basins of Central Asia, with the exception of the Turfan depression, which is actually *below* sea-level. Several deep-cut valleys drain the waters from these highlands into the gorge and supply the waters of Lakes Zalanash and Ala Kul. On the east the exceedingly arid and denuded slopes of the Barlik rise at an easier gradation than do the ranges to the west. The country immediately facing the depression on the east is barren, rugged, and scarred with dry ravines; farther back it rises eventually to about 5,000 ft. in altitude. The actual floor of the depression consists of a smooth, level, gravelly steppe, swept clean of all loose material by the winds which unceasingly rush backwards and forwards through the trough. At the northern end of the gorge reed-beds extend over the swampy southern end of Lake Zalanash; there are also reed-beds and a little grass close to a small spring of water near the centre.

The general aspect, however, is "an abomination of desolation," the scene of perpetual storms and great extremes of climate. During the winter the choice of a bad day to cross the depression may cause disaster to both man and beast, while in summer the intense heat experienced in this low hollow is almost as dangerous. Our own experience of crossing in June was not of the most comfortable nature, our horses and dogs being lamed by the roughness of the surface and exhausted by the heat.

As a geological and physical phenomenon, the Dzungarian Gate is as unusual as that of the Jordan depression. They are both examples of a rift-valley caused by the movement of the earth's crust, not by the action of water. This valley once formed the connecting link between the drainage of Dzungaria and that of Southern

Siberia. The chain of lakes at either end of the valley (Balkash, Ala Kul, Ebi Nor, etc.), are the remains of the great Asiatic Mediterranean Sea ; if their waters were to rise a few hundred feet they would break through the Gate, flooding the plains to the north and south. Even within the historical period it is probable that some of these lakes, now quite isolated, were then connected. Rubruck mentions that, when passing Ala Kul in 1254, he could see " another big sea " through the gorge, and that the two were connected by a river ; Rockhill, in his translation of Rubruck, suggests that the other " big sea " is Ebi Nor. This is improbable, however, Ebi Nor not being visible from the Siberian side of the gorge ; my own opinion is that it was the Zalanash Lake—in the northern mouth of the gorge—that Rubruck saw.

In prehistoric days the Dzungarian Gate must have presented a still more wonderful sight. It then formed a narrow strait joining the Dzungarian inlet with the vast seas of Western Siberia. " This was probably in the recent Quaternary and also in the Tertiary times. Deep deposits of fine mud, now carved out by streams into rolling downs, are to be seen on the north side of the Barlik Mountains. There deposits containing marine shells, which will probably prove to be Quaternary, rise to the altitude of 3,100 ft. Near the Barlik Range there is abundant evidence of marine glaciation,—the debris of icebergs from a frozen sea. Nearer to the gorge the mud-deposits begin ; they contain seams of pebbles,—false-bedded, showing that the currents and tides must have been strong.

" One can picture the Dzungarian Gate in the Ice Age : a narrow strait through which the Arctic-Aralo-Caspian Sea ebbed and flowed into the seas of Central

Asia, scoured by icebergs descending from ancient glaciers on the Ala-tau and Barlik Mountains and forested perhaps down to the water's edge,—not unlike the Straits of Belle Isle at the present day. Now a change has been wrought ; earth-movement has drained the sea. But away to the north there still remain the lakes of Ala Kul, Sasik Kul, and Balkash, and on the south Ebi Nor,—pools left in the desert—all that remains of the great icy sea. The alluvial plains, once its bed, are now covered by desert grasses, while the forest clings only to the shaded slopes and gullies on the northern slopes of the mountains." [1]

The Dzungarian Gate, however, is not such an important dividing-line as might be expected, for although the Barlik—on the one side—was at one period geographically cut off from the Ala-tau portion of the Tian Shan mountain-system—on the other side,—yet geologically they appear to be the same, and, judging from the observations we made during our visit to these ranges in the summer of 1911, we find the Barlik is really also linked to the Tian Shan group by ties of similarity of flora and fauna. For instance, the spruce-pine peculiar to the Tian Shan (*Abies schrenkiana*) grows on the Barlik group but does not extend farther to the east; these mountains forming also the north-easterly limit of the Chukar Partridge (*Caccabis chukar*). " The real dividing-line between Tian Shan and Altai types probably lies somewhere between the Barlik group and the Sair Mountain, and not, as might be expected, in the rift-like depression called the Dzungarian Gate.' [2] The Sair Moun-

---

[1] Price's brief summary of his observations, as published in the *Geographical Journal* for February 1911.

[2] The question of the easterly continuation of this dividing-line between the Tian Shan and Altai is dealt with in the Appendixes.

tains—an easterly extension of the Tarbagatai—were not explored by our party, but it was noticed that they formed the southern limit of the Siberian larch. Between these ranges, the Barlik and the Sair, are other mountain-groups which must at one period have formed a chain of islands in a wide strait, connecting the northern sea with the seas of Central Asia ; the Dzungarian Gate was merely a strait between one of the islands (the Barlik) and the mainland of Ala-tau."

Remarkable as are the geological and geographical features of the Dzungarian Gate, its historical aspect also lays a claim to our interest. Such a scene as the Dzungarian Gate presents to the onlooker appeals most strongly to the imagination. One is tempted to look back into the past, and conjure up the scenes of which this great natural highway must have been a silent witness. This special route must have been the one through which the invading hordes of Asiatics marched westwards; every succeeding wave of migration that swept across Asia must have passed through these narrow "straits." This was the natural route for merchants, caravans, and for all nations on migration bent ; no small part has this deep-cut gorge played in the history of Asia and even of Europe. It requires but a stretch of imagination to recall the thundering tramp of passing armies and to hear the strain of wild barbaric music, as savage hosts of Huns, Mongols, and Turks— filled with lust of conquest—moved westwards, eager for the spoil of the great cities of the Turkestan plains lying beyond the mountain-barrier, the Dzungarian Gate alone allowing these mounted troops to continue, unhindered, their conquering way. Samarkand, Bokhara, Persia, Russia, lay beyond ; the plains, their own free, open plains, led them irresistibly onwards to the very gates of Europe!

A peculiar feature of travel in Central Asia is the sudden manner in which a new country opens up before the traveller. Through gaining the summit of a small pass, or the rounding of some, it may be, insignificant shoulder, he may come within view of an immense stretch of country never seen nor even guessed at by him before. Such a view was obtained as we left the Dzungarian Gate and climbed the foot-hills of the wind-worn granite range situated to the north-west of Ebi Nor. Over the lake, and appearing to rise out of it, the chain of the Tian Shan—the great mountain-system of Central Asia—was spread out in long array, its snow-clad summits stretching unbroken across the whole width of the horizon. All this had been completely hidden from us up to this moment, and this sudden introduction gave us a clearer understanding of the vastness of Central Asia.

We now followed an easy route across the lower portion of the Borotala Valley, over the Kanjik Range by a nine-thousand foot pass, into the basin of Sairam Nor and joined the Chinese Imperial High-road at the wayside station of Santai, which connects the towns of Dzungaria with the Ili Valley. Once on the road we made fair pace and reached Kulja on November 14th, nineteen days after leaving Chuguchak.

Kulja and the Ili Valley are too well known to need description. They are outside the regions we had undertaken to study; in fact, we were only induced to visit this locality by the opportunities it gave us for reconstructing our caravan, for despatching our collections

EARLY MORNING BY SAIRAM NOR.

to England, and, incidentally, for resting a short time after seven months of continual travel.

Our stay in Kulja was made pleasant by the hospitality afforded us by Father Raemdonck, a Belgian missionary, who placed a house at our disposal and gave us such help as cannot be adequately acknowledged by words of thanks. On November 26th our party was broken up by the departure of Price for England. Travelling by way of Tashkent, Transcaspia, and the Caucasus, he reached England in March 1911, and has since written an account of the social and political condition of Siberia, from impressions he gained during this journey. He took with him Makandaroff, our interpreter, whose place was filled by John Pereira, a Cingalese—of great parts—who had lived at different times in Pekin, St. Petersburg, Chinese Turkestan, and England, who could not only speak several languages, but cook a good dinner.

From Kulja I wished to send home my maps and notes, up to date, so as not to run any risk through carrying them over thousands of miles of country. This was arranged through the kindness of Mr. T. P. Miller, who was on his way back to England after a hunting-trip in the Tian Shan, and who undertook to convey them home.

All were delivered safely to the Royal Geographical Society, but the maps and notes did not reach their destination without some risk, as well as giving considerable trouble to the bearer, for immediately Mr. Miller crossed the frontier into Russian Turkestan he was arrested, and maps, diaries, and note-books were confiscated. To all intents and purposes the results of the last seven months' work were lost; however, owing to the apparent inability of the secret-service officials to read the various papers they had got hold of, and by a display of bluff on the part of Mr. Miller, all were eventually returned intact.

In arranging a programme of exploration in Central Asia, the traveller has one great difficulty to contend with—namely, the winter. Some, having experience of lower latitudes, may be prone to criticize ; but let them remember that in these regions the explorer has practically to stop work for four months owing to the cold. From November to March we found it impossible to do any survey-work ; the forming of scientific collections was out of the question, and it was with difficulty that we gained any knowledge of the character of the country, for all was hidden under snow. On the road through Southern Dzungaria we hoped to get an idea of the number and size of the rivers ; but we were baulked in our efforts, for we could not locate them ; ice covered the rivers, and snow hid the ice. The land-relief was equally deceiving ; small depressions assumed gigantic proportions, and low ranges of hills had the appearance of high mountains.

During December and the first half of January we amused ourselves in various ways. Miller went off, in spite of the cold, to the Kok-su Valley in the Tian Shán to try for wapiti, where he remained for two weeks without getting a chance of securing that most valued of trophies. I remained in Kulja the greater part of the time, plotting out my plane-table sheets, in preparation for next summer's work. I prepared, on a scale of 1:400,000, large sheets of all the Russian maps of the regions we hoped to visit, on which I intended to sketch in all the fresh detail that I obtained. This work was varied by duck-flighting,—various hot springs allowing many wild-fowl to remain in this ice-bound country,—which gave me amusement for about twenty minutes every evening ; while a visit to the valley of the Kash, right affluent of the Ili, supplied all the specimens of the pheasants of the locality that I desired for my collection.   On Miller's return from the Kok-su we began to arrange our plans for our journey to the far east of Dzungaria.

CHAPTER XV

A WINTER JOURNEY IN SOUTHERN DZUNGARIA ; ALONG THE " IMPERIAL HIGH-ROAD " FROM KULJA TO KUMUL

SNOW had fallen on several occasions since our arrival in Kulja. Not in the great, slow-falling flakes of an English winter, but in a steady, continual fall of minute particles. These fell swiftly, and lay or drifted, as the case might be, whether in sheltered valleys or on open steppe, causing the immense Central Asian land-scape of endless plains and gigantic ranges to be under a mantle of glistening snow-fields. The white expanse lay unbroken, except where black lines of dead vegetation defined the river-courses or where dark blue shadows on the mountains proved the existence of " riven ravine and splintered precipice,"—where snow found no resting-place. Central Asia—always a land of immensity—is seen at its best and in its truest character in midwinter. The countless leagues of " white silence " then produce an awe-inspiring impression, but during the hot, dusty summer the dreary monotony of the region dissipates this impression, and although its vastness dwarfs all one's previous ideas of sameness, no sense of attraction remains.

The dreary winter began at the end of November in the Ili Valley. It commenced with a series of snow-storms accompanied by a hard frost; by the first week in December the Ili River was frozen stiff, and the whole land was frost-bound. Snow occurred every ten or twelve days, the intervening period bringing bright and sunny weather with a very low temperature. So long as the air was still, the 50 degrees or so of frost were not much felt; but when the wind rose the elements were too severe for man to face.

Across the frozen landscape moved occasional natives, Kalmuks and Kirghiz, wrapped in great sheepskin coats and wearing fox-skin headgear, or Chinamen in quilted jackets and quaint, but most practical, ear-caps. For the most part the inhabitants of this dreary land had gone into winter quarters,—hibernating, in fact,—and would not appear again until the following spring. The groaning ox-wagons gave place to silent sledges, and men used this easy mode of transport to move their grain and merchandise; consequently, the noisy bazaars of Kulja —trade centre of the Ili Valley—became silent owing to the wheelless traffic.

The great trade-routes of the world are now almost entirely superseded by railways or lines of steamships. The tea-trade of China is carried to Europe by ship, and men go to Mecca by railway. In far-distant and exceptionally isolated regions alone are the old caravan-tracks still in use as they were a thousand years ago. It is to Asia, with her civilization of immense antiquity, that we must look in order to find this state of affairs; Asia, where men are still "plunged in thought," still heedless of the West, where commerce and transport are still solely dependent upon beasts of burden, where the old routes, which always carried the trade between Europe and Far Cathay, are still in use, where the same difficulties beset one and the same old caravanserais give one shelter.

Not until we reached Southern Dzungaria did we come in contact with the great high-roads and caravan-routes which connect East and West, and which are to-day as they ever have been since the Far East first attracted the attention of the West and the two sought each other's company. North of this zone little intercourse has been carried on. What trade could flourish between China and Siberia, and what could the cold north-land send to China with the exception of a few furs ?

We can well visualize the varied scenes that the high-road granted in the old days, before modern methods of transport diverted the trade. In those early days the markets of China exchanged their wares for those of Western Asia, traffic poured in and out through these landward gates of the Empire, and endless caravans bore the wealth of Cathay to Western bazaars. A vast internal trade between town and town added to the throng of transport-animals and foot-passengers on the highways. Thousands of donkeys pattered along the road, and strings of groaning ox-wagons moved at even slower pace than the stately lines of great Bactrian camels. The gorgeous cortège of a Chinese official,— with an armed escort, moving on the Emperor's business,—was surpassed by that of some great Mandarin, borne in a high-wheeled mule-cart at gentler pace, relays of transport animals taking him from post to post; following in his wake was a slower-moving cavalcade composed of his wives and concubines and a host of retainers. Amongst all these travellers and caravans of merchandise, by the road-side in the dust moved a host of foot-passengers,—colonists, pedlars, and beggars.

The outlying provinces of the great Chinese Empire are even now only connected by roads with the heart of the Empire, and it will be long before the shriek of the locomotive replaces the bells of the camel-caravan. It requires months for a despatch from the capital to reach the Governors of these regions, officials travel by cart for four months from Pekin to take up their posts, while emigrants think nothing of eight months on the road before arriving at their destination.

Ili, one of the richest as well as the most remote of Chinese possessions, is linked up with Pekin by over 2,000 miles of roadway, the track owning the high-sounding title of the " Chinese Imperial High-road." " Imperial " in name, but not in design ; for at its best it is a mockery of a high-way. In its varying degrees of excellence it corresponds to the different stages through which the " Great Wall " passes on its course of 1,500 miles. This typical Chinese monument, which at the Pekin end, under the eyes of the Emperor, is a magnificent brick-built structure, dwindles eventually into a broken mud wall, and, farther away, degenerates to occasional, isolated watch-towers. In the same way the Chinese Imperial High-road deludes the traveller at the Pekin end, but becomes a sad reality farther west to those who are unlucky enough to travel over it. No one would do so of choice, for in summer the traveller is smothered in dust, choked by heat, or poisoned by brackish water, whilst in winter he is lucky if he survives the cold and the filthy caravanserais which render his life intolerable. Nevertheless, in blissful ignorance of such things we made our preparations, and arranged for transport to carry us over 800 miles of the worst section of this road, from Kulja to Kumul on the edge of the Gobi.

Being winter, this route alone was open to us, and we had no choice but to follow the high-road, which passes out of the Ili Valley over the Boro-Khoro range by the Talki Pass, and, entering Dzungaria, leads by a route of unrelieved monotony along its southern borders. This is the Pei-lu—the " great North Road " of the Chinese ; it runs along the northern side of the Tian Shan Mountains, and is thus called in order to distinguish it from the Nan-lu, or South Road, which runs the entire length of Chinese Turkestan on the *south* side of the Tian Shan. Had it been summer we might have varied the tediousness of a continuous cart-journey along the high-road by taking a mountain-track for a portion of the way ; but even in the best season these hill-tracks in the Tian Shan are difficult and dangerous, while the time occupied in traversing them would be far greater than that entailed by the journey along the main-road.

The season of the year, which limited us in our choice of routes, also permitted only one method of transport. The deep snow and the bitter winds rendered exposure dangerous even to the inured and hardened natives ; transport by camel or horse-caravan would have been impossible in the face of such intense cold, with so great a distance to cover ; the only other means of getting to Kumul was by cart.

The Chinese officials and merchants—all, in fact, who can afford to do so—travel over the roads of the New Dominion by wheel-transport. They come from rail-head at Honan in China Proper to these far western dependencies by cart ; when they have served their

CHINESE ROAD-GUARDS.

428]

appointments or made their "pile" they return by cart, thinking nothing of the time occupied by such a slow method of transport so long as it does not entail any undue exertion on their part. In Kulja we found a useful adaptation of the Russian " telega," or springless, four-wheeled cart, which was far more useful and considerably lighter than the high, heavily built, two-wheeled carts generally used by the Chinese. The Dungan owners—for the Mohammedans appear to have the monopoly of the carrying-trade in Western China—ran these " telegas " from Kulja to Urumchi in eighteen or twenty days. They charged 55 tael (about £6) for a winter's journey when fodder was scarce and dear, but slightly less during the summer months. The actual distance between the two towns was 432 miles, divided up into eighteen stages. The stages averaged 90 li each, which corresponds to about thirty miles ; we found, however, that the Chinese mode of reckoning distances was very unreliable; an easy downhill stage of about 90 li often being found to consist of 120, or even more ; whereas a sandy track, without water, would be considered 90 li because it felt like 90, when in reality it should have been 60 li.

On January 14th we rattled out of the familiar old bazaars of Kulja, and, to the "Hoa-hoa-hoa" of the drivers, drove out across the melancholy, dreary landscape of the Ili Valley. In six hours we made the Chinese town of Sweeting, a "rabbit-warren" of a place, a maze of mud-walls, a city risen out of the ashes of destruction, and repeopled after horrible massacres. The history of the Ili Valley is somewhat like that of the valley of the Hoang Ho. Periodically nature has let loose floods,—either of water or human floods of fanatics,—over these two luxuriant valleys, with disastrous results to tens of thousands of Celestials. No sooner, however, do the floods recede, or are the insurrections quelled, than the Chinese swarm again into the valleys, where they live, as it were, on the slopes of a volcano. No other fact shows so well the remarkable tenacity of the race. The Yellow River overflows its banks and drowns millions of human beings, but immediately the dykes are rebuilt the Chinese go back to cultivate the soil, heedless of the future, until once again catastrophe bursts upon them. So with the Ili Valley; its fertility attracts them to such a degree that they shut their eyes to the possibility of annihilation. It has been said of the British, that they are like ants: if one finds a good bit of meat, a thousand will follow. I think this applies equally to the Chinese, that slow, persistent race, to whom neither the Ili Valley nor the valley of the Hoang-Ho will ever be lost,—not even in the face of the greatest of calamities.

The next day we reached Lao-tzao-gou, a small village now, but formerly one of the six towns of the Ili Valley. The old walls and parapets, showing its former size and ancient importance, were now merely the haunts of owls and foxes, while the rich lands around them awaited the hand of the cultivator. So we passed on, out of the Unhappy Valley, up through the winding Talki Gorge, where the highway first shows any signs of actual road-making. This track alone gives access to Turkestan from China, and all who come or go must pass by this route; of necessity, therefore, the road has been built up to some pretension of a highway.

That night we spent in a miserable serai at the foot of the pass, and as bad weather came on we had to make the best of a whole day in our very draughty, cold quarters, being afraid to negotiate the pass in such rough weather. The wind grew to a hurricane, the snow drifted accordingly, whilst we smoked ourselves out of our mud-built room in vain attempts to keep warm. A few inhabitants of the miserable place came to stare at us, and their dogs in turn fought my dog ; and so we spent a somewhat melancholy day. In winter these serais are the very essence of discomfort, and most unattractive. Men do not choose these cruel months in which to travel, for food is scarce and dear ; all who have business to transact accomplish their work during the summer.

The inevitable carts, laden heavily with merchandise and goods from Pekin, are, of course, always encumbering the road, and, now and then, the retinue of some Chinese official moving to a new post ; these, together with caval-cades of Kalmuks, Chinese soldiers, and nondescript foot-passengers, make up the list of winter travellers. Yet we saw this same portion of the road in late autumn, when the Talki Pass was literally blocked with traffic, and the serais were full to over-flowing. Here, in this veritable Suez Canal of Central Asia, crowded the entire trade and traffic that exists between Cathay and Western Asia. There were Chinese horsemen, well-mounted and proud of purse, and miserable foot-sore emigrants bound for the Ili Valley—the El Dorado of the Celestials. There were long caravans of camels laden with grain, cotton, and felt ; lumbering carts and fast, three-horsed coaches, which came in a cloud of dust—carrying passengers between the few and far-removed towns. All these crowded the high-road in summer, as well as slither-heeled Tartars, slouching Mongols, Mussul-man merchants, and crafty Dungans.

II—8

When we eventually tackled the Talki Pass we found it so bad for carts that we feared a long delay. Snow had drifted across the track, and our spades were in constant use. Streams, which flowed across the road, had frozen solid in flowing, and the white track presented the appearance of a miniature glacier. But with five horses to each cart we succeeded in reaching the summit of the pass—hot and panting in spite of 40° of frost and a biting wind. Below the pass was a guardhouse, occupied by Chinese soldiers whose business it was to keep the road open. Their laziness, no doubt, accounted for the hopeless state of the track, when very little work would have kept it free from ice-floes.

We now entered upon the wide plain of Sairam Nor, whose immense sheet of water lay under ice, and whose panorama consisted of an unbroken snow-field. A long; downhill " rough and tumble " brought us to Santai, a rather more numerous collection of hovels and inns than usual, situated on the edge of the lake. Close by here the road was built out round a rocky promontory which jutted out into the lake and which, by the nature of the ground, formed a strategical point. Here the ponderous Celestials had built mud fortifications to guard the road, a sign of strength, no doubt, but quite inadequate. A group of twenty-four grave-mounds, near by, suggested a conflict at some time or other. Leaving Santai, we passed through the gaps between the Kanjik and Kuzimchik ranges, by means of which the whole of the basin of Sairam Nor must, at one time, have been drained, before a land-movement blocked the passage.[1]

Once out of the Sairam Nor basin we made good pace into the plains of Dzungaria. The next stopping-

[1] See Appendix B.

THE CHINESE IMPERIAL HIGH-ROAD NEAR SAIRAM NOR.

place, Sutai, we considered to be a still more melancholy spot for a halt ; not a blade of grass or scrub, nor even water, was to be found, while the foul mud-huts, and the evil-looking rascals inhabiting them, did not make the place more inviting. We found gazelle near by, but, failing in our attempts to hunt them by driving, we once again resorted to our old occupation of smoking ourselves warm.

Later we decided, since there was a good moon, to make a night-drive, and accordingly, after a good meal, hitched up and started off. The road was simply a stony waste, over which we bumped and rattled to the " Hoa-hoa-hoa ! " of the drivers, till the dawn flushed the sky and we turned out, lit a fire of scrub near the road, and warmed ourselves.

Thus we journeyed, day by day, across Southern Dzungaria. It would be tedious, and vastly uninteresting, to describe every stage of the forty that lay between Kulja and Kumul; it is hard, however, to give a true impression of the region without undue monotony of description.

We usually drove for about seven or eight hours, and averaged twenty to thirty miles a day; sometimes we drove all night, but we gave this up after losing two horses from frost-bite. If, when travelling at night, we pulled up even for a few minutes, to let the sweating horses gain their breath, they ran the risk of freezing as they stood.

At this season of the year the track was comparatively good, for the hard frozen snow had filled up the inequalities of the ground and made the going easy ; there was no dust, and the air was glorious.

The location of the stopping-places controlled our

stages ; these were sometimes a farce, as frequently neither food nor water could be procured, and occasionally we sent our men a mile to cut ice with which to cook, and even this we had to buy !

The same type of cheerless serai offered us a resting-place each night, the same skin-clad native bade us welcome, and tried to cheat us on the bill when we departed next morning. The serais were always quadrangular structures composed of many small rooms, like cubicles, boasting paperless windows, and no chimney ; some possessed a larger (and colder) guest-chamber for the use of Chinese officials when on the road ; but we nearly always used the smaller ones, being the more easily heated.

On arrival a sleepy, " huddled-up " native, looking twice his natural size owing to the number of sheep-skin coats he was wearing, would kindle a smoky fire, whilst our servants commandeered every egg the village could produce. The food-supply was sometimes an important question, for the markets seemed to disappear like the inhabitants during the winter months, and we could not always rely upon getting the most ordinary articles of diet. Nights were often made hideous by the quarrelling animals; there were always dog-fights ; and I remember, on one occasion, the whole inn was kept awake by the mad ravings of a holy man, a Dungan lunatic at large. If the serais were too uninviting, or the smoky rooms impossible to rest in, we were always able to resort to our carts for the nights.

One advantage alone seemed to result from a winter's journey along the Imperial High-road, and that arose from the fact that everything was frozen solid ; the insanitary conditions of our surroundings were thus without danger. Even dead camels lying about outside our quarters did not matter under these conditions; but we scarcely dared to imagine what would have been the effect in summer.

We sought, in vain, for interest or romance in the surroundings of the sordid villages and mud-built caravanserais, which staged our route along Southern Dzungaria. All were stamped with the unrelieved monotony of Central Asia.

On reaching the low plain of Dzungaria the road-side scenery was varied by a zone of vegetation caused by the presence of much water, which, at this altitude, approached closely to the surface of the ground, and either rendered it moist or actually appeared as streams. This fact accounted for a string of villages lying along the route.

Takianzi, the first of these settlements, was typical of them all. A group of ancient elm-trees surrounding a Chanto, or a Dungan mosque, is generally the most prominent feature on approaching one of these villages, which, on entrance, has the appearance of a long, straggling street composed of mud-built houses, small bazaars, and a few inns. In summer, life and colour are added to the scene, nomads from the surrounding country are haggling with the shopkeepers and crowding the serais; but in winter even the benumbed yet inquisitive inhabitants have not the energy to turn out and form a crowd, as is their habit on the arrival of strange travellers such as ourselves.

The population was composed largely of Chanto emigrants from the overcrowded oases of Chinese Turkestan, such as Turfan, Aksu, and Kashgar, in all of which there exists a surplus of inhabitants. They had, in many cases, been ousted from their homes by the iniquitous methods of Chinese usurers, whose one aim is to ruin the Chanto land-owners and so gain possession of their wonderfully fertile farms. Here the Chantos eke out a poor livelihood as small shopkeepers and agriculturists, and, it was said, were freed from taxation in return for settling on the Pei-lu, or North Road.[1] Besides the Chantos there were always Dungans and Chinese, who farmed small holdings, kept the inns, and carried on a certain amount of trade. The villages, indeed, presented a curious mixture of races and creeds. It was instructive to notice that the Chanto, Chinese, Dungan, and Kalmuk mixed freely and even fraternised here, where all Asiatics are of one brotherhood and the European is altogether outside the circle. Religion seems to be of secondary consideration, when it is a question of Europe *versus* Asia; these being far more distant from each other than are Buddhism, Islam, and Agnosticism—as represented by the Mongols, the Chantos and the Chinese.

Takianzi showed signs of recent increase, as proved by

---

[1] These Chantos, however, do not make very good colonists. From the day they arrive they are in the hands of Chinese money-lenders. Even the grain necessary to sow their fields is borrowed, for each sack of which they must return two, and in some cases three, in the autumn. It is said that half the population of Kulja live by lending to the other half. The Chinese settlers in Sin-Kiang are in many cases bad characters who have emigrated by necessity and not by choice. They work their way across the desert to Hami and other outlying oases, make a little money, and gradually move on westwards to Urumchi and Manas; but their goal is always the Ili Valley. Some succeed, but many fail, judging by the fact that only 20 per cent. manage to make enough to return to their own country. In the far west they are a lazy lot compared with what they are in China Proper, spending most of their time in riotous living and gambling—climate or lack of competition being probably the cause. In the Ili Valley a labourer gets as much pay in a month as would satisfy him for a whole year in the home provinces.

newly built houses and bazaars ; an exploration of the surrounding country, however, showed that there were not only large areas of an earlier cultivation now overgrown with reed-beds, but the remains of many old irrigation canals. For six or eight miles to the east of the village I noticed disused canals and fields overgrown with reeds and scrub showing no traces of recent cultivation. There was ample water in this locality ; the present state of the country being probably an example of what it must have been formerly, before Dungan rebellions and Chinese massacres swept away prosperity and left the land destitute.

It was difficult, at this season, to tell the amount of water these settlements were dependent upon, for the streams were frozen and the water-courses hidden under snow. Even the largest rivers, which issued from great valleys in the mountains to the south, could hardly be traced where we crossed their wide beds on the plain. The villagers depended on deep wells, and the nomads used ice, which they cut out, in great blocks, from the rivers and transported on camel-back to their " yurts."

From Takianzi the road led us to Djinko, a town of rather more than usual importance, situated at the south end of Ebi Nor. It was a busy centre for the Kalmuks from the Borotala district, and was inhabited by about three thousand Chinese and Chantos, who traded salt procured near Ebi Nor. Djinko was in a well-watered region ; miles of reed-beds standing 10 to 15 ft. high, scrub, and small forests of gnarled and stunted poplars showed that nearly all this country could be brought under cultivation. As it was, the district only supported a small population of Kalmuks, whom we occasionally saw making use of the points of vantage granted by the mounds which alone allowed a clear view over the reed-beds. These circular mounds of earth were a special feature of the landscape, and the appearance of Kalmuk shepherds on their summits suggested to me that they were probably constructed for the very purpose of "spying," either for their flocks or on their enemies.

Beyond Djinko we entered upon a heavy stage of our journey, the track passing over the belt of sand-dunes which lie to the south-east of Ebi Nor. The sand-hills, of no great height, were irregularly formed, and were for the most part covered on the leeward sides with small tamarisk-scrub. There appeared to be very little movement of sand by the wind, though at a Chinese guardhouse, called Kum Chaza,—where there were a few Kalmuk soldiers who were supposed to look out for travellers or caravans in distress, as often happens when the winds are very high,—the sands were encroaching on the high walls from the direction of Ebi Nor and the Dzungarian Gate, whence come the strongest winds. These dunes were high and free from vegetation. The ground—where the sands left it exposed—seemed to be composed of very fine lake-deposits, ploughed up into the finest dust, thus making the going very heavy.

The distribution of snow was very peculiar; the high, windy basin of Sairam Nor was deep in snow, the country to the east of it was comparatively clear, here again snow was lying, while the reed-beds and jungle were altogether free. After leaving the sand-belt we immediately entered a forest of poplars, which continued —with small breaks—all the way to Shi-Kho. The trees were evidently effected by the severe climatic conditions and a none too abundant supply of water,

KUM CHAZA, A GUARD-HOUSE ON THE NAN-LU, OR NORTHERN HIGH-ROAD.

438]

for they presented a most weird appearance, with twisted, gnarled trunks and branches, and dwarfed growth, few of them being more than 20 ft. high.

Shi-Kho we found to be a thriving and busy centre of trade and transport, with a "moving" population of about three thousand. Even in January the four big inns were full to overcrowding, for here converges the entire trade between Siberia and Urumchi, and constant traffic passes through. From Shi-Kho a road runs northwards to the frontier town of Chuguchak, which the traveller may reach in ten stages. It traverses a bleak and inhospitable country, without habitation, and with a poor water-supply ; in time, no doubt, it will be superseded by another track following the line of the Manas River, which, besides easing the discomfort of the journey, will open up a country at present awaiting development.

There being no inducement to halt at Shi-Kho, we continued our journey for another stage eastwards to the village of Yandzhikhai, where we stopped a day, as Miller wished to hunt the surrounding country. The exceptional conditions imposed by the rigid winter on the fauna of these regions were shown by Miller's discovery that, on the low hills to the south of the road, wild-asses and wild-sheep actually ranged over the same ground. These hills were scarcely a thousand feet above the plain, and formed an isolated ridge separated from the main range of the Tian Shan, which started some miles farther to the south.

Another two days took us to Manas, the centre of an important district. As a town it did not impress us, the bazaars being small, and the walled "city" little else but an empty enclosure. The passer-by

might be easily misled as to the population and importance of this region ; for Manas itself is merely the trade-
centre of a large agricultural district, the population
being scattered over the surrounding country in small
villages and isolated farms. This is the best and richest
farming country of the Pei-lu, for here is an unlimited
area of the finest soil extending along the banks of a
big river, at the point where it leaves its mountain-
gorge and spreads itself out in many channels over the
plain, thus rendering irrigation easy. The water-supply is
reliable; even in the driest season there is a surplus of
water, which finds its way to the deserts below and
there evaporates. At the most critical season of the
year, when the crops most need water, the alpine
regions of the great ranges to the south send down
their melted snows in such abundance, that the river
assumes almost dangerous proportions. We could
scarcely believe that the mile-wide shingle-bed we
crossed just outside the town,—almost without realizing
that it was the bed of a river,—could later on be transformed into a flood which would hinder traffic and
cut off communication for days together. Yet in July
and August the Manas River rises to this extent, and
passenger traffic is only kept up by the employment of
high-wheeled carts especially built for the purpose.
These ferry travellers across the river so long as the water
does not run too deep for the horses to find the bottom ;
when this happens the blocked traffic causes the town of
Manas to become the centre of a busy scene, until the
flood lessens.

The Manas region forms an area suitable for development in the future, but irrigation works on a large scale
are necessary. There is land and water, an equable

climate, and a market for all produce close by. It is, even now, the granary of Urumchi, and its cultivators have the advantage of a large and ever-increasing population at their very doors. Wheat, rice, and maize are a speciality, while grapes and apples grow to perfection.

During our journey down the Manas River at the end of the month of May, we found that cultivation extended for about twenty miles along its right bank; beyond that, the nature of the river-channel made irrigation works impracticable, the river having carved out for itself a deep bed in the soft clay and being bordered by steep cliffs of 50 and 100 ft. in height. The bed of the river was constantly changing, the cliffs being continually cut away ; in several places we found this had resulted in the destruction of the irrigation-canals which had been dug at immense cost and labour. We saw, too, a place where the Chinese Government had endeavoured to cut a canal which would carry water to lands 50 or 60 ft. above the level of water at its start; but even this had been left unfinished, and the farmers had set about irrigating their lands on their own account by damming the river at suitable places, so as to minimize the labour of making long, deep canals, and leading the water thence by comparatively small channels. We saw one of these dams in the course of construction. It was built entirely of bundles of willow-branches and straw, and, it was said, was always destroyed beyond repair by the summer floods and had to be rebuilt every year. For a month or six weeks the entire village turned out and built the dam, on which depended their harvest.

Thus, it will be seen that the real cultivated areas on the east side of the Manas River come to an end twenty miles to the north of the town, beyond this point there being only small farms dependent upon separate canals. On the west side there appears to be more cultivation. Apparently the ground here was easier to irrigate, for we discovered a very extensive area of country, well watered, both by canals from the Manas River and from other sources farther west. The water-supply must be ample, as the main produce is rice. Rice is being introduced more and more; it is of the best quality, and is in great demand. The natives get a living so easily that they idle away most of the time in gambling.

The whole of the lower Manas River, except where hemmed in by sand-dunes or where running in a deep ravine, is capable of being extensively used for irrigation purposes. Truly Manas, itself, is well situated. As we rode out on the road to Urumchi and saw its inspiring background of snow-mountains rising to 20,000 ft., the lands awaiting the hand of man, the fields already "laid out,"—lined with old irrigation-canals needing only to be redug, we marvelled at the starving millions of China who leave their own country for Australia and America, when they have this fertile land awaiting them.

On leaving Manas the atmosphere became more *alive*, and our impressions more interesting. We were now only a few days' journey from the capital, as was shown, even if we had not known it, by the increased amount of traffic on the road. Many a monotonous day's journey had been relieved by counting and tabulating the traffic *en route*. For instance, between Kulja and Shi-Kho we passed three hundred and fifty laden camels going westwards and a hundred returning "empty" to Urumchi, but after leaving Manas we had our work

DUNGAN BOYS.

cut out to keep the record without a break. The first day we passed seventy camels on their way to Manas to fetch grain, six wagons of merchandise bound for Kulja, and three average-sized caravans carrying cotton and wool to Chuguchak. Farther on we counted twelve wagons of grain going west and seventeen going east, two camel-caravans of seventy and ninety camels each, numberless foot-passengers—mostly colonists from the home provinces, long strings of coal-carts bearing an- thracite from the mines situated to the south of Manas, besides two theatrical companies " on tour."

Although the country appeared to be busier and the roads more full, the region between Manas and Urumchi presented a spectacle of ruin. The destruction caused by the disturbances of 1865–75 defies all description. Ruined towns dotted the landscape ; we encountered only two villages where the old maps marked five. For this district was, and still is, the centre of Dungan coloniza- tion, and it was here that the hand of the destroyer worked with the most disastrous results. The traces of earlier irrigation-canals were to be seen on lands now lying idle. The country was, however, slowly recover- ing, for small villages and farmsteads were springing up alongside the road, and in time it may assume a more normal aspect.

Immediately on leaving Manas we sighted the peaks of the Bogdo-ola Mountains, which mark the position of the capital. Our first view of this remarkable alpine summit was that of a single ice-clad peak showing its crest over a far horizon, but on reaching Urumchi we found that it formed an imposing background to the city lying close under its slopes.

Urumchi, Ulu-muchi, or Tihua-fu, the provincial

capital of Sin-Kiang, or the New Dominion, is situated in the midst of attractive surroundings, in a bay in the mountain-wall at the point where the Tian Shan dips before joining the Bogdo-ola. Tucked away close under the mountains, in a sheltered locality, and with an ample water-supply, it presents a pleasing aspect to the traveller after the bleak and featureless deserts.

The position of Urumchi, although not practical from a strategical point of view—being commanded by the surrounding hills, is well chosen, for the capital is situated in the heart of its administrative area, and also at the junction of two great trans-continental trade-routes, and of many local lines of communication. At Urumchi the two main roads from China meet, namely, the northern route across Mongolia and the southern route through Lan-chow and Hami; Urumchi is, also, on the road to Ili, the most fertile and valued portion of the New Dominion. As the capital of Dzungaria and Chinese Turkestan, its position is admirable, being close to the only point at which the great mountain-chain of the Tian Shan drops low enough to permit the easy passage of caravans between the two countries. The internal trade, therefore, of these regions and all traffic between Chinese Turkestan and the north must pass through Urumchi.

Although only the recently named capital of a newly incorporated province, Urumchi[1] has already grown to be a town of size and importance. It forms the residence of the Governor of the province, a Fan-tei and Nea-tei

---

[1] Urumchi appears to be a corruption of the Mongol name Ulu-muchi. Tihua, Tihua-fu, or Tih-hua-fu is the Chinese official name; but the locals always speak of the capital as Houng-miao-tze—" Red Temple," a name which originated from the existence of a temple built on a red hill, close by the town.

(Provincial Judge), a Tartar General, and a considerable garrison, some of whom have been drilled under European instruction and armed with modern weapons. The population is said now to stand at 70,000 ; Bonin, in 1900, estimated it at 40,000 ; and in 1905 it was placed at 50,000. These figures show the advance Urumchi has made during recent years. Of this number of inhabitants, one quarter are said to be Chantos, some of whom are Russian, and some Chinese subjects. Outside the walls of the city there exists a quarter entirely composed of Russian subjects, represented by Chantos or Sarts, Tartars, and a few Siberian merchants, to advance whose interests a paternal Government has placed a Consul-General, a Vice-Consul, and a guard of fifty Cossacks.

Here alone does the traveller in the New Dominion encounter a real Chinese town. Urumchi is typically Chinese, its streets lack nothing of the atmosphere of a town in China Proper. You may see the retinues of high officials, and Chinese ladies in the latest Pekin fashions ; you can buy Pekin goods—at three times the original cost, and encounter men from every province in the Empire. Urumchi is the centre of trade and fashion ; there are several theatres, a gunpowder factory, an electric-light plant ; and a far better choice of goods in the bazaars than one could find in any other town in Central Asia.

An innovation, which has recently brought Urumchi and Sin-Kiang into greater prominence and into closer proximity to the outside world, is the wise employment by the Chinese Government of Europeans to reconstruct and manage the postal system. Mr. Petersen, to whom this work had been entrusted, was our host whilst staying at Urumchi, and we owe a great deal to his hospitality. After two years' work he has organized a complete postal system from this most out-of-the-way corner of China to all points of the compass. Urumchi, by this new system, is brought within forty-five days of Pekin, and letters will reach London, via Siberia, within thirty days. The local post is carried to Kulja, a distance of 430 miles, in four and a half days, and to Chuguchak in the same length of time. In earlier days, under Chinese management, the post took *three* times as long, and even then safe delivery was uncertain. This is the result of careful organization, by means of a systematic staging of the route into regular distances, and by the enforcement of a time-limit. Well-mounted riders, in relays, carry the mail-bags for stages of 80–90 li each ; the service being kept up day and night across the whole width of China. A combined, local, passenger and mail service has been organized on this same principle between the capital and Guchen, and the journey, which formerly took from five to six days, is now accomplished in a day and a half.

In spite of the distance from Pekin, caravans of merchandise creep across from China to Urumchi, taking eight months or a year on the road. These caravans generally come direct by the northern route across Mongolia, for they carry wares especially for the Urumchi market. The capital thus laid out, however, obliges the merchants to charge at the rate of 200 to 300 per cent. on the Pekin price. On the other hand, we bought cigarettes of the " Aden Tobacco Co." at the rate of 3s. per hundred ; whether they were Japanese " fakes " or not we cannot say, but they seemed uncommonly good to us after a year's experience of all kinds of local products—both Russian and Chinese. They were, in any case, cheap enough, after being transported 1,500 miles

BACTRIAN CAMEL IN SUMMER COAT

BACTRIAN CAMELS IN WINTER COAT.

by camel to a town where only a small demand could be made for them.

At Urumchi we paid calls on Governors, Generals, and Provincial Judges, and we enjoyed for a season grotesque Chinese dinners and polite society, but our desire was to move on, so we did not rest long. Some days were occupied in arranging money matters, for, although the Russian rouble has penetrated thus far into Middle Asia, beyond Urumchi we found it necessary to use Chinese coinage. We needed, however, money which was current over the *whole* province, a *local* coinage being useless to us; so we carried paper-money in 1-tael notes, silver pieces of the same value, and very bulky copper coins which filled a sack and weighed seventy pounds, the exchange working out at a loss of 30 per cent.

On February 12th we set off on the second stage of eighteen days, following the northern road to Guchen. We decided to go direct by the Guchen route to Kumul instead of by the southern road, which passes through Turfan, in order to confine our attentions, as far as possible, to Dzungaria. In spite of the cold and the deep snow the north road seemed to us the more worthy of traversing, it being less known than the southern, or Turfan route. From the point of view of time the two routes are about the same during the winter months, the hindrances caused by a heavy snowfall on the north being more than counterbalanced by those resulting from the sand on the southern road ; but in summer the Guchen route is greatly to be recommended, the traveller thus avoiding the excessively hot basin of Turfan. The difference in the height of the passes over to the Nan-lu is of little consequence, for, although the Guchen route leads over a

II—9

6,000 ft. pass, and a pass of only 3,500 ft. lies between Urumchi and Turfan, yet the higher pass is the more easily approached from either side.

A misadventure during the first day's journey from Urumchi, the loss of a tent-bale, which fell off the cart, and was apparently stolen from the road before our men could pick it up, as well as the attempt on the morrow, made by a member of our escort, to steal one of our horses, showed that, even close to the capital, no great amount of law and order prevailed. In former days this road was feared by Chinamen on account of highwaymen and thieves, and even now it is customary for foreign travellers to be provided with an escort of two mounted men, road-guards, who are picketed at intervals along the route, and are responsible for the safety of travellers over their particular portion. The danger, however, is more imaginary than real, owing to the prompt action taken at the start by the Chinese officials. Their method of dealing with the robbers was most effective, for they immediately hamstrung those they caught. The pickets are supplied from the Kalmuk reserves, or the Chinese rabble, in accordance with the Chinese principle that " you do not turn good men into soldiers any more than you make nails out of good iron."

Skirting close under the foot-hills of the massive Bogdo-ola Range, across unbroken snow-fields, we passed onwards to Guchen, which we reached in three days of actual travelling from Urumchi.

Guchen, or Ku-ching—the ancient town—appeared to be a large and busy place, which might be described as the " port " of Urumchi, for it entirely owes its existence to the position it holds as the terminus of all trans-Gobi trade. Here, the overland trade from Kalgan and

Kho-Kho-Koto,[1] first finds rest after a continuous trek
—one long desert stage—of fifteen hundred miles. Here
the caravans, which outfitted at the " Blue " city on the
northern bend of the Hoang Ho, deposit their loads, and
wait until a sufficient quantity of goods has been collected
for transport eastwards; the merchandise they bring
being here stored and sorted for further distribution by
fresh caravans, which work the transport of the regions
westwards of Guchen.

It is a far cry from the Pacific, or even from the
industrial centres of China, to Guchen, yet a sufficient
trade exists between them to call a regular caravan-
trade into existence and to employ a whole army of men
as transport-riders. Far Western China is, in fact,
in closer connexion with the European markets by way
of Chinese ports than she is by way of Russia. Man-
chester goods compete with Russian wares in the bazaars
of Urumchi, and it is noteworthy that the goods coming
to Sin-Kiang from the east, *i.e.* from Pekin or the coast,
are distinguished by a name which signifies the " Best,"
as opposed to those which come from the west, or Russia ;
Urumchi merchants crack up their wares as coming from
the East. Mr. Hunter, of the China Inland Mission, who
has resided a long time in the capital, told me that he
thought more English goods reach Guchen via Pekin
than reach Kashgar via India. It might be supposed that
the cost of transport would be prohibitive ; the tariff
being, according to Petersen, 20 tael per 167 lb. A
camel carries about 500 lb. on such a journey ; the cost
would, therefore, run roughly at 60 tael or £6 10s. per
camel-load ; but the Urumchi merchants charge quite

---

[1] Ku-ku-koto, or Kou-kou-koto, also called Kwei-huaching, the start-
ing-place of the caravans.

enough to realize a handsome profit on all they sell. The rate is rather high, for even on the easy road from Guchen to Kulja the rate is 15 tael per camel-load, and the distance is about one-third of the journey from Pekin to Guchen.

Time, of course, is no object ; the caravans move at the rate easiest for the camels ; they travel continuously over the barren, fodderless region, stopping to feed and to recuperate when they reach a locality with ample food and water. Any time between six months and a year may be occupied with the journey; this depending on the quantity of fodder the desert produces at the season they make the passage,—if there is little food they move more slowly,—and on whether they decide to take a direct line from the Hoang Ho to Guchen or to call *en route* at Uliassutai and Kobdo in Northern Mongolia. The reason is obvious for using the trans-Mongolian route for the transport of heavy goods. Large caravans can find nourishment, no cost is entailed on account of food, the track is level, crosses no mountain-ranges, is not encumbered with other traffic, and does not pass through towns where delay or expense can be incurred.

Chinese officials, when in haste to return to Pekin, sometimes travel by this northern route in preference to the southern. By using carts drawn by camels, they can make the entire distance between Guchen and Kho-Kho-Koto in fifty days. The discomfort of the desert journey forbids all except those in great haste to take this line, the eight months spent in loitering along the southern road being much more after the heart of the Celestial. It proves, however, that there is a good, hard, direct route suitable for wheeled-traffic between Sin-Kiang and the capital of the Empire, practicable

DZUNGARIA IN MID-WINTER.
The Basin of Sairam Nor.

THE LEADER OF THE CARAVAN.

on account of the presence of food and water, and which, in the event of an opening up of Northern Mongolia, would become a well-used track.

The first part of the route is the same as that which connects Urga with Pekin ; this part will shortly be superseded by a railway. In Mid-Gobi, half-way to Urga, the track branches off towards the north-west, passes along the northern edge of the Gobi, and skirts the lower and most easterly spurs of the Mongolian Altai. Water, draining from these ranges, flows out and eventually loses itself in the Gobi, and the caravans must keep in touch with them. A more northerly line may be taken, to include Uliassutai and Kobdo, in which case ample fodder and water will be found ; but the crossing of the eastern part of the Mongolian Altai necessitates an ascent to 8,000 ft. above sea-level ; caravans, therefore, more frequently take the direct route leading to Guchen.

Guchen is now the terminus, for it appears to have superseded the town of Barkul, which lies a hundred and seventy miles to the east, and was formerly the old " port " for steppe-bound caravans. According to the Russian maps, the trans-Gobi route leads from the Southern Altai to Barkul and thence to Guchen ; there is no signification on them of any track leading direct to Guchen without touching at Barkul, yet this track exists, and though for ten days' journey there are no habitations, it is a well-worn road over hard steppe, and is staged by guard-houses.

In winter, when food is scarce along the high-road between Guchen and Barkul, and when snow forms a water-supply on the desert to the north, the caravans may well take a bee-line from Guchen to the southern spurs of the Altai ; but in summer they must needs go due north on leaving Guchen, until they pick up the wells of the Baitik Range; they then turn eastwards, eventually joining the winter route near the Koko-undur and Aji Bogdo Mountains.

In these days, caravans invariably take one of the desert tracks and never include Barkul in their itinerary; yet we were told that they did so in the old days. It has been said that this route was abandoned in consequence of the Dungan riots, but I think a far more likely theory as to the cause of this change is that Guchen alone, at the present day, possesses a neighbourhood suitable for the feeding of large herds of camels, during their enforced stay in the vicinity of the town where they deposit their loads, and where the freight for the return journey is collected and made up. Barkul, for instance, possesses excellent grazing in the near neighbourhood, but the Barkul basin supports a Government stud of horses, the grazing being thus monopolized by thousands of horses. Urumchi, on the other hand, is surrounded by cultivation, and there is no place for camel-herds. Guchen, then, alone remains, and when approaching this town in the month of May, on our urnetr from the steppes to the north-east, we had reason to appreciate the facilities afforded by that region as a resting-place for the camel-caravans.

Here, at about twenty miles' distance from the town, was a land covered with high grass, with plenty of water at a depth of ten feet below the surface; many wells had been dug, and around each we found two or three encampments of caravaneers. Each was represented by a blue or white canvas tent, the temporary home of the caravan-bashi, or leader, around which were piled the bales of merchandise; we counted the signs of twenty separate " outfits," the whole country being dotted with the camel-herds feeding vigorously on the excellent grass. Here the caravans rest until they receive from the agents in Guchen sufficient loads to enable them to start back on the return-journey. The caravans never actually enter the town of Guchen, but remain outside, where the bales are gradually collected until a caravan-bashi has his full complement. Then the slow freight-train starts on its journey eastwards.

The long, snaky, camel-caravan is such a feature of the trade-routes of Asia and so large a number of men gain a living by caravanning and occupy their whole lives in moving to and fro across the heart of the continent with their charges—the camels, that this allusion to camel-transport would be incomplete without a description of a caravan on the march. We met many of a prodigious size, slowly moving along the well-worn routes, and all presenting much the same appearance. The approach of a caravan was heralded by the far-away sound of low-toned bells, wind-borne across miles of desert, and mellowed by distance ; an hour might easily elapse before any sign of it would appear. First prowled the dogs—guards of the camp—of a breed kept and highly valued as watch-dogs ; they were black, shaggy animals of a sturdy build. All day they roamed at will, but at night their duty was to watch over the bales of merchandise ; after dark they became uncommonly savage, and any one foolish enough to approach an encampment on foot and unarmed would be certain of a bad mauling. Even when on horseback, it is often necessary to tuck one's legs well up to escape their teeth. Following the dogs, at the head of a string of camels, slouched a big Mongol, with hands behind his back, eyes on the ground, and apparently with no thought beyond his feet. He had slouched all his life, across Asia and back again, and would probably continue to do so until he could slouch no longer. He was clothed almost entirely in sheepskins and felt ; even his trousers were made of sheepskin—with the wool inside, and these our interpreter persisted in calling " mutton-trousers."

These caravan-men are of a hardy breed, their faces burnt to the colour and consistency of a walnut by constant exposure to the fierce heat, biting cold, and continuous winds of the Gobi. They have a character-istic movement peculiar to their calling : the body is bent slightly forward, and they drag their legs with an effortless scrape at a pace which would kill an English-man ; so slow, indeed, that they seem scarcely to move their feet at all, and so dully and so hopelessly that it is easy to understand why Asia has lagged behind in the world's progress. It is nearly always possible to pick out these men amongst the cosmopolitan crowd in a Central Asia bazaar. The monotony of their lives would be hard to exaggerate ; it consists of trudging at the head of a string of camels for months over a barren country—desti-tute of towns or habitation, with every feature of which they must be thoroughly familiar. All they have to look forward to is a short stay in the neighbourhood of a town, while the bales are being collected for another journey. The only occupation we saw them indulging in was the spinning into coarse twine of the camels'-hair, which they collected in the spring when the animals cast their long, woolly winter-coats.

The work of the men, however, must be heavy, in spite of their slowness on trek, for the entire caravan has to be loaded and unloaded every twenty-four hours,

BACTRIAN CAMEL.

and the camels have to be taken out to graze in the bitterly cold nights. There were generally twenty camels to the charge of each man, an average caravan being made up of a hundred and twenty camels, under six cameleers and a caravan-bashi, who alone was mounted and who rode at the rear, armed with an old "blunder-buss."

After the leading cameleer came the camels, slow, stately and cynical, twenty in a string—tied nose to tail, and carrying full loads of 500 lb. The heavily built Bactrian,—the weight-carrier, the freight-train,—compares poorly with the fast dromedary—the desert-express ; yet amongst all the various means of transport used in Asia the Bactrian camel holds first place. You may find him from China to the Caspian ; you may safely depend upon him for the crossing of a terrible sand-desert, and you may meet him at 18,000 ft. above the level of the sea, on a Himalayan pass. He is ubiquitous, adaptable, and, in fact, indispensable to the traveller and merchant in Asia. The Bactrian camel is in his true home in Mongolia. The finest breeds, according to Prjevalsky, come from the Ala Shan district in the south ; but I am doubtful whether equally fine types do not exist in the excellent pastures of the north-west, on the slopes of the Mongolian Altai. Heavy loads and short stages is the order for caravans bound for far-distant regions ; and whenever food is found in exceptional quantity a halt of several days is often made, in order to rest and feed up the camels.

I have diverged from my narrative, by describing the ways and means of communication between Guchen and the Far East, for it is the camels and the caravans which are essentially the features of this town situated on the edge of the desert. There was little else of interest to be noted, the town itself existing, for the most part, as a sorting-house for goods in transit. Its surroundings were exceptionally fine, with the illimitable plains stretching to the north, east, and west, and with a background composed of the giant peaks of the Bogdo-ola. It was up to this point that the most recent traveller, Professor Merzbacher, had carried on his systematic exploration of the Tian Shan, but beyond this point eastwards he had not worked ; here, therefore, I intended to take up my surveying in order to continue it to the furthermost limit of the Karlik Tagh, some three hundred miles to the east. The season of the year, and the deep snow, compelled us to put off any idea we had of travelling in the mountains until a much later date. We had to content ourselves with the wonderful spectacle which this range—under fresh snow—presented to us with a desert foreground of forty miles ; we determined, therefore, to penetrate its upper valleys and visit its sacred lake on our return to these regions during the following summer.

In strange contrast to the snows on the south of Guchen were the sands on the north. Since leaving Urumchi we had noticed a long line of sand-dunes, running parallel to our route on the north, at a distance of about fifteen miles. These belonged to an outlying portion of the great sand-belt of Central Dzungaria, which here approaches to within a day's journey of the southern border-ranges. The heart of Dzungaria had been crossed by the Russian explorers Prjevalsky and Kozloff, but we had little information as to the character of the central plains or as to the type of sand-desert found in their midst ; we knew nothing as to the extent of sedentary life and cultivation towards the north, nor had we any knowledge of a nomadic population in those regions.

We vaguely imagined those central deserts to be untenanted by nomads, there being no indication of a water-supply; we had not counted, however, upon the possibility of the existence of *winter* residents, dependent upon snow for their drinking-water. In Guchen, noticing many Kirghiz in the bazaars, we inquired who they were, and they told us proudly that they were of the Kirei clan, supplementing this information by adding that they were " Kum dan "—from the sands. This led us to make further inquiries, and we eventually made friends with their representative in the town. Each different tribe or race in the cosmopolitan towns of Inner Asia has a head-man to represent it and to look after its interests in all matters; the nomads of the surrounding districts have also a similar figure-head whose duties partake of those of a " consul." The " Shangea," or representative of the Kirei in Guchen, was a man of wealth and importance, who showed us hospitality and furthered our plans for a visit to the " sands."

On February 19th, in company with a Kirei, whom we had to " mount," for the desert nature of inner Dzungaria does not allow the nomads to bring their horses with them on their winter migrations, we rode out of Guchen to the north-east, and in five hours reached the edge of the sand-belt. Here was a guard-house called Kuntiza, and here the track divided, one going north across the sand to the Baitik Mountains and on to the Irtish and the Altai, while the other followed along the edge of the sands to the north-east. The former of these was a level road, practicable for carts, with forage, fuel,

and water in sufficient quantity, and formed a regular
way of communication between the Irtish district and
Southern Dzungaria. We noticed that it was well used
by camels and carts carrying coal to Urumchi, from
some mines situated three stages from Guchen on the
road to the Baitik, the coal being found in great quantity,
near the surface, on the northern edge of the sands.

Between Guchen and the sands is an area of semi-
cultivated land. Many small streams, unfrozen even
at this season, flowed across the steppe and ended in
the sand-belt, beside which were situated a few scattered
farms and Chinese villages. None of these streams
flowed into the Olon Nor basin, to the north-west of
Guchen, but lost themselves in the sand. Irrigation-
canals and water-courses could be traced amongst the
outermost dunes, while the amount of vegetation and
trees on the sand-hills showed that water was close
under the surface. The sands seem to have encroached
on the cultivated area, for we found a few ruined
houses surrounded by sand-hills; this made us pay
rather more attention to the story told us by a Chanto
who had lived twenty-five years at Sin-tai, a small village
on the high-road near the south end of Olon Nor,
who said he knew of an old Kalmuk town called
Khopuza, to the north-east of the lake, which was buried
in sand

Trees existed only around the villages, and near the
water-courses ; the country as a whole was barren, forming a pasture-land suitable only for the feeding of camel-
herds as described earlier in the chapter. The scattered
nature of the farms, which were all Chinese, showed
the difference in character between the Celestial and the
Chanto. Here were Chinese families living ten miles

TYPE OF KIREI KIRGHIZ.

KIREI AND BRONCO.

458|

away from their nearest neighbour, when apparently there was ample room for them nearer the villages. Had the colonists been of Chanto race they would have worked together and formed small communities; but the independent Chinese, possessing more initiative, started ranches on their own account.

On entering the sand-belt we found that the dunes were well covered with tamarisk and small saxaul; as far as the drainage extended were reeds and small poplars in the hollows; the dunes lay across our track, having been formed by south-westerly winds. We rested at a solitary Kirghiz yurt that night, and the next day passed over a similar country for several hours, until reaching the northern edge of the sand-belt. At this point the sands were about twelve miles across,—in a direct line north and south; farther east the zone narrows down to three or four miles, and then runs out in a wedge-shaped tongue until it ends abruptly about thirty miles east of the Karaul Kuntiza; we noted at once that this sand-area was wrongly defined on the existing maps.

On reaching the northern edge of the sand we entered a dense forest of saxual; travelling through this for several hours towards the east, we reached a group of ten yurts, one of many small encampments of Kirei, snugly ensconced amongst the saxaul trees or in hollows in the dunes. This was the home of our guide, who in his official capacity was "over fifty yurts," he being responsible for their good conduct and the payment of their taxes. The people presented the usual aspect of healthy, clean-living, well-to-do nomads of Mussulman faith; not fanatical, nor, on the other hand, showing any desire to offer their services to travellers unless tempted by the hope of a large reward, or unless compelled to do so by order of a superior. They seldom came in contact with the sedentary people, since the whole extent of their territory touches on only two settled localities—Guchen in the south, and Sharasume in the north.

A description of the Kirei and their range has already been given in Chapter XII. This branch of the clan belonged rightly to the Baitik Mountains, and migrated southwards only under stress of bad seasons. According to report, the last few winters had been exceptionally severe, as was the case with the present winter, snow lying deeper than had been seen for years ; consequently the Kirei had come southwards in larger numbers, and had even tried to establish themselves permanently on the Bogdo-ola Range ; in this attempt they had been frustrated by the Chinese. From this encampment I explored the sand-dunes, while Miller hunted the " kulon," or wild-ass, on the steppes to the north.

This sand-area was chiefly composed of small, stationary dunes, well covered with growth ; but on the eastern edge it had thrown out a narrow tongue of high, *moving* sand-hills. These hills, with their back, as it were, to the stationary dunes, ran out eastwards until they faded away to nothing. Immediately to their north, along the edge of the sand-hills, was a zone of fine saxaul forest, where the trees grew to a height of 20 ft. The forest did not extend far on to the dunes, nor were the trees so well developed there. Whether the existence of this heavy growth had caused the gradual heaping up of the sand to the south and south-west it is difficult to say for certain ; the prevailing wind and the size of the dunes suggest it, for, contrary to the observations of other travellers, I noticed that the dunes showed the prevalence of a west, and not an east, wind. The moving dunes were all steep-sided towards the east, and long-backed towards the west, and during the three days we were on them the wind came from the south-west or west. The early mornings were often characterized by strong south winds, which veered round to the west during the day.

Although the nature of the stationary dunes was the same throughout, that of the moving sands varied considerably. Some dunes presented the phenomena of enclosed, crescent-shaped pits, the sandy hollows of which lay 50 ft. below the average level of the sands. There was rarely any trough between the lines of the dunes, for the arms they had thrown out had joined up with other dunes, and I was thus enabled to travel "up-stream," as it were, or transversely to the lines of the sand-hills, without any effort. It seemed to me that the formation was often due to varying winds. I noticed repeatedly that the hollows between the dunes had been banked up by miniature dunes formed from the south ; and on one occasion I found a high dune formed by a *south* wind, situated on the top of an ordinary dune formed by a *west* wind.

A considerable movement of sand was in progress— for while the stationary dunes were snow-covered, these moving dunes were practically bare ; a careful examination showing that the snow had been blown as the sand was blown, and that in certain places where it had collected were successive layers of snow and sand. On the crest of some of the highest dunes were several strata of snow and sand, showing how each fall of snow had been covered up by a succeeding movement of sand. The stationary dunes were all of an insignificant size, and very malformed ; the moving sands were heaped up to a greater height,—I estimate the highest dunes at 100 ft. from crest to hollow,—these keeping their ranks and preserving their form with the monotonous precision peculiar to wind-blown sands.

Other information we acquired through this visit to the Kirei related to the first spurs of the Altai Mountains, which gave us some conception of the nature of the gap of a hundred miles which separates these mountain-systems, namely, the Altai and the Tian Shan, as represented by the Baitik and Bogdo-ola ranges. From our encampment, on a clear morning, we could just discern the snows of the Baitik Mountains, an outlying range belonging to the Altai group. This range, according to the information given by the nomads who call it their home, is an isolated mass, not actually reaching to a summer snow-line, but sufficiently high to afford good grazing ; water is found in small springs, rising in the valleys, and flowing a short distance before drying up ; the forests on the northern flanks consist of poplar and alder in the valley bottoms, and larch on the heights above. Taken altogether the description of the home of these Kirei seemed most inviting, and did not in any way tally with the manner in which it was depicted on the maps, as, lacking in names, in waterings, and in everything that suggested an inhabited area.

The water-supply, the Kirei told us, is ample for the nomads who live there during the dryest months, and is even sufficient to support a small population of Torgut-Kalmuk residents, who never move as the Kirei do. The Torguts live a semi-nomadic existence, growing a little barley, and grazing their flocks, but still occupying yurts in preference to houses ; they are sufficiently well off in flocks and herds, but are by no means on an equality with the Kirei. We find, therefore, that the plains which separate the Tian Shan from the Altai are, at this point, composed of a hard, barren steppe, broken by a narrow zone of sand-dunes; on the south of this is the agricultural district, while on the north lies a partially used nomads'-land. The average altitude of this section of the gap between the Bogdo-ola and Baitik Mountains is 2,200 ft. above sea-level.

On our return to Guchen we engaged carts from a Chanto owner and set off eastwards for Kumul. It being now February 24th, the thaw had set in, and we realized the time and trouble we had saved by accomplishing the greater part of our journey eastwards in midwinter. East of Guchen the snow lay very deep, and it was as much as the three horses could do to drag the heavy Chinese carts up the long incline to the Tou-shui plateau, across which lay the road to Kumul.

On reaching the small town of Mu-li-kho, two stages to the east of Guchen, we endeavoured to get some knowledge of the mountain-region to our south by making a lateral journey from the high road, and we actually spent an entire day trying to get round an official who refused to supply us with a guide, on account of his being quite certain that we should succumb if we attempted to travel in the mountains at this season, and that he in consequence would be beheaded! After a dinner given in our honour, at which he consumed prodigious quantities of Chinese spirit, he became sufficiently affable to supply us, on our own responsibility, with two mounted men as guides. Sending the carts along the high-road, we rode southwards into the hills which lie within a short

distance of Mu-li-kho; then, turning east, we traversed
the region between this point and Ta-shih-tu, following
a chain of farms which are to be found in the mouths of
the valleys some ten to fifteen miles to the south of the
road. Farther into the hills we could not go, owing to
deep snow and lack of inhabitants; but even these
few days on the foot-hills gave us a clearer insight into
the nature of the eastern Bogdo-ola and its varied inhabitants, the region appearing to be a sort of Tom
Tiddler's ground.

A wide expanse of out-lying foot-hills shut off from
the high road the main Bogdo-ola and all signs
of existing habitation; but, on crossing the first spurs,
pleasantly situated settlements and farmsteads came
into sight. We first visited Bain-kho, a small Chinese
village where we found a little cultivation, and later
in the same day we reached Borstan—a few scattered
farms belonging to Chantos and Chinese. The Chantos
were emigrants from Turfan; but, as nobody would
emigrate of choice to this region in preference to a life
in Turfan, we asked an old Turfanlik what brought him
to these parts. The old man replied that he had lost his
land in Turfan through a Chinese money-lender, into whose
clutches he had fallen during a bad season. He bewailed
the fate of having to live in a country more or less
dependent upon rain, whereas in the Turfan there was a
constant supply of water from wells and kariz. Yet the
rainfall on this portion of the Bogdo-ola must be considerable, for the forest-zone continues in a broad belt along
the main ridge half a day's journey to the south. The
water-courses, however, had the appearance of being full
only at spring-flood. Ice formed the winter's water-supply,
in order to accumulate which the farmers led off water

TAMARISK MOUND.

4641

from their irrigation-canals and filled up any depression that chanced to be handy, allowing the water to freeze solid.

East of Borstan the main ridge of the Bogdo-ola sank to a lower altitude and lost itself in a jumble of wild, formless hills which stretched eastwards as far as the eye could see. To have entered the hills at this season would have greatly increased our difficulties, so, skirting along under the foot-hills, we rested another night at the house of a Chanto, or rather a Sart, for our host had found his way hither from the Ferghana of Russian Turkestan. Living a semi-nomadic existence in a yurt during the summer, and in a house during the winter, herding cattle and growing grain, our host was probably making a small fortune on which he would retire eventually to his own country. He had several advantages, for being a Russian subject, he could not be turned out by the Chinese, and, having taken a Kirghiz girl to wife, he received much useful aid in matters relating to cattle and sheep ranching, besides being thus placed on good terms with the Kirei nomads.

Truly these ranges are inhabited by a nondescript lot of people ; near to our host, who hailed from across the Russo-Chinese border, was a settlement of discontents from the kingdom of Kumul,—Kumuliks who had escaped from the serfdom of their Khan, and who preferred a freer if somewhat harder life in this region ; besides these were occasional encampments of Kirei Kirghiz, wanderers from the far north, already beginning to start on their march back to their real home. No wonder these nomads attempt to settle permanently on these ranges,—forming, as they do, the most remarkable winter resort for shepherds and their flocks, these rolling foot-hills being free of snow at a season when the plains below were deeply covered. This favourable district, although scarcely used at the present time, is capable of supporting a far larger population. Its value in earlier days is attested by the presence of many old tumuli, as well as a few grave-mounds surrounded by upright stones.

On reaching the main road at Ta-shih-tu, and finding that our carts had not yet arrived, we decided to spend a few days in the neighbourhood, Miller hunting wild-sheep, which were fairly numerous, while I mapped the most important features of the plateau to our south. The thaw, which had set in a few days previously, was now increased by a strong, hot wind from the south, its effect on the country being magical; the roads became quagmires, streams began to flow down the valleys, snow-fields—previously hard enough to support the traveller—now became serious obstacles, and the bare, frozen soil changed into mud. We were not surprised, therefore, when the carts turned up two days late, having taken three and a half days to do two ordinary stages and having lost one horse, which died on the road.

Ta-shih-tu consists of only a few houses, but the name will often occur in these pages, there being no other by which to identify this locality, where the northern high-road turns to the south-east and crosses the water-shed between Dzungaria and Chinese Turkestan, and where a side-track leads onwards to Barkul. The actual plateau which the high-road crosses, and which is an important geographical feature, is also nameless; I shall, therefore, call it the Tou-shui plateau, from the halting-place of that name on the southern side of the watershed.

Ta-shih-tu stands at an altitude of 5,000 ft., and

from this point the plateau rises in an easy incline to its average altitude of 6,000 ft. ; the plateau is crowned with a bewildering maze of isolated crests and summits which form in themselves a wild turmoil of hill-country, most difficult to map ; I found it hard to gain even a broad idea of the essential features. Looking westwards, a higher ridge showed where the first spurs of the Bogdo-ola rose out of the plateau ; eastwards the jumble of hills continued as far as eye could reach without any indica-tion of the existence of the Barkul range.

To climb on to the watershed necessitated only a rise of 1,000 ft., but the track was in so bad a condition that the carts had to be taken up one at a time with the aid of five horses. We crossed the watershed,—character-ized by a broad, open, plateau-like summit,—and began immediately to descend into a gorge surrounded by rough hill-country of most amazing barrenness. The whole of the next day we were passing through a winding gorge between naked crags, remarkable for their tilted and sometimes even perpendicular strata. Not a tussock of grass, not a vestige of growth relieved the blank landscape, which was composed of black shale slopes, sterile ridges, and valleys choked with denuded matter. In spite of the thaw we found only one tiny spring of water. This sudden change of climate and of the physical conditions was emphasized by the fact that we were now beyond the snow-zone ; quite unexpectedly we found ourselves surrounded by a landscape of intense blackness instead of glistening white. During one day's journey we passed out of Dzungaria into Chinese Turkestan, and on entering the latter we immediately came across an example of its most important characteristic, namely, the gradual process of desiccation to which it is subjected, and which stamps the entire region with an undeniable character of its own.

The change was so sudden, so complete, that we did not hesitate in forming an opinion that the desiccation at work on the south side of the Tian Shan does not extend into Dzungaria. By a curious chance our route at first led us into a small, self-contained basin, a kind of miniature Turkestan, with its special features and peculiar conditions reproduced for us on a miniature scale.

This isolated basin, which I will call after the guard-house and inn situated in its centre—Chi-ku-ching, lay immediately below us as we left the gorge in the mountains and entered the plain. It is a small basin; its area could be covered by that of Middlesex. On the north it is bordered by the declivities of the Tou-shui plateau —where a small amount of water drains into the basin at certain seasons of the year; on the south a semicircle of low desert hills connect up with the northern wall and render the basin complete. The road from Kumul to Turfan crosses it from east to west, Chi-ku-ching forming the junction of the Guchen road. The group of three or four houses and the rather brackish water-supply found at a depth of 20 ft. interested us little, the chief feature of the basin being the unmistakable signs of desiccation in actual progress.

The centre of the basin, at its lowest level, was covered with tamarisk mounds. These mounds stood as high as 20–25 ft., and were perfect types of æolian action— cut away underneath by persistent winds, and increased above by the deposition of blown sand, with a scanty growth of tamarisk on the summit. According to Professor Huntington's theory as to the approximate age of

DEAD POPLAR FOREST IN THE BASIN OF CHI-KU-CHING.

468

tamarisk mounds, these should fall under the category of mounds of from 500 to 1,000 years old.

In addition to the tamarisk mounds was a forest of stunted, unhealthy poplars with the dry stumps of many dead trees,—another obvious proof of a deficient rainfall. Many trees were already dead, others were giving up the struggle, for the stamp of decay was on them, and they were doomed to a slow and lingering death. In comparison with the desert surroundings the forest seemed out of place; it was as if the earth had been blasted, and some of the vegetation alone had managed to survive. Those that had succumbed stood like ghosts, their withered stems and twisted branches preserved by the dry atmosphere. It was a depressing scene, and we gloomily picked our way in and out amongst the crooked, white-trunked giants which must once have given welcome shade to the traveller.

The poplar forest, which had once covered the greater part of the basin, was now restricted to the northern edge, where there was still a small number of living trees. The living poplars were small, of about 30 ft. in height, with a meagre growth of branches at the summit of a bare trunk; the dead stumps, however, showed an immense girth, far surpassing any of the great poplars of Russian Turkestan. The present condition of the tamarisk mounds and the dead and dying forests of the basin of Chi-ku-ching made us realize that no such factors producing such devastating results were at work in Dzungaria. We recalled the poplar forests near Manas as being in a comparatively healthy condition; we could not remember even one tamarisk mound; and when, during our subsequent journeys in the following summer, we reached the central plains and the limit of the water-

flow from the mountain, we found that even in the
localities where the slightest variation in rainfall would
make itself first felt, there were no indications of a
changing climate such as existed south of the Tian
Shan.

Leaving the basin, we entered a black, stony desert,
destitute of fodder and water, this sterility continuing
until the level dropped to 4,000 ft. We there entered
the zone of grass and water, villages and cultivation,
a pleasant land inhabited by Turki Mohammedans, or
Chantos, who appealed to us as more picturesque, of
greater historical interest, and certainly more enter-
taining than the nondescript population of Dzungaria.
Chinese Turkestan is a continent inside a continent; it
is secluded, and barriered from the outside world, its
inhabitants having been moulded into a peculiar people
by their unique physical surroundings.

As we passed eastwards and water became more
abundant, pretty mud-built villages staged our route.
These were surrounded by orchards irrigated by rivulets
of clearest water; there were picturesque mosques
standing on sacred ground, half hidden by gigantic elm-
trees; and we heard once again the mellow voices of
the Mullahs calling the faithful to prayer. All this was
delightful after the restless atmosphere of Dzungaria.
We were treated here as honoured guests, and the dark-
eyed Chantos, with the hospitality for which they are
famed, entertained us as travellers in a strange land.
Beyond our immediate surroundings our view was en-
hanced by the wide panorama of the Barkul Range,
which, emerging out of the Tou-shui plateau, now ran
parallel with our route on the north, the snow-clad
summits and forested flanks forming a pleasant con-

trast to the dusty plains across which our carts now plied their way, and giving rest to the eyes from the aching yet fascinating deserts which, in long, flat sweeps, broken by occasional escarpments, extend southwards into the unknown.

There were many, indeed, far too many, matters to occupy our thoughts, and to stimulate our ambitions as we drew near to our goal. In a wayside village we found the tomb of some long-dead Chanto, decorated, as is the custom, with the horns of wild-game, such as wapiti, ibex, and wild-sheep ; the proportions of some of these horns gave Miller hopes of finding ampler and hitherto unknown hunting-grounds in the ranges to the north. A few days later, too, when the highest summits of the Karlik Tagh hove into view, and I drew the first lines across my plane-table on to its virgin peaks, we felt a considerable satisfaction in having accomplished the long winter journey of 800 miles, and we pressed forward eagerly towards the dark line of vegetation that shimmered in the dusty desert ahead of us and indicated the position of Kumul.

CHAPTER XVI

HAMI, OR KUMUL

" CAMUL is a province which in former days was a kingdom. It contains numerous towns and villages, but the chief city bears the name of Camul. The province lies between the two deserts ; for on the one side is the great desert of Lop, and on the other side is a small desert of three days' journey in extent. The people are all idolaters, and have a peculiar language. They live by the fruits of the earth, which they have in plenty and dispose of to travellers. They are a people who take things very easily, for they mind nothing but playing and singing, and dancing, and enjoying themselves. And it is the truth that, if a foreigner comes to the house of one of these people to lodge, the host is delighted. . . ."

Thus Marco Polo—the great Venetian traveller—some 600 years ago, briefly described Camul, or Kumul,[1] the Hami of the Chinese. Although it is certain that he himself never visited the locality and that his information was gathered from hearsay, or, as Yule suggests, from the personal experiences of his father and uncle, who may have passed through Kumul, yet our descriptions will show the accuracy with which Marco Polo's account tallies with the Kumul of the present day. It is true

---

[1] Kumul appears in a variety of forms. According to Yule (*Travels of Marco Polo*, p. 211) Kamul is the Turki form of the Mongol name Khamil ; it is also spelt Komul, while Khami, or Hami, is the Chinese form of the word. The inhabitants are called Kumuliks.

that there are certain marked differences, the cause
of which can easily be traced to radical changes in the
lives of the people, but on the whole the people are
the same ; they remain as an interesting proof of the
stagnating effect of living in the far-away and secluded
desert-basins of Central Asia.

Kumul is still the capital of this same little Khanate
" which was once a kingdom " and which is, in fact,
an independent native state—tributary to China, under
the direct rule of an hereditary Khan, or Prince. Re-
membering, therefore, Marco Polo's remarks about the
hospitality of the inhabitants, and knowing that Kumul
was sufficiently far away from the " world " to have
avoided contamination, we despatched a rider ahead, with
orders to deliver our visiting-cards to the Khan. On
approaching the first trees of the oasis we found a messenger awaiting our arrival who took us in charge and
led us to a house especially prepared for our recep-
tion. These quarters were situated outside the walls
of the town, overlooking the oasis, and with an uninterrupted view of the snow-mountains to the north ;
a large walled fruit-garden surrounding the house added
to its sense of comfort.

On arrival, we found a whole retinue of men awaiting our orders ; these unpacked the carts as we sat on the
carpeted divan at the end of a cool and exquisitely
clean room, drinking green tea brought by the head-
servant who had been told off by the Khan to attend to
our wants. Other retainers ran to fetch food, fuel, and
water ; but before these returned another batch of
messengers arrived, bearing the cards of the Khan with
inquiries as to the success of our journey and to our
comfort ; these messengers brought cart-loads of coal

and firewood, food for the horses, and two sheep for ourselves. Obviously Marco Polo had not exaggerated the inborn hospitality of the people of Kumul ; and, as will be noted in the following pages, the oasis, though situated on the main road between North China and Western Asia, still lives up to its former reputation, and remains unspoilt by over-taxation or misuse of its good-will.

In these delightful surroundings we rested a week, making the acquaintance of the feudal chief of this curious little kingdom on the edge of the Gobi, who showed us much hospitality and courtesy ; and here we prepared a plan for the exploration of the Karlik Tagh Mountains, which comprise in themselves the greater portion of the Khan's territory.

Marco Polo called Kumul " a city," and gavè the impression of the existence of many other towns and villages in the neighbourhood ; but, at the present day, Kumul is the only town that remains, and the capital itself can hardly claim to rank as a city. Kumul is not large, and its surrounding oasis covers a relatively small area ; it is so small, indeed, that in other parts of Chinese Turkestan Kumul would pass unnoticed. The geographical position of this oasis is alone responsible for its boasted importance, for Kumul owes its prosperity entirely to its location as the *last* town in Chinese Turkestan for desert-bound caravans, and as the *first* resting-place for travellers and for traffic coming from China. Beyond Kumul all is desert ; whether the caravans come or whether the caravans go, this town is to them of immense importance ; it represents either a goal safely reached after a hard and trying journey of eighteen days from An-hsi-chow on the southern side of the intervening

THE WALLS OF KUMUL.

THE KHAN'S RESIDENCE.

Gobi, or it partakes of the nature of a "taking-off" place where travellers outfit before entering on this same food-less and uninhabited stage.

When weary travellers from Cathay sight the cool snows of the Karlik Tagh they know their toils are at an end. The peaks which lift themselves from the central mass and are the culminating points of this insular mountain-group are also a landmark to wanderers on the plains below, and towards them converge the ancient trade-routes connecting China and Mongolia with Western Asia. Mongol nomads of the nameless region to the east and north "pick up" these snowy beacons from across the plains, and recognize that they form the boundary-point of their territory—the end of the pasture-zone. As a lighthouse on some far-flung promontory, guiding ships from across the ocean, so the snows of the Karlik Tagh shine as a guide to the caravans that cross the Gobi; and under their shadow lies the safe port of Kumul.

Those who have come hither for the first time wonder at the native inhabitants, with their Aryan features and strange garb; at the quaint, mud-built town and "covered" bazaars. Everywhere are new impressions, sights, sounds, and above all a new religion, for Kumul is the eastern outpost of the Turki-Mohammedan world,—all unite to prove to the newly arrived traveller from China that he has reached a foreign land, Chinese only in name.

Kumul introduces the traveller to Turkestan; it is the first Chanto oasis on the Nan-lu, or southern high-road. Westwards the Mohammedans hold all the fertile centres that encircle the desert heart of Turkestan, but in any other direction beyond the territory of the Khan extend unsettled steppes, the domain of Mongol chieftains and

Kirghiz shepherds. Karlik Tagh might be described as the meeting-place of three great territorial divisions, Mongolia, Dzungaria, and Turkestan. For, in point of fact, the territory of the Khan actually touches on all these countries.

This unpretentious oasis has taken an important share in the affairs of Inner Asia owing to its unrivalled position, and for this same reason it has experienced a long and chequered career.

In the early days, between the ninth and twelfth centuries, Kumul formed a part of the Uigur dominion, and it is probable that the first cultivators, and, indeed, the actual creators of the oasis, were the ancient Uigurs, who, coming in this direction when driven out from Mongolia, made large settlements on both flanks of the Tian Shan in the neighbourhood of the present-day Urumchi and Turfan. In the Kumuliks we may see the remnant of that ancient race whose migrations, and success as agriculturists, have so materially altered this part of Asia.

During the Mongol supremacy the oasis fell to the portion left by Jenghis Khan to his son Chagatai ; but there was small mention of Kumul in those days, for it lay to the south of the pasture-zone which formed the main resort of the Mongol hosts. Later, during the period that China held no very strong hold over her far-western dependencies, Dzungaria and Turkestan being in constant revolt, Kumul was more in evidence, for she was frequently in trouble and constantly changing her suzerain. Kumul formed the base of Chinese military operations not only during the crushing of the Dzungar Empire and the Dungan insurrection, but during the suppression of Yakub Beg.

Kumul is the key to Dzungaria, and is therefore of

immense strategical importance. Its resources must have been taxed to the utmost when vast and ponderous Chinese armies, after crossing the foodless Gobi, suddenly poured into the town. The oasis itself suffered much during the Dungan rebellions, for Turki and Chinese Mohammedans fell out amongst themselves ; Piassetsky, who visited Kumul in 1875, spoke of the town as being in ruins and used only as an encampment for Chinese soldiers. It is surprising to find this same town in such a flourishing condition as it is at the present day.

The Khans of this little kingdom have been wise enough to recognize the suzerainty of China, and for the last two hundred years, by careful diplomacy, the ruling chiefs have steered a clear course through the intrigues and entanglements that beset the heads of outlying native states in Central Asia ; consequently the individuality of the oasis has been preserved intact.

The most interesting side of Kumul is its status as a convert to Islam from Buddhism. In the days of the Uigurs the whole of this region belonged to the Buddhist world ; even up to the fourteenth century, when Marco Polo wrote of them, the Kumuliks were still " idolaters," or Buddhists. Signs of the prevalence of Buddhism are still to be found around Kumul in the presence of many shrines and temples such as those excavated at Togucha (to the west) by Prof. Grünwedel, and such as the remains of images and colossal seated Buddhas of which Stein was the first to record the existence at Ara-tam, a small oasis to the north-east of Kumul, which has always been the summer resort of the Khans.

In the middle of the fifteenth century it is evident that the two faiths were striving for the mastery, for there is record of a mosque and a great Buddhist temple standing side by side. Kumul is now, however, a veritable stronghold of Islam, and its inhabitants keep more strictly to the law than do the greater number of followers of the Prophet.

At the present day Kumul consists of a native Chanto [1] town, surrounded by high mud-walls and dominated by a great mud-palace—the residence of the Khan ; to the north-east is a walled Chinese town, containing yamens, quarters for the garrison, and bazaars, where most of the business is transacted. The population of the capital is probably about ten thousand, the native Kumuliks being in a slightly greater majority than the Chinese, the Dungans, and the garrison combined. It is probable that in recent years the Chinese element has increased, represented, as it is, chiefly by traders and small shopkeepers ; but the Chanto farmers cannot have increased much, owing to all available land being already under cultivation. Any further increase would undoubtedly cause either discontent or a desire to emigrate.

Around the town lies the oasis, a veritable Garden of Eden in the midst of a howling wilderness. The inhabited zone of cultivation is very small, extending only for about seven miles north and south, and five miles east and west ; but such is the richness of the soil, and with such care is the ground terraced and watered, that it supports a considerable population in proportion to its size. Kumul lies in the midst of a salt-encrusted plain, and its existence depends upon the drainage from the highlands of the Karlik Tagh lying some fifty miles away. The water which drains southwards from these ranges is for the most part lost

[1] See footnote, p. 397.

A STREET SCENE IN THE CHINESE QUARTER.

below the surface of the ground after leaving the mountains. The torrents sink below the surface in the piedmont gravel slopes at the foot of the hills, but appear again twenty miles out on the plain in the form of copious springs, which ooze up and form the irrigation-supply of the oasis.

No existing map gives a true idea of the hydrography of this region. Rivers, intimated by continuous blue lines, flowing out into the waste where they form lakes (called Kul), are common errors on the maps. As a matter of fact, the water which escapes being used for irrigating purposes generally disappears below the surface of the ground ; though in a few cases, when there is a sufficient supply from the mountains, it may reappear again in some depression far out in the desert in the form of small saline springs.

The Narin River, for instance, the main source of the water-supply that feeds Kumul, disappears into the ground a couple of miles from the point where it leaves the rugged sandstone foot-hills of the Karlik Tagh ; eighteen miles farther on, five large springs appear in what was once its river-bed. This water is used for irrigating the oasis.[1] Twenty miles below the town the water is too

---

[1] Although these springs are the main irrigation-supply, they are not the only ones. The eastern half of the oasis we found to be dependent upon small springs, of the same type, which originated from the drainage of the Edira Valley, the next valley eastwards of the Narin. Apart from these, all the cultivation at the north-east of the oasis, which extends for some four or five miles, relies upon a water-supply obtained from melting snows or rain in the mountains, arriving by way of the Edira Valley, or by the canal, which has been led with great labour for some twelve miles across the plain, from close below Toruk, where it catches the surplus of the spring and summer floods. Failing this supply, the crops would be ruined. " Kariz," or subterranean canals, as employed in other parts of Turkestan and Persia, only existed in a ruined state to the west of Togucha.

salt for irrigation. Beyond this point there is no continuous flow, the drainage is spasmodic, regulated by the supply from the mountains. In summer, when the snows melt in the highlands, there may be a flow of water above ground to the lakes of Shona Nor, which the Russian maps mark as forming the terminus of the river of Kumul. This would be, however, for a very short period only, and I think it probable that these "lakes" are in reality only marshy ground containing a few stagnant pools, formed by the residue of the drainage oozing up at this level,—which is the "water-table."

These imaginary lakes have crept into the maps and are religiously copied from edition to edition, no one having visited them since the time of the early Russian explorers who located them, in most cases, by hearsay. Thus, the illusive problem of Lake Toli,—that mysterious patch of blue in the desert to the south of Kumul,— had long attracted my attention and made me desirous of solving its mystery. Lake Toli remains unvisited, but from information I gathered at Kumul I am in a position to give a satisfactory explanation of its character ; and its existence, in a somewhat modified form, may safely be accepted.

The Kumuliks have a somewhat unusual rendering for the Turki words relating to water, signifying springs, lakes, rivers, etc.; the meaning they attach to the ordinary Turki words for these being, in some degree, responsible for the supposition that Toli was a lake. They give a very exact interpretation of such words as "daria," "bulak," and "kul." For instance, a river is only a "daria" for a short time in early summer, when the channel is full ; they speak only of "daria" when the melted snows from the mountains send a stream in high flood across the plains. The remainder of the year the water-supply is called " bulak," meaning springs. All ordinary watercourses on the plains around Karlik Tagh, even good-sized streams used for irrigation purposes, are called " bulak," because they originate from springs, and do not come continuously from the snows. Now, a large group of strong springs, such as is often found issuing out of old river-beds at a distance of about fifteen to twenty miles from the mountains, or in the depressions still farther away on the desert, are invariably called " kul," a word like the Mongol " nor," generally used to denote a lake or large sheet of water, but here used to describe a spring-head or a terminal marsh which may, or may not, form an area of standing water. Iti Kul near Togucha, Shona Nor at the end of the river of Kumul, and Toli Kul in the desert to the south, are examples of Kumulik nomenclature.

All these are localities of the same character, namely, water-tables where the land-surface drops to the level which permits water to appear above the surface. I believe that the use of the word " kul " caused early explorers to locate lakes, by hearsay, in a region where merely springs exist. It is not too much to suppose that Toli Kul is in reality a depression, in which, if there were sufficient water, there would be a lake. The water is never sufficient in itself to form a lake, as only a meagre supply issues from underground, this being the residue of occasional drainage from the higher land to the north and east ; nevertheless, according to the Kumulik idea, it is a " kul." No doubt, in former days, when the climate was damper, a lake existed. For the same reason that the lake has disappeared, the old route which led thence from Kumul, across what is now the most inhospitable desert, and joined the great trade-route that ran between Su-chow and Lop Nor, has also sunk into disuse.

This peculiar subterranean system of drainage creates areas of luxuriant cultivation in marked contrast to the barren stony plains surrounding them. The fruits of the earth are so abundant that, as Marco Polo remarks, the inhabitants have even sufficient to dispose of to travellers. The fame of the oasis for rice, melons, and grapes has already spread to China. The melons are a speciality of the Kumulik cultivators, the preserved skin being exported in large quantities, and actually forming a part of the tribute sent to the Court at Pekin. Wheat, barley, and oats occupy the larger area and form the staple supply; while the influence of the Chinese is shown in the neat little vegetable patches close to the walls of the town.

The chief interest lay, however, in the people themselves—both the townsfolk and the cultivators—for the strange mixture of race and religion, of Turki and Chinese, of Islam and Buddhism, has given rise to many peculiarities, and laid the foundation of many unusual characteristics. The position the oasis holds on the outskirts of the Moslem world, and as the last of the Chanto settlements of Turkestan, renders it liable to invasion by foreign customs. As a result the inhabitants, although of pure-blooded Turki descent, have been so influenced by Chinese elements during the last two hundred years—as to make them adopt the same dress, speak the same language, and in many cases even eat the same food. The Kumuliks, indeed, are a people undergoing a rapid process of assimilation by the

A KUMULIK GIRL.

Chinese, and were it not for the determination of their Khan to preserve their "nationality" (in order, no doubt, to preserve *his* chieftainship), his subjects would already have lost their individuality, and, perhaps, have broken away from his rule.

In a great many cases the men wore a strange mixture of Chinese and Chanto dress, replacing the Chanto "khalat" by a Chinese coat, but always retaining the typical Turkish skull-cap as head-gear, this being worn in winter without, and in summer with, a turban. Sometimes complete Chinese costume was worn; this was especially noticed at the Court of the Khan, in deference no doubt to Chinese officialdom; and in these cases the "get-up" was duplicated even to a mock-pigtail. The women-folk on the other hand, had not taken so readily to Chinese ways, for, although they copied the Chinese custom of painting their faces, and occasionally donned coats of gaudily coloured Chinese silks in preference to their own more picturesque "chapans," this was chiefly the case in the town of Kumul and amongst the more wealthy class. In the mountains and outlying oases the Chinese influence had not affected them.

The women did not veil their faces, but guarded their good looks from strange eyes with equal success by the judicious use of their coat-tails. The excessive shyness of the ladies of Kumul appeared strange to us after the easy manners of the Mongols and the Kirghiz and even of the Chanto emigrants in Dzungaria. In Kumul it was almost impossible to catch a glimpse of a woman in the streets. They were as shy as rabbits, and dived into their houses when they saw us approaching, and even locked the doors until we were well past! It was obvious that the reputation which Kumul possessed in the days of Marco Polo had been entirely changed ; this change cannot have been the result of their conversion to Islam, and can only have taken place in recent years, for Prjevalsky, who visited the oasis in 1879, said that " the women were free and easy in their manners, just as they were in Marco Polo's time." Now, however, morality is a feature—a strange paradox indeed, a moral town in Chinese Turkestan ; a profound contrast to olden days, in order to produce which some very strong cause must have been at work.

As Chinese influence is responsible for the mixture of customs which the Kumuliks now exhibit, so is it indirectly the cause of their morality and good behaviour. Formerly the rapid advance of the Chinese element was viewed by the Khan with apprehension ; he foresaw the degeneration of his people into a mongrel type—half Chinese, half Chanto, and, as a good Mussulman, fearing the effects that might follow, he determined to keep his subjects so closely to their religious principles that they could not slip away from Islam. The Khan, no doubt, also suspected the possibility of discontent amongst his subjects, and perhaps even a desire for freedom from his rule ; eager, therefore, to keep his people from being contaminated by the Chinese, realizing that he might lose his hold over them, he strictly enforced the tenets of the Mussulman faith. The fact of this very small but extremely strict Mussulman community situated at the very end of the Islamic world and completely under Chinese influence is, indeed, a paradox. Herein lies the chief peculiarity of Kumul. It is cut off from any other strongholds of Islam, and lies outside their sphere of influence, few Mohammedans pass through it, and its inhabitants are environed by Buddhists and Chinese possessing no definite faith. Moreover, it has been so greatly influenced by Chinese elements during the last two hundred years that it has adopted many Chinese customs and even Chinese dress. Yet, in spite of this, or perhaps *because* of this, the Kumuliks represent a type of Mohammedan people hard to beat for strictness of conduct, and exact upholding of the letter of the law.

The position which Kumul holds in this respect is entirely due to the strength of character of the Khan and his ability in enforcing a form of narrow Puritanism which prevents the Kumuliks from breaking away, and makes religious principle the foundation of their good behaviour. The Khan sets an example, which is followed by his retainers and copied by the people. Men have to pray at the mosque, whether they like to or not, and for those who offend large whips are kept, hung up in the courtyard of the castle, and, according to report, are used without mercy. The drinking of spirits is forbidden, and all Moslem laws as regards the seclusion of women are carried out without relaxation. Such are the reasons for the one great change in the customs of the Kumuliks which has taken place in recent years.

This tyranny has had an irritating effect on the inhabitants, who seem to suffer from over-legislation. They have no longer time or opportunity for " playing and singing and dancing and enjoying themselves," as in Marco Polo's day, although, no doubt, the desire for amusement is as strong as it is amongst other Chantos. Their status is that of serfs under a feudal lord, who owns the best lands, the largest flocks and herds, who employs forced labour, levies a considerable tax, and even takes upon himself the responsibility of posing as their spiritual leader. Even in this out-of-the-way corner of the world there existed a strong desire for freedom from an autocratic rule ; we noticed a general feeling of discontent amongst the Khan's subjects, who appeared eager to come directly under Chinese rule. Up to the present the Kumuliks have possessed neither the initiative nor the enterprise to take a decided step in any direction ; the man who has " ideas " is immediately exiled, we met many such in the outlying villages of the far corners of the Khan's dominion. We found, too, that the hunters had been deprived of their guns, these being forfeited on account of an attempted rebellion the year before.

The discontents endeavoured to emigrate ; this move had to be carried out secretly and with a loss of their possessions, for it was considered the worst of all crimes to desire to leave the fatherly rule of the Moslem Khan and to dwell in a heathen land. If Kumul were situated nearer the Russian frontier, she would no doubt seek Russian protection and thereby escape from the harsh rule of the Chief.

In addition to Kumul there are several small oases on the plains,—Taranchi, Togucha, Astine, Lapchuk, Toruk, Ta-shar, Khotun-tam, Karmukchi, Tashbulak, Bai, Adak, Nom,—besides others hamlets composed of a few farmsteads, but hardly worthy of the name of village. These are all subject to the Khan ; but the main bulk of the population who owe allegiance to him,— outside the town of Kumul,—is made up of Taghliks, or mountaineers, who live in small villages tucked away amongst the rugged valleys of the Karlik Tagh ; here they are left in greater seclusion, but pay their taxes in

KUMULIK MUSICIANS.

A TAGHLIK OF KARLIK TAGH.

grain, kine, or labour to their overlord at Kumul. We have knowledge of no less than thirty villages and groups of farm-houses belonging to the Khan, twenty in the plain and ten in the high mountain valleys, all of these being inhabited by agriculturists. On the northern slopes of the mountains only, where grassy plateaux replace the steep-sided, rocky ridges of the southern side, are people to be found who might be described as nomadic shepherds; even these are in reality merely Taghliks who live a semi-nomadic existence in more or less permanently pitched tents, tending the flocks and herds.

Over these ruled Mahsud Shah, hereditary Prince of the Khanate of Kumul and eighth of his line, bearing the complimentary Chinese title of Tsing Wang, or Prince of the First Rank. Kumul remained as an example of that system whereby the Chinese were enabled to leave the affairs of the western dependencies in the hands of local chiefs, the status being that of a protected native state. The Khan had absolute power over his subjects, except in the exercise of the death-penalty; in such a case the sentence imposed by the Khan had to be sanctioned by the Chinese " political agent " in residence at Kumul, who managed the affairs of the Chinese colony, and acted as adviser to the Khan in matters of any importance.

The Khan treated us with much kindness and honour. The British, he said, were friends of Islam, and he was glad to meet them. He knew of Hindustan, and, as a Mussulman under Chinese suzerainty, he appreciated foreign rulers who showed respect for the religion of their subjects. During our stay in Kumul and our journeys throughout his dominions we experienced such wholehearted hospitality and such genuine good-will from this Eastern Prince, that no written words can sufficiently convey our appreciation. After the first short complimentary visits which he paid us, and which we returned, the Khan invited us to dinner, and the five hours spent in his company in his palace gave us a real insight into the life of a Chanto ruler.

Overlooking the town of Kumul was the group of buildings making up the Khan's residence, picturesque in the possession of several stories, high walls, great gateways, and a paved road leading up to them. Sending a messenger in advance, we rode first through a portion of the Turki town, which, with narrow alleys between flat-roofed mud-houses, street corners overshadowed by fine old trees,—under which groups of gaudily dressed Kumuliks lounged and talked,—with mosques and minarets, presented a choice of rare pictures to the eye of the artist. As we approached the palace and passed under the numerous vaulted gates into the inner courtyard we felt as if we were approaching the stronghold of some medieval baron. On our arrival servants were awaiting us; some seized our horses, while others led us on through the last gateway into the outer hall of the Khan's abode. Here was drawn up a double line of armed retainers,—a bodyguard of Chinese soldiers, mercenaries in the employ of the Khan. The Khan himself came down to meet us, and led us, with much ceremony, into the inner chamber, where we sat down and drank tea.

The palace was a quaint structure, a composition of both Chinese and Turki architecture, the interior being well furnished in Chinese style. Here in Eastern luxury lived the Khan, surrounded by his retainers and

A BY-LANE IN THE CHANTO TOWN.

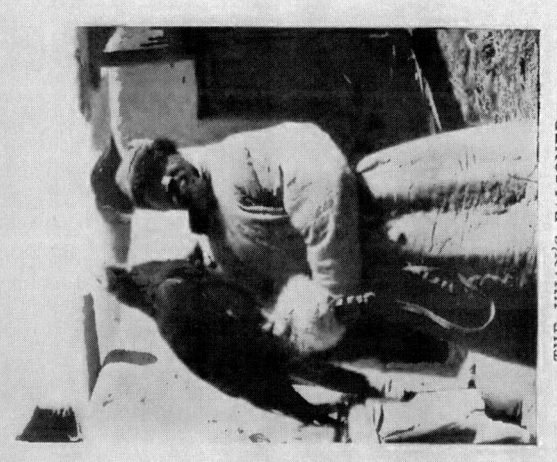

THE KHAN'S FALCONER.

488]

courtiers ; he kept up considerable state, which befitted
his position as ruler, but tended to increase the strain on
the resources of the Kumuliks. He possessed stables
for his horses, mews for his falcons, and a three-storied
harem for his womenfolk, while surrounding the palace
was spread a garden of extraordinary luxuriance.

Mahsud Shah, as a vassal of the Emperor of China,
visits Pekin every sixth year, where he acts as personal
servant to the Emperor for forty days, in proof of his
allegiance. These visits had considerably enlarged his
ideas, and were responsible for the introduction of many
innovations, quite beyond his means, into the ceremony
of his Court. Hence, no doubt, the growing discontent
amongst his subjects, for we gathered that the Prince was
more feared than liked, and therefore unpopular. Treated
with respect and honour by the Chinese, who upheld his
authority, in receipt from the Government of 2,000 tael
a year, besides twenty-five bales of silk, etc., with his
people in comparative serfdom, he has a very good
time and is presumably very wealthy. He certainly
upheld the reputation of Kumul for liberal hospitality.

After an hour spent in talking and drinking tea, the
Khan showed us his garden. Followed by an escort
of attendants, we paraded the paved walks which led
in and out amongst orchards and flower-beds; crossed
little bridges built in Chinese fashion over running streams
irrigating the land; passed several miniature mosques,
and finally reached a summer-house which lay under a
group of giant elm-trees. Here tea was again served and
we rested a little, for the Khan was not used to long
walks. Later we visited the shooting-range where the
archers practised, and then continued our walk to the
iris-beds. Here was an artificial lake, and on an island

in the midst of irises and overshadowed by a ring of tall poplars was built a cool pavilion for use during the midsummer heat.

On our return to the palace we sat down to the *real* dinner of thirty-courses, served up in Chinese style. We had eaten Chinese dinners before, so the entertainment was no novelty; but the peculiar circumstances under which it was given made it interesting. For, although our host lived in a Chinese house, entertained us with exact Chinese ceremonial, gave us a Chinese dinner, was dressed himself, as were all his servants, in Chinese costume and wore mock pigtails, yet, on the other hand, there was much in the Khan that was not at all Chinese. The Prince was almost European in features; he had the dignity, the ease, and the charming manners of a Mohammedan gentleman; he talked in Turki in the most friendly way, and seemed to understand the aims and objects of wandering Englishmen in Central Asia. His real character showed up in contradiction to all that he had copied from China, when, for example, he would only touch the spirit from a bottle he had opened in our honour, and when he left us half-way through dinner in order to pray at the mosque! He much wanted to make the pilgrimage to Mecca, but was doubtful of obtaining the necessary permission from the Emperor of China, perhaps also fearing to leave his people under the present unsettled conditions. He took great pride in showing us the extent of his resources and the variety of his belongings. A crowd of courtiers were on duty in the adjoining room, and at the expression of the slightest wish half a dozen men would cry, " Khosh! " and hasten to obey his commands. We chanced to ask if he had any falcons, and the falconers appeared as if by magic,

one with a peregrine, another a goshawk, and a third
bearing a magnificent golden-eagle. His guns were
brought for our inspection—a Mauser and a Winchester
rifle, a Browning automatic-pistol and a 12-bore shot-
gun; he showed us his camera, which he could not
work; while his gramophone played to us English,
Russian, and Chinese music.

Besides his residence in the capital, the Khan had two
country-seats, one at Ara-tam at the foot of the mountain,
and another in the high valley of Bardash ; both of these
we visited in the course of our journey through his
territory. As a landed proprietor, he had some of the
finest orchards in Central Asia, a considerable acreage
of corn-land, and large flocks and herds, these latter
being tended by forced labour, for the Khan exacted a
tax of five days' work out of every month, or two
months a year, from all his subjects.

We asked him how far his territory extended, and
with a sweep of the arm he said, "All that you see is
mine, and more that you cannot see—behind the mountain." This was more or less correct, for although a
portion of the Barkul Range which is visible to the north-
west of Kumul does not actually belong to him, yet it is
an uninhabited country and not of much consequence.
All that is of value within view of the capital is under
the Khan. The plains are dotted with occasional oases—
miniature Kumuls, which are situated wherever water
approaches the surface and allows irrigation ; but the
Karlik Tagh Mountains really compose the greater part,
as well as the most important part, of the Khan's dominion. About 7,500 square miles lie under his rule, and
of this nearly one-half is taken up by the rugged ranges
and high plateaux which provide pasture for the flocks and

herds, small areas for cultivators, and—most important of all—the entire water-supply on which depends the existence of the oases on the plains below.

The combination of physical and climatic conditions comprised within the dominions of the Khanate of Kumul renders it a complete, self-supporting, and independent region. There exists every variety of scenery, temperature, fauna and flora. There are dry deserts below, granite ranges above, mountain torrents, pine forests, alpine pastures, snow-fields and glaciers. There are rice fields and vegetable gardens ; luscious fruits, such as melons, grapes, and apricots from the plains, and apples and pears from the hills ; there are corn-lands and fine sheep pastures. From cool glaciers one can look down on to dusty plains at a distance of only a long day's march ; and the haunts of such mountain-loving fauna as ibex, wild-sheep, and snow-cock margin closely on those of gazelle and wild-horses ! The region is one of peculiar extremes even for Central Asia, where, as Curzon has remarked, "nature seems to revel in striking the extreme chords upon her miraculous and inexhaustible gamut of sound."

It was the Karlik Tagh that was the real object of our visit, for, although we traversed some 3,000 miles of country in Dzungaria both by plain and mountain, this portion alone offered the chance of making additions to geographical knowledge. The region between the Altai and Tian Shan had been fairly well mapped ; new ground alone remained on the south-eastern border-ranges— the Bogdo-ola, Barkul, and Karlik Tagh. To speak of this region as being a part of Dzungaria is incorrect, for the watershed of these ranges forms the boundary between that country and Chinese Turkestan ; but, in this case, the boundary of the region to which we devoted ourselves was of necessity a political one, the Karlik Tagh on both north and south belonging to the Khan of Kumul. This was the only point where our work extended outside the natural boundaries of Dzungaria.

The area of country over which the word of the Khan is law, includes the entire mountain-group of Karlik Tagh and the plains to the north, south, and east, as far as Karlik Tagh water flows. The Tur Kul basin on the north side of the range, and the eastern half of the Metshin-ola, an offshoot of the main group, is included, as is also the eastern portion of the Barkul basin, beyond Kou-si. The Barkul range, as far north as the watershed, is the Khan's, while the western boundary of his territory is determined by the town of Lodun, or Liao-tun, three stages along the high-road to Turfan.

The fact that our goal lay entirely within the jurisdiction of the Khan greatly simplified matters for us. When we informed him of our plans he answered that he and all his belongings were at our disposal; we could ask all we needed, and should lack nothing so long as we were within his territory. Consequently, orders were given to enable us to travel at our pleasure and view the whole of his country; whilst letters were sent ahead and the way prepared, we had time to enjoy the beauties of the mountains which it had for so long been our ambition to visit.

CHAPTER XVII

THE KARLIK TAGH

ON a clear day the view from Kumul is inspiring. Southwards stretch the yellow deserts to the fabulous Lake Toli, and still farther away to the gates of China Proper. Across these runs the track connecting Sin-Kiang with the home provinces. A desert-stage of eighteen days would take the traveller to An-hsi-chow, on the farther side of the Gobi, and two more would allow him to rest his eyes on the Hoang Ho—the Yellow River. Northwards rise the snow-ridges of the Barkul range, linking up farther east with the Karlik Tagh, which culminates in several fine summits. The mountains rise abruptly, straight from the plain, superb in their setting of far-flung Gobi, lifting their crests in triumph above the haze and the dust of the low-lying deserts.

It was early spring when we first sighted the Karlik Tagh, the abundant snows that lay on the high, flat summits and spread themselves out in smooth fields over the plateaux lending an enchantment to the somewhat barren plains of dust and stone that lay around. Here the mountains end and the deserts begin, for at this point the great Tian Shan mountain-system, after extending from west to east for close on sixteen hundred miles, finds at last its limit. Dropping, as before described, into a low, rounded plateau-country at the eastern end of the Bogdo-ola section, it then rises again in one last effort, attains a worthy altitude of over 14,000 ft., and drops sheer into utter desert. This solitary group of snow pinnacles stands as a sentinel guarding the marches of Mongolia, of Dzungaria, and of Turkestan. Day after day, during our tramps around the range, those peaks were our land-mark, and for weeks during our survey-work our " sights" rested continually on them. Far out into the deserts beyond, they guided us and put aright our erring calculations. They were a source of wonder, whether sulphur-yellow as dawn flushed the sky, or caught at evening by the rose-gleam when the flats below were already dusky; scarcely a day passed without our being treated to some new impression of the Karlik Tagh.

A word as to our forerunners in these regions and the extent of their discoveries.

In 1872 we received the first accounts of the way thither from Russian territory, through the means of a trading expedition, which a Russian merchant despatched into Mongolia, and which touched at Barkul on its wanderings. It was not until 1875, however, that the first true explorers, coming across the Gobi Desert from China, roughly recorded the topography of Kumul, Barkul, and the neighbouring mountains. These were Russians — Sosnovski and Matussovski, who came through to Kumul by the high-road from Western China, and, crossing the passes to Barkul, visited Guchen on their way home to Siberia. A member of the expedition, Piassetsky, left us an account of this journey, one of the few records of Russian travel which has been translated into the English language.

To these travellers must be assigned the honour of

being the first visitors, but the following year more systematic work than theirs was accomplished, and finer results obtained, by the expedition under the celebrated Potanin, who, with Rafailow as surveyor, came down to Barkul from Kobdo and the Eastern Altai. The expedition crossed the Barkul Range, paid a short visit to Kumul, and returned by the same pass (the Kosheti-dawan), by which they had come. The travellers then explored the northern flanks of Karlik Tagh as far as Adak and Nom, and returned to Siberia by way of Uliassutai. The maps of Potanin and Rafailow stood for many years as the standard survey of those regions, and, as a matter of fact, up till the time of our visit there had been no additions to their original survey of the northern flanks of the Karlik Tagh. Rafailow determined the astronomical positions of Barkul, Adak, and Kumul ; but, although his observations still hold good for the two former places, more recent work by Stein's surveyor and Mr. Clementi has placed Kumul slightly farther to the west. The retention on the maps of the work of these early explorers shows how few other travellers have visited this region during the time which has elapsed since its first discovery.

The next visitor was Prjevalsky, who seems to have included visits to most towns in Central Asia on his itinerary of exploration. This experienced traveller, on his third scientific journey through Middle Asia, (1879–80), passed by Barkul—without entering it, and rested for a short time at Kumul on his way to Tibet. He gives a short description of the famous oasis, but has nothing to say about the Karlik Tagh or neighbouring ranges.

Although Potanin gave us the first ideas of the

THE HIGHEST PEAKS OF THE KARLIK TAGH.

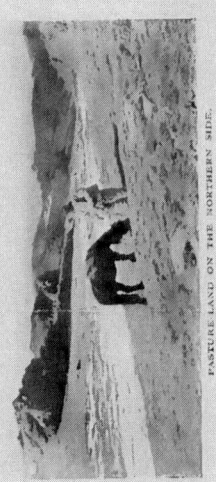

PASTURE LAND ON THE NORTHERN SIDE.

DENUDED SLOPES ON THE SOUTHERN FLANKS OF THE RANGE.

[268]

geography of the Karlik Tagh Mountains and the basin
of Barkul, it remained for two other explorers, the
brothers Grum Grjimailo (1889–91), to show the
nature of the country between the Barkul and the Bogdo-
ola groups and of the desert region to the south-east of
Kumul. The topography of these regions, as represented
on the maps predating their explorations, was mere
imagination. These travellers, who were chiefly interested
in natural history, were the first to put forward a theory
that the Karlik Tagh had certain affinities with the Altai
mountain-system, instead of, as expected, with the Tian
Shan. They were the first to explore the famous Bogdo-
ola Mountains and the Tou-shui plateau, which they
crossed and recrossed in several different directions. They
also visited Kumul and the southern flanks of the Karlik
Tagh, before striking east-south-east into the unknown
Gobi.

In 1887 the first Englishman visited Kumul; this
was Captain (now Sir Francis) Younghusband, who, in
the course of a trans-continental journey from Pekin to
India, came to the Karlik Tagh from the north-east,
having followed the northern Gobi trade-route from
Kalgan. He crossed the eastern spurs of the Karlik
Tagh from Mogai to Kumul, and, staying there four
days, passed on to Turfan and Kashgar. In the same
year Colonel Mark Bell reached Kumul from the south
and crossed the ranges to Barkul, thus being the only
Englishman in advance of us to visit this town.

The map of the Karlik Tagh region remained un-
revised until Kozloff arrived in Kumul, at the termination
of extended journeys in Chinese Turkestan and Tibet,
accomplished between the years 1893–5. In those days
Kozloff was working under the experienced Roborovsky,

but he was entrusted with the management of many lateral expeditions. From Kumul, for instance, he made an excursion into the Karlik Tagh, and gave us the most up-to-date map of that region as a whole, which still stands on the Russian " 40-verst " sheets as the most correct survey. Kozloff's journey was the most scientific, and gave finer results than any other traveller's in those regions. He visited Narin, Tur Kul, Adak, Nom, and Bai, and made an ascent into the alpine region, describing his experiences with remarkable ability.

After Kozloff's visit twelve years elapsed before the next explorer set foot in these regions. This was Dr. (now Sir Aurel) Stein, who, in his itinerary of archaeo-logical research, made the complete circuit of Chinese Turkestan. Stein arrived in Kumul in the autumn of 1907, and spent two weeks in the oasis itself and on a visit to Toruk and Ara-tam ; there he investi-gated the ruins of certain Buddhist shrines, while Rai Lal Singh, his Indian surveyor, explored the southern flanks of the mountains between Khotun-tam and the Barkul passes. Stein's work considerably altered the configuration of this portion of the range as shown on previous maps, and a certain amount of material from his maps is embodied in that published at the end of this volume.

During Stein's visit to Kumul another traveller, Mr. Cecil Clementi, passed through on his way across China. Success in the laborious undertaking of making a com-plete series of astronomically fixed positions right across China from Kashgar to Hong-Kong has caused the acceptance of his position for Kumul, in preference to those of others, in the reproduction of my plane-table survey ; beyond this his work has not affected mine. The antiquities of this region have been investigated by Dr. von Lecoq and Professor Grünwedel, who explored those they considered worthy of excavation, near Togucha, to the west of Kumul, where they found interesting remains belonging to Buddhist times.

Many other travellers have, no doubt, passed through Kumul on their way east or west, but none, except those here enumerated, have, so far as I can ascertain, visited Karlik Tagh or Barkul. The object of our visit was to complete the survey of the region and to bring out a detailed map of the whole mountain-group, as well as to gain some idea of its fauna, so as to be able to decide the exact place the Karlik Tagh holds in the life-zones of Central Asia. A lateral journey to the far east, which should have included a visit to the Ati Bogdo, was planned, but this most important portion of the programme had to be given up, owing primarily to the extreme difficulty of finding transport or guides into a region to which men never go—from this quarter, as well as to lack of time. By making a complete circle around the range, however, by penetrating to its uppermost valleys, and clambering (with no small amount of difficulty) over its rugged sandstone foot-hills, we gained a reliable idea of its physical features and a rare insight into the conditions of life on this insular mountain-group.[1]

The panorama of mountains spread out to the north and north-east of Kumul was instructive. North of the oasis, at a distance of about twenty-five miles, lay the Barkul Range, running east and west, in a narrow ridge. The western part of this range presented the appearance of a flat-topped block-mountain, but in

[1] See map at end of volume.

the neighbourhood of the highest peaks the ridge became rough and serrated. Farther east the Barkul Range dropped in altitude, thus allowing free intercourse between Kumul and the northern steppes, over several cols of between 8,000 to 9,000 ft. in height. At this point the Karlik Tagh began,—a long, table-topped ridge which gradually inclined from 9,000 ft. to the summit of the highest peak in the centre of the range.

The western Karlik Tagh showed a large expanse of deep-lying snow-fields, which added to the grandeur of this panoramic view, and emphasized the peculiar, blocked-shaped formation of the range. Its plateau-like summit was seamed by deep-cut, steep-sided ravines, which led off the drainage. Even the highest peaks visible from Kumul were of a rounded type, and did not do justice to their height ; but immediately to the east of the culminating point the formation changed, the plateau broke up and fell off into excessively rough country, with lofty, tooth-like pinnacles and jagged peaks, well worn, razor-edged ridges, splintered precipices, and V-shaped valleys. The snow-line extended for over thirty miles in length, and over this area, even in summer, no pass or track is known by which man can cross the range from north to south. Barren, stony plains led up to the foot-hills, which rose suddenly in the form of a rough, steep ridge of sandstone. This the desert had waged war upon and successfully overrun, but beyond these outlying foot-hills the higher slopes showed welcome green of forest, above which naked rock and shale-slopes led up to stainless, untrodden snow-fields.

Whilst waiting for our transport arrangements to be completed, we made a short trip to the foot of the mountains, which gave us a good impression of the nature

ROUGH CLIMBING IN THE KARLIK TAGH.

of the ground and of the condition of the Kumulik cultivators in those parts. Leaving Kumul on March 12th
with one man as guide, we rode to the north-north-east.
Immediately on leaving the cultivated areas we found
that the sandy soil, deprived of its moisture by irrigation
works, was threatening to overrun the oasis ; the land had
perished, and the desert was encroaching on the "sown."
Beyond this, a bare gravel "sai" led us, for twenty
miles, up to the rocky girdle of sandstone which forms
the first foot-hills of the range. There was nothing to
note during this long ride except one great watch-tower
which stood alone in the plain, about half-way between
Kumul and the mountains. Being massively built, it
formed a landmark for a great distance, and was evidently
intended as a place of refuge. Stein says that it was
reputed to be of great age, and he questions from what
marauding tribes of the north was it meant to offer
shelter.

On approaching the foot-hills we found a small river
issuing from a gorge in the sandstone range, and
forming a tiny area of fertile land at the point where
it entered the plain. The river had cut a deep trench
in the gravel fan, and terraces a hundred feet high
margined the little valley, in which were ensconced the
fields and village of Toruk. Toruk was apparently a
typical village of Kumuliks, whose progress is limited
by the amount of land at their disposal and the amount
of water they are allowed to use for irrigation purposes.
This locality supported only some twelve or fifteen houses ;
these were crowded together in the space of less than
half an acre, and formed a circle, completely walled
in but for one wide gateway. Boulders from the river-
bed and mud formed the building material. Naturally

the houses were mere hovels, but we were entertained by the friendly Kumuliks in their homely way, and given the best that the village could offer.

Their land scarcely extended for a mile down the valley, which was half a mile wide; but even this small area was not all available for cultivation, the growing of crops depending upon the amount of soil left amongst the rocks and boulders. Every available spot was used, and I strongly suspect the artificial making of fields within range of the irrigation canals, by the laborious means of bringing soil from the terraces above. This example shows how closely the economic possibilities of Karlik Tagh are put to the test by the Kumuliks and what amount of labour is expended in order to sustain their simple lives. The river, the main source of the water-supply of Kumul, must bring a considerable flood at times, for it was spanned by a good bridge. At the time of our visit it was frozen over, but water was flowing under the two-foot coating of ice. Two miles below the village it disappeared altogether below the surface of the ground, and three miles farther even the high river-terraces spread out and lost themselves in the wide fan of the river-bed, which farther still became scarcely discernible.

Above the village rose the sandstone foot-hills of Karlik Tagh. This outlying range of sandstone was perhaps the most peculiar feature of this side of the mountains.[1] It extended as a barrier between the plain and the high-lands all the way from Toruk to Khotun-tam, and con-fined the Taghliks, or mountaineers, and their villages to the secluded upper valleys which lay behind. Toruk, for instance, was quite cut off from direct communication with those numerous settlements of Taghliks which

[1] See diagram, p. 521.

GORGE IN THE SANDSTONE FOOTHILLS OF KARLIK TAGH.

502]

find ample room for cultivation on the middle course of the river, between the sandstone and the main range. The rivers invariably pass through this sandstone ridge in deep-cut, impassable ravines, the lower valleys rarely giving access to the upper. This rendered travelling exceedingly laborious, it being necessary to make big detours in order to reach the mountain villages situated at the back of the foot-hills.

We returned to Kumul by the way we had come, and set about making the final arrangements for our move eastwards. By command of the Khan, men and horses were provided for us, and such orders were given as would enable us to travel at our pleasure, and see the whole of his territory. An old Kumulik Beg, a gentleman of most courtly manners, was especially deputed to accompany us and to arrange all our affairs whilst travelling within the Khanate. Relays of horses were to take us from place to place, wherever our work led us, whilst our heavy baggage could go by cart along the plain, at the foot of the mountain. Lodgings were to be prepared for us at the villages and food supplied, and injunctions were given that, as we were travelling under the Khan's orders, no remuneration should be demanded of us. It was only by a careful and secret distribution of presents to those who had been called upon to supply food, lodging, or transport, that we were able to accept, with a clear conscience, the hospitality of the mountaineers of Karlik Tagh. In this manner we traversed the whole of the Karlik Tagh until leaving the territory of the Khan at Barkul.

We finally left Kumul on March 15th, and travelled eastwards to Ta-shar, a village which proved to be another example of the admirable use the Kumuliks make of good soil, lying within play of a river as it issues from the sandstone range and before it sinks into the ground. Ta-shar was a tiny hamlet, but seemed to be able to supply all that we needed:—a warm, clean, and comfortable lodging, excellent Chanto food, and pleasant people to deal with. The following day we sent our heavy baggage on to Khotun-tam by the plain, whilst Miller and I, escorted by our friend and guide—the Beg, made a detour and worked our way round by a mountain-track. Ta-shar was situated at the end of the Bardash River, which came out from a sandstone gorge a few miles above, a foaming, laughing, racing stream, watering on its way the famous orchards and gardens which surround Ara-tam, the summer residence of the Khan.

From Ta-shar we picked our way over a boulder-strewn fan, where the hardy cultivators had endeavoured to make their fields, and presently found ourselves wandering amongst the luxuriant growth of the Khan's gardens. Gigantic poplars towered above the groves of walnut, apple, peach, and apricot-trees; under these, running brooks, bordered by dense scrub, tumbled their way over the steep descent to the plain. It was an approach as charming as if laid out by Nature herself, our chief regret being that the trees were not yet in leaf. The Khan's country-house lay close under the sandstone ridge, half hidden by fine old trees. Here we rested and drank tea provided by the caretakers, before exploring the ruins which, although in a much dilapidated condition, still remain. The cellas, the remains of seated Buddhas carved out of the rock, and the frescoes have been described by Stein, who placed them as belonging to the time of the Uigur dominion, *i.e.* between the ninth and twelfth centuries. Great destruction, due to fire and moisture, had robbed the excavator of what might have been of great interest, and the existence of these shrines was little more than a proof of the former religion of the inhabitants of Karlik Tagh, besides showing that this locality must have been a favourite summer-resort of the old Uigur Khans. Their collapse is a sign that Karlik Tagh lies on the edge of a region of greater precipitation than is the Tarim basin, where, owing to lack of rainfall, such antiquities have remained intact.

The Bardash Valley, whose waters irrigate Ara-tam, is typical of the whole southern side of Karlik Tagh, so I may as well give my impressions, as they came to me, of the contrasting features of the entire length of the valley, from sandstone barrier to glacier-snout. Leaving the plain, we faced the abrupt wall that formed the first foot-hills. The river-valley itself was not negotiable,—the stream winding its way through a steep-sided ravine and allowing no space for a track,—so for some hours we toiled painfully over barren red ridges, destitute of everything but thorn-scrub. Occasionally from the crest of a ridge we got a view of some peaks far ahead in the heart of the range, and of the immeasurable desert that lay below and behind us; but later, when we dropped down out of the sandstone border-ridges into the main Bardash Valley, our views were impeded by the surrounding hills. Here, beside the mountain-stream, grew thickets of willow and rose, and we passed under groups of tall poplars, elms, and walnuts which in summer would grant welcome shade to these hot, shut-in valleys. At convenient and picturesque places our friend, the Beg, would produce a "dastarkhan" of bread, dried apricots, and raisins, and persuade us to rest a little.

He had evidently been told to show off the beauties of his master's possessions, having already led us around the Khan's old country-seat with an enthusiasm that would have done justice to any professional showman.

For the twelve miles of mountain which lay between Ara-tam and the settlements on the middle Bardash there was neither room nor facility for human occupation, but later in the day we came to a place where the hills receded, the valley-floor widened, and men had space to cultivate. In these secluded upper valleys, such as the Bardash, the Taghliks, or mountaineers, lived a peaceful existence. Their settlements were scattered, and the villages never large, their size depending entirely on the amount of land left at their disposal by somewhat harsh physical conditions. Most valleys supported but one village ; only in the Narin Valley, where two rivers united before breaking through the outer-range, were there several villages and a considerable extent of cultivation. Often, too, we came across isolated groups of three or four farmsteads located in a place where the nature of the country afforded only such an area of cultivatable land as to just support them. Every available patch of ground was made use of, and I do not believe there are many spare acres on the mountains. With an increasing population, the land available for cultivation does not increase, and, since the Khan forbids emigration, there is " overcrowding " in the pleasant valleys of the " snowy " range.

After the impoverished aspect of the plains these high valleys seemed pleasant enough. We rode through fields which had been cleared—with infinite labour—of rocks, and crossed brooks of clearest water margined by dainty willows. Chukar and brown partridges called from the

THE VILLAGE OF BARDASH.

A typical mountain hamlet in the southern valleys of Karlik Tagh.

[3965]

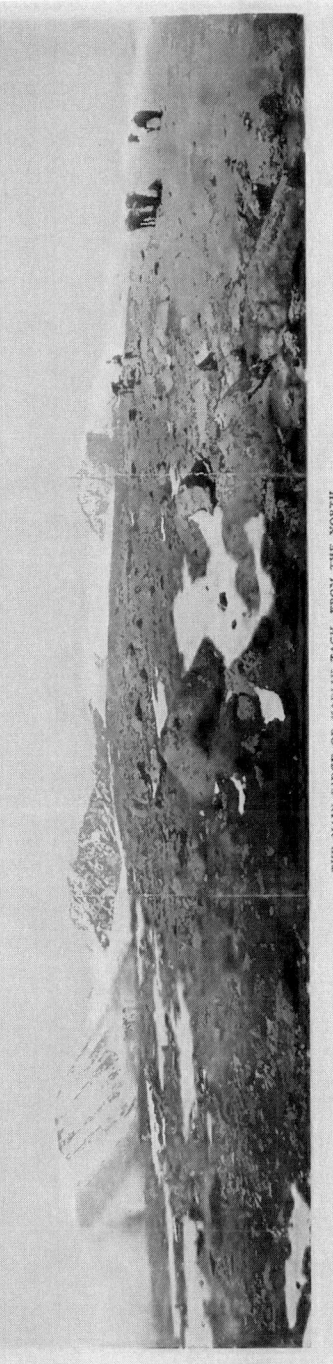

THE MAIN RIDGE OF KARLIK TAGH, FROM THE NORTH.

hillsides, and small boys herding the flocks of goats sang more joyous songs in their mountain-home than did their confrères of the melancholy plains. Pleasantly situated, too, were their houses of stone and mud, which were, in many cases, perched on the rocks so as to avoid wasting land capable of growing crops. In no less a degree did the people attract us. They were essentially mountain-folk; their environment seemed to have so branded them that we imagined we could trace a likeness between them and the Tadjik mountaineers of Bokhara or Hunza, rather than the lethargic Chantos of the Turkestan plains. The lives of these mountain-folk were certainly harder than those of the Kumuliks in the hot oases below. The ground had to be cleared of rocks before ploughing was possible, and, even then, there was not overmuch land.

Bardash was a scattered village of about twenty farmsteads, and had additional importance owing to the presence of a disused country-house belonging to the Khan. In former days this had always been the summer resort of the ruling chiefs, but the present Khan was too old to accomplish the journey over the mountains, and his "shooting-box" had now fallen into disrepair. It was, however, a "show place" to visitors like ourselves, and we were escorted over it with much ceremony, apparently by the orders of the great man himself. The house was charmingly situated in an orchard, surrounded by fine walnut-trees; but, being built largely of wood, in Chinese style, it had fared badly from wet and winter snow.

The chief man of the village set aside for us a room in his home, killed a sheep, and made a real Turkish "pillof" in our honour. They were a gay, happy lot at Bardash, free of intercourse and outwardly friendly with us non-Mussulmans, owing no doubt to the distance which separated Bardash from Kumul and placed them beyond the influence of their hard task-master, the Khan.   For this separation the sandstone range must be accounted largely responsible.   The men were well-made, clad in half-Chinese, half-Chanto costumes, and wore moccasins over thick felt stockings.   The women, too, were more independent than their friends "in town"; they made no attempt to hide their faces, and behaved with a freedom and natural inquisitiveness which was denied to the Kumulik ladies.   Their good-humoured merriment was cheering after the morosity and stolid indifference to amusement to which we had become almost accustomed; their hospitality and friend-liness were a real pleasure after the reticence of the surly Chinamen; and their neat little houses gave one some impression of a true *home* after the cold welcome of inns and the draughty abodes of wandering nomads. The Taghliks much impressed us, for we had travelled for close on a year without coming across sedentary mountain-dwellers; nomads in the high mountains were common enough, but only in the Karlik Tagh did we find villages inhabited by a settled race.

Later in the course of the expedition I again visited Bardash and explored the valley up to its source under the highest peak of the range.   Cultivation and farms I found extending up the valley for several miles,—as far as the foot of an immense old moraine, which reached for a distance of some six or seven miles below the existing glaciers.   This moraine choked the valley, the main river and a tributary passing through deep gorges on either side of it; yet even here the natives had

THE TAGHLIK SMILE.
Natives of Bardash.

508

cunningly led irrigation-canals from the streams on to the top of the ancient moraine, where they cultivated small fields of barley.

In this naked land, denuded of vegetation, every geographical feature was demonstrated with diagrammatic clearness. The former extent of glaciation was clearly shown. I travelled for two hours over this old moraine before coming to more recent ones, typified by hollows filled with little lakes ; and after toiling several hours through deep snow-drifts arrived at impregnable country close to the glaciers which hung below the highest peaks. The Bardash River had three heads; these drained the southern side of the highest points, all of them having their sources in glaciers. The largest of these was at the source of the tributary which rose on the south-western side of Peak No. II., but I did not measure it ; the glacier on the south-eastern side was about a mile in length, and that at the head of the other source half a mile long. All the glaciers were very steep ; and, as far as I could see, were in a state of retreat. Observations on the northern side of the mountains, however, seemed to point to a recent advance in the snouts of the glaciers.

The uppermost portion of the valley should afford fine summer pastures, and is, no doubt, made use of by the Taghliks, but at the time of my visit (April 8th) it was deep in snow, which lay everywhere above 8,000 ft. The arid nature of this valley was proved by the fact of it possessing no forest ; I saw only one little group of larch trees. This is strange, because forests of considerable extent exist on the southern flanks of the far eastern end of the range and on the northern flanks at the north-western end, yet the

Bardash Valley, situated close under the culminating point of the range, should possess a more abundant rainfall, and, therefore, heavier vegetation.

In the Upper Bardash I found myself in a trench-like valley, with wide, open bottom and steep sides, up which it was necessary to clamber in order to obtain a view. Climbing, however, was no easy task, for the snow was soft and let me in up to the knees—and often up to the hips—at every step, but four hours of stiff work over snow-covered boulder-skrees took me up on to that table-topped ridge, so distinctly seen from Kumul. The view repaid me for the strenuous climb, for, at a fair distance, I had spread out before me a complete panorama of the highest peaks (from No. I to VIIª), which taught me the topography of the alpine regions of Karlik Tagh far better than if I had ascended the highest peak itself, which at this season was impregnable. The panoramic view I obtained is reproduced on page 496 ; it clearly demonstrates the plateau-like summit of the western end of the range, and the deep-cut gorges of which I spoke. The culminating point of the range shows as a rounded summit, and to the east of it are the serrated ridges and pinnacles of the eastern portion of the Karlik Tagh.

The excessive roughness of the country made travelling laterally along the range very difficult. The valley of Bardash was so cut off that, in order to reach another valley, one needed to toil over transverse ridges for a day's journey. A break in the formation, however, allowed a track to run east and west along the north side of the sandstone range, between it and the higher spurs. We followed this route from Bardash, and, passing the forested valley of Karchamak, arrived at Khotun-tam, a village situated in a boulder-strewn locality at the foot of the mountains, where our main caravan awaited us. Khotun-tam marked the end of the sandstone foot-hills and the limit of the plateau-like summit of the main range. Above this village the Karlik Tagh lifted up its knife-like and deeply serrated main ridge, and deep-cut valleys gave a direct approach to the highlands from the plain. The spurs of the range retreated, the distance between the desert plain and the alpine region shortened, and the marked contrasts of the scenery were intensified.

The absence of the border-range and the shortness of the valleys allowed the Taghliks to live in their villages on the plains, and at the same time to make what use they could of the highlands to which the valleys gave easy access. Thus the eastern Karlik Tagh was portioned off between the various villages lying on the high smooth plain at the foot of the mountains. Khotun-tam, for instance, monopolized the two valleys to its north; Ulu-tai had its own valley; the Koshmak valley was used in summer by the Chinese farmers from Tashbulak—a village some miles away to the south, while the Little Koshmak belonged to the inhabitants of Shopoli.

Khotun-tam, although at the foot of the real hill-country, had an altitude of over 5,500 ft. Beyond was a high, smooth plain which swept away to the south-east, never dropping much below 4,000 ft., and finally merging into higher country. Much water rendered a large area suitable for cultivation; in fact, a string of farms and small fields extended all the way east to Tash-bulak. In this zone the population concentrated, and, consequently, we found the mountains quite deserted.

Travelling now became more pleasant, spring being already in evidence in these sheltered localities. Although the Khotun-tam River was frozen over, the poplars were bursting their buds and the willow-stems were red ; summer-birds were fast arriving, and on April 16th the first butterflies were seen. Up the valley, small fields,—off which a crop would be taken during the summer months,—extended to an altitude of about 8,000 ft. Indications of the summer-resorts used by the Khotun-tamliks were not lacking, for besides the kraals for cattle we noticed a curious kind of dwelling which seemed to be a reproduction of a nomad's yurt. This consisted of a circular wall of stones, on the top of which was erected a roof of spruce-poles in the form of a wigwam or tepee, over which, during the summer, was spread a covering of felt.

The valley itself was a good example of the great denudation to which the Karlik Tagh has been subject. The lower half of the valley was a V-shaped gorge ; higher up its floor was choked and barriered with more matter than the stream could carry away; the ascent was very steep, and in seven miles along the valley-bottom we passed from 5,500 ft. to 9,000 ft. Grass grew where possible, and poplars extended along the stream up to 8,000 ft. ; above this altitude scrub filled the bottoms, and spruce forest appeared on the slopes facing north and north-west. The ascent of a ridge, to an altitude of 12,800 ft., helped me to place a large area of unknown country on the map, which now grew in importance as we approached the quite unsurveyed eastern end of the range. This ascent proved to me clearly that all previous estimates of the height of the culminating points were at fault.

From Khotun-tam the survey was run eastwards over hill, hollow, and plain to Shopoli, a small village situated in a region possessing many interesting characteristics. This village was the most easterly Taghlik settlement on the southern side of the mountains, and the last we were to visit for some time to come.

The impression left by Shopoli was one of wind, dust; and rain. We had imagined that; the farther east we travelled, and the nearer we approached the Gobi, the greater the aridity would become ; yet, for some peculiar reason, we found this particular region to be rich in forests, pasture, and wild-game, all of which pointed to a considerable precipitation. The proximity of the Gobi was merely brought to our notice by the prevalence of dust-laden winds of great violence. The winds commenced immediately on our arrival, and during the first two days our work was delayed by a strong east wind which filled the air with dust and hid all distant views. The inhabitants took it as a matter of course, remarking that the air always became thick and hazy on these occasions. Frequent winds of this kind would be exasperating to the explorer, outdoor work being rendered impossible.

That this region had a phenomenal rainfall was first suggested to me by the sight of the forested slopes to the northward ; this was confirmed by the remarks of the natives, who being asked why their houses were built with *slanting* roofs, in Chinese style, replied that it was on account of the *heavy rains*.[1] The Turki inhabitants may have found out that a slanting roof has

---

[1] The natives of Shopoli said that there was an ample summer rainfall. The snowfall must also be great, for even at the end of May it lay a foot deep on all slopes with a northern aspect.

the advantage, over a flat one, for turning rain; but I do not myself think it was the rain which determined the shape of the roofs so much as the fact of a Chinese village being close by, and that Shopoli had once been inhabited by Chinese. Many ruined shrines and buildings showed traces of former Chinese settlers, now restricted to Tash-bulak; yet the Chinese influence remains strong, and the kingdom of the Khan of Kumul is in as much danger of being assailed by the foreigners in that quarter as it is in the capital itself.

The natives of Shopoli showed that love of amusement which old writers have described as being the chief characteristic of the Kumuliks. They treated us to some of their local songs, sung to the accompaniment of a *Chinese* violin; but we cannot refrain from thinking that, since these people have given up their own peculiar musical instrument, such as the Chanto guitar, and use a foreign one, they show signs of becoming denationalized. Many of the men were clothed in the Chinese manner, and all spoke the language, yet they kept with worthy persistency and strictness to their Mussulman exactitudes of food and cleanliness. The Chinese element approaches by way of the highlands which stretch south-eastwards to An-hsi-chow and Suchow. This region averages over 5,000 ft. in altitude and supports Chinese ranchers in small numbers. They come up to the very borders of the territory of the Khan, and at one place, Tash-bulak, have actually established themselves.

The region lying to the east of the trans-Gobi route, which leads from Kumul to China, is very little known. A couple of Russian explorers have crossed it, and from their map we understand the country to be one of

A TAGHLIK GIRL.

desert hills, apparently without much rainfall, for no drainage is marked; small springs alone showing that it is capable of supporting human life. Yet this region rises in some places to as much as 7,400 ft., and unless I am altogether mistaken as to the character of such hill-country in this particular part of Inner Asia, I strongly suspect that it is not such " bad-land " as the Russian map represents it to be.

By making a wide circle over the hills to the south of Shopoli I obtained a definite idea of this region as a whole. The altitude averaged 5,500 ft., with summits rising to 6,200 ft. It was a broken hill-country, somewhat formless, with dry *wadis* winding vaguely in and out amongst the hills, but having a general direction of south and south-east. In the wadis grew fine dry grass, tamarisk, and small saxaul trees, showing the reason why the natives rear camels in preference to other beasts. There was no sign of a permanent water-supply, and therefore no habitations, yet, according to report, it was used by herdsmen who wander over it feeding their flocks so long as the frozen snow supplies them with water. The pasture was evidently good, for we found that wild-sheep inhabited these somewhat arid ranges; were there occasional springs coming to the surface, the country to the south-east of Karlik Tagh would become of some economic value to herdsmen acquainted with its topography. The grazing on the outlying spurs around Shopoli was responsible for the semi-nomadic condition of the inhabitants, which was emphasized by the curious appearance, such as Shopoli boasted, of houses built on to yurts, and yurts pitched in the courtyards of houses.

North of the village were several charming valleys.

Our first expedition was to the Little Koshmak Valley, to which we were attracted by a fine rock-peak, capped by a beautiful snow-cornice, that stood up alone—the last summit of the range. The Little Koshmak introduced us to the forests, every lateral valley with a north aspect being covered with spruce ; higher up larch[1] crept in, and finally predominated.

A pleasant and unexpected surprise it was to find forests of such luxuriance so near to the barren Gobi. The remarkable beauty of these south-eastern spurs of the Karlik Tagh, with their grassy tops, forested slopes, and poplar-choked valleys,—with the immense views that they afforded of the desert ranges beyond,— attracted us as much as anything we had seen. The forest extended down to about 7,000 ft. and grew as high up as 9,000 ft. ; it was much influenced by aspect, showing no signs of life on slopes that did not face north. Thus it was that the Narin Valley, with its bending course, held an exceptionally large area of suitable ground, all of which was densely forested, groups of larch and spruce clinging to every rock-girt summit, and thickly crowding the more easy slopes. Here we found traces of " maral,"—the great stag of

[1] The presence of the larch (*Larix sibirica*) gave the first sure sign that the conditions of the Karlik Tagh are not entirely those of the Tian Shan system. Here was a northern tree, the southernmost range of which we had already determined to be in the Barlik group and in the Mongolian Altai ; yet this larch had extended its range southwards to the Karlik Tagh and Barkul Range. Here it lived and thrived, growing to a height of 40 ft. and 50 ft. with trunks from 1 ft. to 2 ft. in thickness. There was no sign of degeneration ; the forest was a healthy one. The pines, on the other hand, were of a variety peculiar to the Tian Shan Mountains (*Abies schrenkiana*) ; these grew to a height of between 30 and 40 ft. Thus, the forests of Karlik Tagh were composed of two varieties, one peculiar to the Tian Shan and the other to a more northern zone ; this proved that the flora of the Karlik Tagh had affinities with that of the Altai.

the Tian Shan, and of wild-pig, while the grassy slopes above the forests supported large herds of ibex, some of which carried remarkably fine heads.[1]

The existence of these forests will seem the more peculiar when the distributions of other forested areas of the Karlik Tagh are enumerated. The northern side of the range, where one would most expect forests, is bereft of trees of any description. The nature of the ground—an exposed plateau—being quite unsuitable. On the southern flanks, the Shopoli forests cover by far the largest area : occasional groups of pine or larch are found in most valleys, but the only other large extent of forest is in the upper Edira Valley. Not till one reaches the Barkul basin are forests encountered of any considerable extent. The whole length of the northern flanks of the Barkul Range has a forest-belt, especially at its eastern end in the neighbourhood of the cols that lead over to Kumul; the rounded hills to the east of Chagan-bulak Pass being very extensively forested. The Barkul forest-belt runs westwards for some seventy-five miles, and finally disappears.

To return to our exploration of the valley of the Little Koshmak. From a camp at 8,500 ft. we made an ascent to the head of the valley, mapping its course and attempting an ascent of Peak No. IX.,—the pinnacle of the snow-cornice which had shown up so well from Shopoli. We steadily climbed up the ridge dividing the two sources of the river, until an altitude of 12,988 ft.

---

[1] A head, picked up in the Little Koshmak Valley, measured 47½ in. The wild-sheep of the Karlik Tagh must also run large, for Miller found some horns on a tomb at Togucha which measured 59 in. in length—with the tips broken off,—while Younghusband picked up several old horns lying on the eastern spurs of Karlik Tagh which measured 54 in., and one gigantic pair of 62 in. in length.

was reached. Finally, the extremely broken nature of the rock-country, which consisted of strata of flaky slate flung up perpendicular to the ridge, and which came away with every step, stopped us ; but not before we had found the miniature—quarter-mile-long—glacier at the foot of No. IX., and traces of old moraines extending as far as a mile and a half below. We failed to make the ascent of the pinnacle, but the clinometer readings were sufficiently consistent to made up for the loss of a boiling-point reckoning, and we were not out to climb untrodden peaks for the love of mountaineering. Should a member of the Alpine Club ever chance to come this way I recommend him to make a start on No. IX., for, although not the highest point, it will try his skill and give him a rare view of snows and deserts.

From summits of 12,000 ft. and 13,000 ft., at the eastern end of the Karlik Tagh, we enjoyed views that fully repaid us for the expenditure of time and for the extraordinary rough climbing entailed. From these points of vantage, within sight of herds of ibex and within call of the snow-cock, we looked out over a region that seemed to embrace the whole of desert Cathay, and it was easy to grasp its essential features. Through narrow, deep-cut valleys, clothed with larch and pine forest, opened up beautiful vistas of the Gobi, for the Karlik Tagh has the character of an island set in a wide sea, the views from its summits being always terminated by the ocean-like plain that lies around and washes up to its very foot-hills. On a clear day in winter or early spring, before the summer heat-haze begins to hide the distance, and when no south wind, with its complement of "loess," darkens the air, one can stand aloft on some pinnacle

or spur, and gaze till the eyes ache, over infinite space.
One can search the southern deserts, where yellow flats
indefinitely extend to a far horizon, broken here and
there by pyramidal hills of carmine and yellow ochre.
Eastward one's gaze is mystified by the regions of colour,
shown by the succeeding ranges of desert hills as they
pass from yellow to dun, and from dun to purple, till
they tone to the softest ultramarine, and fade into space
at a hundred-mile range. Even yet one has surveyed
but half the panorama. Northwards the horizon is
broken by distant snow-ranges—the Aji Bogdo, a
southern offshoot of the Mongolian Altai. These stand
up superbly, their height being intensified by the desert
gap which lies between—" the small desert of three days'
journey in extent," of which Marco Polo wrote.

Within our vision we held the frontiers of four
different Asiatic peoples, different worlds altogether to
this settled region of Chanto farm and Kumulik hamlet.
Far to the north we could just discern the territories of
the Kirei Kirghiz and the Mongol hordes; eastward,
across the intervening zone of uninhabited desert, were
the haunts of Torgut nomads, while from the south
ceaselessly advanced the plodding bands of Chinese
colonists.

On our return to Shopoli we found it impossible to
continue our journey to the Ati Bogdo Mountains. Although this range lay only 180 miles to the east, yet
lack of guides and independent transport made the undertaking of greater difficulty than we expected. It seemed
possible that, with an independent caravan and water-
supply, an attempt might be made to travel eastwards
without guides, taking as landmarks the Emir Tagh and
Mount Jingis, until sighting the summits of the Ati

Bogdo ; failing this, the traveller must needs go northwards to the eastern Altai ranges, where he might fall
in with Mongol wanderers who would perchance be able
to supply transport and guides. A few Khalka—or, as
they called themselves, Mingyn Mongols—who had come
down to Shopoli to trade skins, knew nothing of those
regions, yet the Ati Bogdo is certain to be in communication with Northern Mongolia, although its inhabitants are Torguts,—summer visitors from the Edsin
Gol or Gashiun Nor, in the very heart of the Gobi. The
Ati Bogdo had so far been approached from the north
alone, this being the reason why we wished to attack
it from the *west*.

Although a visit would have been of great help to
us in our work of deciding the distribution of life-
zones,[1] and in tracing the lines of demarcation between
the fauna of the Tian Shan and Altai, yet the topography
of the intervening region was made clear to us without the labour of a desert journey. A climb to the
summit of the pass that led to Tal showed us the
eastern desert-spurs of Karlik Tagh and the configuration of the region between them and the Ati Bogdo.
A day's journey away to the east rose into sight
the red sandstone pyramid of Emir Tagh, which sloped
desertwards in a long-backed ridge until lost to view.
There seemed to be no connecting range between the
Karlik Tagh and the Ati Bogdo, but rather a genuine
break consisting of hard steppe and stray sand-dunes.
Occasional isolated hills cropped up, such as the Jingis
and Atis peaks, but looking eastwards there was no
suggestion of the pleasant highlands where,—according
to Kozloff, the only visitor,—there are meadows, forests,

---

[1] See Appendix, *Life-zones of Inner Asia.*

and running streams, with herds of wild-game such as sheep and roe-deer.

As we travelled round the eastern spurs we visited Tal, the summer quarters of the men of Mogoi, whilst our heavy kit, packed on camels, followed an easier track along the foot of the hills to Uturuk, on the northern side of the Karlik Tagh. Settlements of Taghliks were few and far between, after leaving Shopoli. A few, such as Mogoi, Bai, Uturuk, Adak, and Nom, existed on streams draining northwards,—the last examples of sedentary life on the edge of the nomad's land of Mongolia. For the most part we had left settled life behind, and, upon

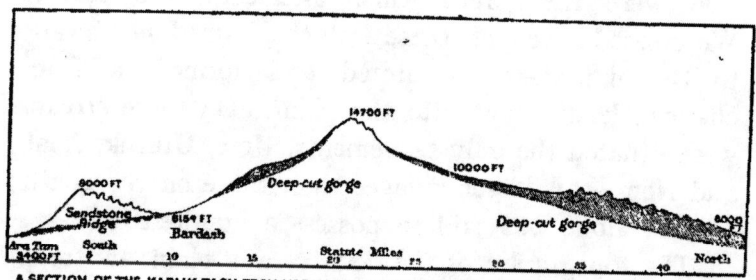

A SECTION OF THE KARLIK TAGH FROM NORTH TO SOUTH THROUGH THE CENTRAL PORTION OF THE RANGE

reaching the northern flanks of Karlik Tagh, found large areas either entirely uninhabited or partially used by nomads.

The different formation of the northern side of the range was demonstrated by the fact of its being a fine pasture-land. The rugged, barren, desiccated rock-region of the southern side was replaced on the north by a smooth plateau of rolling downs, which occupied the whole area between 8,000 ft. and 11,000 ft. In consequence, we were enabled to travel comfortably along the range at an altitude of 10,000 ft. to 11,000 ft. Above us, rounded spurs and shale slopes led up to the main ridge, while below, the plateau swept down at a gentle grade until it ended in a low, rough, rocky girdle which, in some degree, corresponded to the sandstone foot-hills of the southern side. In this plateau the rivers had carved deep gorges, and in travelling westwards we found it necessary to keep as high up as possible, for lower down the gorges deepened to terrific cañons.

By moving slowly along the plateau, and keeping close below the shale slopes, we were able to map the rivers to their sources and to overlook the country below, as far as the point where the same rivers ran dry in the desert. The principal features of the north side were the gorges which intersected the plateau. We crossed seven of these, which drained northwards to Uturuk; there all united and formed a single channel, leading out into the plain. On these streams were situated the only settlements, Urge, Uturuk, Adak, and Nom,—all larger villages than those on the south; Uturuk alone was said to possess a hundred houses.

The topography of the country was plain, and mapping was easy work, as compared with the riddles of the southern side. Ascents, too, were more easily accomplished, and it did not take long to run the survey westwards to Tur Kul. Of special interest were the little glaciers which lay at the head of nearly every valley. They were no larger than those on the south of the range; even the wide valleys leading from the highest peaks did not hold glaciers exceeding two miles in length, but they showed traces of old moraines five miles below their present position.

The plateau was uninhabited at that season, it being still subject to cold winds and snow-storms; later on, the herdsmen drive their flocks up and tent there all

A TAGHLIK FARMSTEAD.
On the south side of Karlik Tagh.

TAGHLIK YURTS.
On the northern pastures of Karlik Tagh.

the summer. Farther west, however, where the plateau swept down to the lower altitude of the Tur Kul basin, we found a permanent population of shepherds. Here the Taghliks had adopted a semi-nomadic existence, living chiefly in yurts ; even the movable tents presented a half-fixed appearance, with kraals for the herds built close by, and hedges of scrub and grass for protection from the wind. Now and then we came across large flocks of sheep, which in most cases belonged to the Khan. The grazing was exceptionally rich, and the plateau could support a very large herd of horses and sheep, but the accessibility of the region hinders it from being reserved as a private pasture for the Khan and his subjects ; in consequence, Chinese herdsmen from Barkul use it considerably.

The scenery of the northern side was varied by the lake of Tur Kul, a small upland basin situated at a height of 6,301 ft. Close by was Tomdun, a settlement consisting of three yurts and two mud-houses, where we rested for a few days owing to bad weather. Cold winds and driving mists made us glad to get off the open plateau into the warm yurts ; snow fell heavily, and when the weather cleared we found that even the desert-spurs of the Metshin-ola to the north were snow-clad. Tur Kul was the water-table for a considerable drainage from the ranges to the north and south. No water from the mountains entered the lake above ground, but it was margined by a wide border of soft, boggy ground, where much water oozed up and formed small springs and streams. Large flocks of sheep and herds of cattle fed on the excellent pasturage sustained by a perennial watering, and many shepherd encampments were scattered along the shores of the lake.

Approaching the lake after a four-mile ride from Tomdun, we discovered that it was surrounded by a treacherous salt-bog, and the water was the most saline we had ever experienced. An analysis of this water from the lagoons at the eastern end of Tur Kul showed that it contained 34 per cent. of salt, and in comparison I may mention that the water of the Dead Sea,—the "most saline of all the world's important lakes,"—contains only 25 per cent. A thermometer boiled in this water made the altitude of the lake at sea-level! and it was not until we found fresh water some miles to the east—where it first appeared above ground, that we obtained a correct boiling-point reading for altitude. The salinity, however, did not appear to affect the bird-life. We chanced to be there, on the first occasion, during a spell of bad, stormy weather, when the lake was alive with myriads of wild-fowl, which had sought refuge there from the more exposed water of Bar Kul. Wild swans, geese, sheldrake, mallard, teal, and pintail were constantly on the move between the salt lake and the fresh-water marshes, from which they were continually harried by native hunters. When we attempted a serious attack on the wild-fowl, a few days later, armed with guns, and accompanied by beaters, we found the lake absolutely deserted! The natives said they came but rarely, and only stayed for a night at the most, for "they did not like the water." I think, however, they only come here under stress of bad weather and depart again at the earliest moment, owing to their cramped surroundings.

At Tomdun we divided forces, Miller travelling with the main caravan direct to the Barkul basin, whilst I turned south in order to finish off my survey of the southern side of the Karlik Tagh. Taking only two men and a horse-load of necessaries, with a paper from the Khan which enabled me to get a change of horses and guides at every village, I made a rapid survey of the country between the Barkul passes and the sources of the Bardash River.

South-west of Tomdun was the Belju Pass, the only track that crosses the Karlik Tagh, and this at a considerable height; at the summit of close on 11,000 ft., snow-storms assailed me, hiding the views and hampering my work. This pass led me down to the Koral Valley, which, with its fine forests and open areas capable of cultivation, and, consequently, its numerous villages, formed one of the most important and beautiful valleys in the Karlik Tagh. Its almost continuous line of cultivation, its hamlets, and the three villages of Temirty, Koral, and Narin, gave the valley an appearance of much industry. The Taghliks had cultivated almost impregnable tracts of land high up the mountain-side, by irrigating them with canals, the building of which showed considerable ingenuity and labour. The hills were subject to such denudation that the canals had to be built up annually, and in some places the water was carried for *miles* by aqueducts of hollowed poplar-trunks. The largest centre of agriculture was at Narin, the junction of the two valleys of the Koral and Narin. Beyond Narin the sandstone border-ridges shut off these highland villages from the plain.

From Koral a climb up a steep face of 3,000 ft. took me across the ridge dividing this valley from the next —the Edira, where I found other small settlements of Taghliks farming in quiet seclusion the small patches of land nature allowed them, and keeping a few cattle, goats, and yaks. This upland valley, shut in completely by the impassable snow-fields above and by the sandstone barrier below, was typical of the environment which has forced the Taghliks to follow an isolated, hermit-like existence. Yet there was no feeling of suspicion nor exclusiveness amongst the natives when I dropped unexpectedly into their villages from the ranges above, or when I set up my plane-table on the roofs of their houses; they were merely amused and inquisitive, and showed genuine hospitality.

A long ride up the Edira Valley and a climb over a 10,000-ft. transverse ridge led me again to the Bardash, which, as described elsewhere, I explored to its source; then, turning back, I covered a wide extent of country lying between my former track and the foot of the range, passing from Bardash to Kara-kapchin, Toruk, and Narin.

Connecting Kumul and Barkul are three tracks, namely, the Kulluk, the Barkul, or Kosheti, and the Chagan-bulak. Traffic mostly goes by way of the Barkul Pass, which, according to Prjevalsky, is feasible for wheeled traffic, but from Narin the nearest route is over the Chagan-bulak, and thither my guides led me by the worst of routes, which crossed and recrossed the Narin River some twenty or twenty-five times, obliging us to make several big detours up and along the hillsides in order to avoid bad ground. Tou-shi,—a village composed of half-yurt, half-house habitations,—supplied me with a change of men and horses, and, on the evening of April 10th, the forests and deep snow-fields of the Chagan-bulak Pass introduced me to the plateau-basin of Barkul.

RIVER TERRACES AT NARIN.

CHAPTER XVIII

BARKUL, THE BOGDO-OLA, AND ACROSS DZUNGARIA

THE Barkul [1] basin is a topographical feature by itself, having nothing to do with Karlik Tagh or Kumul. It is a self-contained world, little influenced by the surrounding regions, for mountains border the basin on the south and deserts fringe it on the north ; it lies, moreover, on the road to nowhere and has little through-traffic. Barkul is neither arid Turkestan nor desert Dzungaria, but a plateau-basin of such equable climate that men can till the soil without the laborious construction of irrigation-canals, and can pasture their flocks without fear of drought. It is not only the unique climatic condition of the Barkul basin that causes us to consider it a separate district, but politically and ethnographically it is divided from the Khanate of Kumul. For although in the eastern portion may be found Taghlik settlements subject to the Khan, the basin is really utilized and ruled by the Chinese.

I shall not forget my first impression of the Barkul uplands. After the horses had struggled, belly-deep, through the snow on the northern side of the Chagan-bulak Pass, and we had picked our way through the deeper drifts which lay in the forest-belt down to the grassy flats below, I eventually reached the friendly shelter

---

[1] I use the form Barkul for the town and Bar Kul for the lake, in accordance with the Russian system.

offered me by some Kumulik herders. It was evening, and a wild sunset hung over the cloud-girt Barkul Mountains; beneath the mists a broad belt of forest showed, and below this, a prairie-steppe swept down and across the central basin until it rose again northwards into the rough-sided, flat-topped ridge of Metshin-ola. The prairies were dotted with cattle, droves of horses, and flocks of sheep; besides the black yurts of the shepherds there were many small farmsteads which gave an air of settlement to the pastoral scene. It was an unusually animated scene for Central Asia; for we had at last found a happy valley free from the blight of desiccation.

The next morning showed in clearer detail the impressionist picture of the previous evening. The upper edge of the basin was good pasture-land, but above the contour-line of 6,000 ft.,—except in the immediate neighbourhood of water,—the ground appeared to be unsuitable for cultivation; below this level, however, abundant water oozed up in all directions. The drainage from the surrounding mountains was chiefly below the surface, the Barkul basin boasting only one river-bed, the Irdi Khe, which carried a stream of water varying according to the season of the year; the course of this river-bed could be easily distinguished on account of the numerous farms situated on its banks. Signs of sedentary life were not restricted to the neighbourhood of water, rains being sufficiently reliable to ensure the raising of crops elsewhere; small settlements of agriculturists were scattered over the whole floor of the basin; in fact, it seemed probable that the lands which Chinese colonists were taking up for corn-growing would eventually curtail the pasture-zone.

In strong contrast to the corn-lands and pastures was an isolated group of high *sand-dunes*, lying at the south-eastern corner of the basin, between the gaps which lead through the surrounding mountain-wall to Tur Kul and Kumul. This is the most remarkable physical feature of the Barkul basin. It should be understood that the entire flora of the basin is more or less saturated with water, being a mountain-girt hollow into which flows a constant drainage from the snow-clad ranges on the south. Nowhere does the land present any sign of being deprived of moisture, and therefore it is not a desiccated area. Yet this peculiar, miniature sand-desert suddenly makes its appearance in the midst of fertility and pasture. The sand-dunes cover only a small area of six or seven square miles, but attain a great height and are a landmark from afar. Neither in the sand-areas of Dzungaria, nor in Chinese Turkestan, nor even in the great sand-belt of Trans-caspia had we seen dunes of a similar height. Miller, who spent some time in them, reckoned the maximum height to be 400 ft. The dunes were very curiously formed, a profile of their summits showing a sharp angle, instead of the long-backed windward and steeply inclined leeward side. In the centre of the dunes was a typical " falj," or circular pit, which went down to the floor of the plateau and supported vegetation in the form of grass and scrub. Here, according to native report, was a sand-buried Mongol village ; and, at night, could be heard the crowing of cocks and the lowing of cattle !

As I travelled westward, the panorama of the Barkul Range spread itself out and showed a long, even ridge, reaching to an average height of 11,000 ft. The dis-

tribution of the rainfall was emphasized by the type
of forest on the range ; in the east it was spruce and
larch, but gradually the spruce was eliminated, until at
a point south of Barkul the larch alone remained. The
maximum rainfall, judging by the distribution and type
of the forest, would be on the easternmost spurs of the
Barkul Range and around the head-waters of the Irdi
Khe River.

After joining Miller and the main caravan, which was
still in charge of the Beg, the transport being supplied
by subjects of the Khan from Narin Kur, we rode, on
April 13th, into the town of Barkul.   From here we
despatched the Beg to Kumul, with many messages to
his master and a suitable present for himself.   With
the help supplied by the Khan of Kumul, a large proportion of the inconvenience and worry which hinder
real work on a journey had been eliminated ; we more
than appreciated the advantages we had been enjoying
when we suddenly found ourselves stranded in Barkul,
a town which boasted an imbecile Governor and an
exceptionally surly population.   It was with real regret
that we parted with the Beg and the willing Taghliks,
who had shown us the many hidden valleys of their
mountain home.

In connexion with the adjacent pastures and corn-
lands the town of Barkul itself was an important centre.
Situated close under the mountains, where ample
forests gave a plentiful supply of fuel and from whence
the melting snows, or frequent rains, perennially saturated the surrounding country and kept the pastures
fresh and green throughout the heat of summer, it constituted the centre of trade for the whole district.   Here
came the Kumulik shepherds and the Chinese farmers,

who found in the bazaars all they needed in the way
of foodstuffs and clothing.   Barkul was little else but a
distributing centre for the surrounding district ; occasional Mongols came in from the far north, especially
from the Mingyn Gobi,—between Barkul and the Altai,
and a few Chanto merchants from the great oases of the
Tarim basin ; but the ordinary aspect of a town situated
on a trade-route, with a moving population—entailing
much coming and going, was entirely absent from Barkul.
As a town it had little to recommend it, while its inhabitants seemed sunk in a state of degeneracy to which it
would be hard to find an equal, even in Inner Asia.   Its
complete seclusion may be responsible for this, even a
degraded Chinaman being influenced by popular opinion
and publicity.

Barkul does not even possess a fair reputation in
spite of its numerous temples and shrines, of which
there are said to be from eighty to a hundred.   Its bad
reputation has probably been the cause for its having
been avoided by many travellers, this being a significant
fact in connexion with a region where towns and bazaars
are rare.   Atkinson, when wandering with the Kirei
Kirghiz, was the first traveller to approach Barkul ; he
actually arrived within sight of the town and then turned
back into the desert.   The Russian trading expedition
of 1872 was refused admittance, the Chinese Mandarins
saying that Barkul belonged to the province of Kansu,
whereas Mongolia alone was opened to Russian traders.
Potanin and his followers in 1876 camped within sight
of the town, but did not enter it.   He sent men to
procure provisions, but even his envoy was not received
in a friendly manner.   Prjevalsky, the next traveller,
passed close by without actually visiting the town,

although it lay right on his road to Kumul. In those days, the disturbed conditions, owing to the Dungan rebellion, may have caused travellers to pass it by; but even now, in these quiet times, one risks trouble by entering the town.

We ourselves found Barkul a delightful locality, with its altitude and fine air of 5,650 ft., the pleasant temperature warming us after the cold of the bleak, northern plateau. After a rest, we inspected several old temples, one of which, according to Piassetsky, dates back three thousand years; in the precincts of this we found and took "squeezes" of the black stone called Tzin-Chen-Bei, where are recorded the victories of a Chinese (Mongol ?) general.

We then attempted to get transport westward; but, in spite of immense droves of horses running half wild over the prairies and very large camel-herds in the vicinity of the town, it took us some eight days before we were able to come to an agreement, and even then we had to "come down" to camels. Barkul is famous for its horses; for this reason we never imagined it possible that we should have to depend on camel-transport in this land of horses. The reputation of the Barkul broncos had been in no manner exaggerated; they were, indeed, the special characteristic of the basin. We had been puzzled as to the kind of animal which had given the name to "Bar Kul" or "wild-animal lake." The neighbourhood possessed, it was true, abundant animal and bird life; we saw wild-fowl innumerable on the lake, and its western shore was the haunt of troops of gazelle and droves of wild-asses; but, we now believe that the real "wild animals" of the Barkul basin signify the great herds of unridable horses

The Kazan Peak.

The Surkul Range.

Sandwoven.

THE BARKUL PASS.

The Kalu Kiver.

323

which roam untamed over the steppes. These form
an Imperial Stud, and are said to number fifteen
thousand, the pick of which are transported yearly to
Pekin.

Barkul was eventually left behind on April 21st; we
then wandered westward with seven camels and a few
horses and camped by the lake-side. Bar Kul receives
the surplus drainage of the basin, and has a fine sheet
of water surrounded by luxuriant meadows bordering
on saline marshes. The lake itself tasted slightly brackish, the analysis showing only 3 per cent. of salt: contrary to the highland lake of Tur Kul, which was too
salt to freeze, this lake, in spite of the advanced season,
had large ice-floes at its northern end. Old strands here
showed themselves at a height of 10 ft. or 11 ft. above
the present level; there appeared to be but one level
for summer and winter,—unlike Tur Kul, which showed
traces of much variation in level during the year.

Westwards the floor of the basin rose in a long, gentle
incline until it merged imperceptibly into the rolling
down-lands of the Tou-shui plateau, and thither we
hurried as fast as the counter-attraction of gazelle and
" kulon "-hunting alongside the track allowed us. This
westward slope of the basin was very dry and waterless
for twenty miles at a stretch, but, at this date, good
grass had already sprung up and the game from the
deserts of Eastern Dzungaria had sought out the early
grazing on these high plains for which man had little
use. Between Bar Kul and the Tou-shui main road we
saw only one Chinese guard-house and a couple of farms;
a few others existed, it was said, nearer the main range
to the south, but, for the greater part, this region is
given over to wild-game and a few shepherds. We,

finally, reached Ta-shih-tu and connected up our route-survey with the outgoing track.

In retracing our steps westwards we again traversed the whole length of Southern Dzungaria, but, being spring, the country presented a very different appearance to what it did in midwinter. Grass and flowers now carpeted the steppe in place of unbroken snow-fields, and the country, which in January had seemed lifeless, now appeared as the home of thriving colonists, possessing busy towns with much traffic.

Our journey now took the form of a hurried review of the remaining portion of Dzungaria rather than a detailed survey of any one part. We visited various localities for the sole purpose of investigating the fauna of regions little known from a zoological point of view, the results of these studies being described by Miller ; while our itinerary included the traversing of those parts of Dzungaria which are rarely visited. A considerable portion of the information we obtained on the return journey, after concluding the exploration of the Karlik Tagh and Barkul regions, has been already embodied in Chapter XIII, which dealt with Dzungaria as a whole. The details of our experiences alone remain to be described.

After Miller had successfully hunted that strange animal—the Saiga antelope ; and a small, but most instructive collection of mammals had been formed on the plains in the south-eastern corner of Dzungaria, where the lowlands merge into higher Gobi, we marched again into Guchen. May 5th saw us outfitting for a lateral journey into the Bogdo-ola in order to visit its sacred lake.

A description of Dzungaria, without reference to

the Bogdo-ola, would be incomplete, for besides its geo-graphical interest, the economic value of the lands at its base, its close proximity to Urumchi—the capital, and the incomparable beauty of its alpine region, the Bogdo-ola is also the sacred mountain of the natives.

The towering summit of Bogdo-ola is *the* feature of Southern Dzungaria. Although not attaining the altitude of some peaks in the Tian Shan to the south of Manas, it shows its height to great advantage, as it rises abruptly out of the plain, and can be seen for an immense distance from every point of the compass. Manas, from where we first saw the peak, is a hundred miles away ; we took its bearings from beyond Ta-shih-tu at the western end of the Barkul Range,—about a hundred and twenty miles to the east of the peak ; while Prjevalsky has mentioned viewing it from the banks of the Urungu River, at a distance of one hundred and sixty miles. Such a pinnacle, standing alone on the edge of the desert, creates wonder and astonishment in the minds of the superstitious natives, who deem it sacred, call it the " Ghost Mountain," and connect it with mythical and mystical traditions. Its triple-crested summit can worthily take its place as the Olympus of Dzungaria.

The Bogdo-ola is typical of the southern borderland of Dzungaria, and compares strongly with the less inspiring northern border-ranges that we visited later in the season. The range lies midway between the Karlik Tagh group and the main Tian Shan, but it belongs wholly to the latter mountain-system. Its altitude is nothing unusual, being the forerunner of mightier peaks to the west ; but no one who has seen the Bogdo-ola can deny that it possesses a certain *character* of its own, leaving an impression rarely given by even higher summits.

This mountain first became known to geographers as a *volcano*, and for some years it appeared as such on the maps; this report was, however, soon proved to have originated from the Chinese myth, that fire and smoke issued from it when the gods visited it once a year! There is, no doubt, an uncanny atmosphere about the Bogdo-ola, for, when other ranges lie basking in the sun, the summits of these peaks are certain to be enveloped in mists and hidden in clouds.

Dull weather is very common, and this conserves the snow which perpetually covers the summits of the Bogdo ranges. Sudden storms of great violence frequently occur, rain falls at intervals throughout the summer months, and the weather is far more changeable than in other localities in Central Asia. Strong winds, blowing to a hurricane, are a feature of the region; the route leading southwards to Turfan being well known for the violence of the gales which blow through the gap in the mountains. Travelling by this route was said to be dangerous, even carts being occasionally blown over; our Chinese informer added, however, that it was "only Treasury carts that were blown over," one of these, carrying bullion, having vanished altogether, the wheels only being found; its disappearance was attributed to the wind, aptly named the "Ghost Wind"!

The uncertain climate is caused, it is said, by the position of the high peaks towering above the low, hot depression of Turfan. Whatever the reason may be, these highlands are the scene of violent climatic changes which overawe the natives and cause them to consider it a suitable abode for "spirits," and therefore holy.

The existence, also, of a romantic alpine lake, at an altitude of 6,625 ft.,—embosomed in the highest forests, close under the silent glaciers and snow-fields,—forms a scene of such beauty as to make it an object of worship by a myth-loving race.

The Bogdo-ola was first explored by the brother-travellers, Grum-Grjimailo, in 1889–90, who mapped the essential features of the range, visited its sacred lake and the glaciers above, but did not penetrate farther into the alpine region. The maps they produced were poor in detail, and are now proved to be inaccurate; but they stood for long as the only survey of the Bogdo-ola. No other traveller came to this remarkable mountain-group for eighteen years; then Merzbacher, in 1908, concluded his exhaustive exploration of the Tian Shan by a visit to the central portion of the range. He thoroughly explored the main valley of Bogdo-ola, made two ascents of about 13,000 ft. on the northern edge of the central mass and achieved a still higher ascent on the south; he then crossed the central part of the range from north to south by the Miskan Pass. A great deal of scientific interest regarding the geological formation of the range and its excessive glaciation resulted from Merzbacher's work, but there still remains much detailed survey-work to be accomplished. East of Long. 89° 40′ the higher portions of the range are quite unknown, and the upper sources of the rivers on north and south have never been visited.

The second week of May showed us, as we rode from Guchen into the foot-hills at the base of the range, what the Bogdo-ola can supply in the way of samples of climate. The early days of May had been hot, the elms and poplars were practically in leaf, wheat was six inches above the ground, and summer-birds were singing; but on the first night after leaving Guchen rain occurred, and on the second a heavy snow-fall. Violent winds got up at a few minutes' notice; nature seemed to be always in the throes of some great cyclonic disturbance. We saw valleys which gave the impression of being cleared by sudden storm-bursts; the river-beds were wide, although, at this season, they contained little water; but dead timber lying high and dry above the ordinary water-level, and great log-jams in the streams, were suggestive of the floods that occur so frequently.

A sparse population of farmers and nomads lived on the lower slopes, but the main valley which drained from the sacred lake,—although a smiling land of grass and flowers, where streamlets ran beneath the chequered shade of elm and willow groves,—remained untenanted, a reserve too holy for the use of man. A day's march takes the pilgrim up the length of this silent valley, and through a frowning gorge, beyond which he will find himself confronted by a great barrier entirely blocking the valley. This wall of moraine deposits, which has dammed the valley and caused the formation of the Bogdo-ola lake above it, was the most perfect I had ever seen. From below it looked almost artificial, with its smooth, unbroken slope and level top. Grass and forest covered it in part, and here and there water, draining through from the lake beyond, burst out and formed cascades down the bank.

On reaching the top of the barrier we came suddenly into view of the long-hidden lake and of the snow-peaks which form its background. Small wonder that the pious natives considered this region sacred and

THE SACRED LAKE OF BOGDO-OLA.

538]

guarded it from the profanity of man ; it was a pleasure we keenly appreciated to be able to enjoy its beauty, undisturbed by the presence of other mortals, with the exception of the aged priests who dwelt in the temples surrounding the lake.   Strangers were rarely permitted, and nomads were never allowed to disturb the peaceful surroundings.   The neighbouring pastures grew rank and wild ; and the wild-game resorted here in numbers from the hard-hunted valleys beyond the sacred precincts.

A previous explorer relates that he found a notice put up near the lake, saying : " It is forbidden, under penalty of instant death, to violate the tranquillity of this holy land.   There must be not only no shooting and no tree-cutting, but cattle may not even be pastured here, that they may not trample underfoot the herbage belonging to God's creatures."

In an amphitheatre of steep-forested slopes lay the lake, tucked in close under the highest summits, backed by a world of snow and ice.   Merzbacher called it "the pearl of the Eastern Tian Shan," and I think it would be hard to find an alpine lake having so perfect a setting as the Bogdo-ola.   Turquoise-blue lakes, pine forests, and snow backgrounds are not uncommon, but the presence of quaint Chinese temples picturesquely perched on the steep hill-sides and mirrored in the lake added greatly to the effect ; as did, also, the sound of muffled drums and deep-noted horns at sunset.

The colony of priests who lived up there in isolated temples spent a life of dull monotony.   In bare cells, existing on bread and water, cut off from the outside world, and never returning to it, they might well be described as having to "live on air and scenery."   They had no intercourse with their fellow-men, and did no work ; even their bread was made in the next valley and brought to them at intervals. One temple was built in such a position as to be unapproachable from the land side; thus giving its inmates the additional advantage of being able to shut themselves off even from other priests, for there was only *one* boat. The priests protected animal life, and were greatly concerned at hearing the reports of my collecting-gun ; but on learning that I was shooting only small birds, and not the deer, they were quite satisfied.

Turning to the purely topographical side of the Bogdo-ola, the range is composed of a single main ridge running, on the whole, due east and west, but in detail bending and varying the direction from east to southeast. The main ridge has a uniform altitude averaging 15,000 ft., which drops off in a sharp decline towards the Dzungarian plains on the north and the Turfan depression on the south. The main ridge is very steep and retains its altitude with such persistency that it can only be crossed in a few places. Out of this 15,000-ft. wall rises another 5,000-ft. block, formed by three distinct peaks, which attain a maximum altitude of over 20,000 ft. These virgin peaks remain unclimbed, but Merzbacher's clinometer reckonings, which he considers fairly accurate, make the east peak 21,356 ft., the central peak 21,240 ft., and the west peak 20,976 ft. The glaciation of this so-called "secondary chain" is unusually extensive, and the traces of the diluvial ice-age are remarkably developed. The glaciers, according to Merzbacher, are more numerous on the northern than on the southern slopes ; on the other hand, the largest glaciers are to be found on the south. The largest glacier he measured on the north is three or four miles, and that on the south six or seven miles in length. All are in a state of retreat, more especially those on the southern side. This glaciated chain extends over a distance of 145 miles.

It was with reluctance that we left the beautiful Bogdo-ola and started on the stage of our journey which led us across the hot, monotonous plains of Central Dzungaria. Passing again through Urumchi and on to Manas, we could well have continued our route by the main road which crosses the plain between Shi-Kho and Chuguchak; but, in order to obtain an idea of the heart of the land, we determined to follow a line north from Manas. The main route is well known; it crosses a low-lying desert-belt, and is remarkable at this season only for heat and mosquitoes; there is little information to be obtained and few physical features to be studied. By going north from Manas, however, and following the Manas River, we hoped to arrive at our goal, the Jair and Barlik Ranges, by a less-known and more interesting route.

The Manas is the chief river of Southern Dzungaria; this river alone, of the countless streams which descend into the plains from the snow-clad ranges, forms a water-way of sufficient size to outlive the toll that is taken of its water in the irrigated area, and to continue to flow on,—a silent, sluggish stream, destined to form many mires and swamps before finally evaporating. The course of the Manas River suggests the most natural route northwards across the arid plains; and in time to come, when the region is more fully developed, this will no doubt become a highway able to compete with the present Shi-Kho road; for it will have not only the advantage of a better water-supply, but will also tap the traffic of a richer country. At present both the Manas River and the highway afforded by its banks are wasted.

The Manas River is a feature of immense importance in a land so barren; this is proved by the fact that no other practical route leads across Dzungaria to the east, the Chinese having taken advantage of the opportunities it offers by planning a route which should connect their capital with the projected new city of Sharasume, or Altai; it also represents the shortest and most direct road to the frontier town of Chuguchak as well as to the important trade-centre of Zaisan. The only signs we found of the existence of communication between north and south by this route were a caravan of a hundred bullock-carts, laden with hides, bound for Chuguchak, which we passed on the road a few days north of Manas; and a line of telegraph-poles lying beside the track in readiness for the line to be carried northwards.

Leaving Manas with a light caravan, we travelled along the east bank of the river. Although, at first, a fast-flowing river, many channels running in over shingly beds, it soon degenerated into a sluggish stream winding its way between mud-banks and bordered by jungle, swamp, or rice-fields. The farther north the smaller and less frequent were the patches of cultivation. Now we passed through the fields of Chinese colonists, and now through sand-dunes alternated by marsh or forests of dwarf oak and poplar, which formed the haunt of stags, pigs, and the small Central Asian tiger. There were many varieties of scenery and changes of weather; thunder-storms broke over us, and rain fell in such quantities that the passage of the baggage-horses across the quagmire, into which the plain was transformed, became a matter of difficulty; later on, the great heat and the ferocity of the mosquitoes reminded one of the tropics. On the third day we found ourselves wandering amongst the sand-dunes which not only surged up to the very edge of the river, but even changed its course, when the winds were sufficiently violent to move the sands. In hollows amongst the dunes were lakes teeming with bird-life, such as ducks, waders, terns, and gulls; and even here small patches of suitable ground were utilized for corn-growing.

The scenery of the central plains, although monotonous and featureless in itself, was always relieved by the panorama which the giant Tian Shan offered until the northern ranges came into view. From this outlying point could be seen the Celestial Mountains, with an unbroken snow-line of about two hundred miles in length, but to the north there was either nothing, or splendour of colour, as the case might be, whether the day were hazy with loess-laden winds or calm and clear. Mirages often shimmered in the distance with such reality and persistency that one could easily forgive the mistakes, made on even recent maps, which placed an imaginary Ayar Nor lake in a desert we actually passed across and an extensive Kizil-bashi Nor to the north-east, where the only water-surface is the small lake of Telli Nor with a few salt marshes.

By slow and tedious marches, often losing the track, and experiencing long delays caused by guides who did not appear to know the way to the next village, we finally arrived at an easy ford and crossed over to the western bank of the Manas River. The vagueness of the country ahead of us, and the difficulty of obtaining information, obliged us to trust a guide to conduct us to a village called Sa-veen. When, after a long, hot trek, with much wandering amongst bogs, jungles, and rice-fields, we eventually arrived there, we appeared to be in altogether the wrong direction. We found travelling in a straight line to be impossible, and moving without a guide in such a country to be folly, so, after resting the horses for a day and bribing a native of Sa-veen,—who appeared to be so well off, owing to returns from rice-culture, that he had no time for anything else but gambling,—we moved westwards, hoping some day to come within sight of the Jair Mountains.

On leaving the vegetation-zone of the Manas River barren, open steppe surrounded us; yet, in spite of the apparent aridity and the easy nature of the country, we experienced considerable difficulty in our attempt to cross these plains. The nature of the ground was, over large areas, an expanse of salt-encrusted, friable earth; at every step the outer crust broke through, and we sank deep into the soft, dusty earth beneath. The fatigue thus occasioned made it most tedious for man and beast; whether wet or dry these soft, salty plains formed obstacles of no small difficulty. Where water approached the surface, dangerously soft ground bogged the horses and made progress slow. It was almost impossible to distinguish between the dry, saline earth and the bog, for both were dry on the top, and for this reason we repeatedly fell foul of them. The horses went down like ninepins when the dry crust proved to hide treacherous ground; then they had to be unloaded, pulled out of the soft, sticky bog, and loaded again; then the bog would be tried in another direction,— with the same result of muddy horses and wet baggage.

THE SALT-ENCRUSTED PLAINS OF CENTRAL DZUNGARIA.

DEEP-CUT RAVINES IN THE DZUNGARIAN PLAINS.

On one occasion we actually had to unload and un-saddle the horses, to spread all the felts we possessed on the soft bog, and to lead the animals and carry the baggage over them to firmer ground.

Travelling transversely to the water-courses, as we were now doing, entailed heart-breaking detours in order to cross the deep-cut gorges which had been carved out by the streams, when once a year—in spring—the melting snows sent down from the lofty border-ranges a flood of *useless* water. The plain, as a whole, looked easy-going and level, but was in reality seamed with sheer-sided trenches, the high, earthy banks of which were difficult obstacles to negotiate. Their existence was not realized until the lip of a nullah was reached; then a way had to be found for the baggage-horses to descend into a bottom choked with a jungle of scrub, tall reeds, poplar, and wild olive; tearing our way through the jungle we were involved in another climb up the opposite cliff. The baggage, as often as not, came off on the descent, and, being once more loaded up, slipped again on the ascent—that is to say, when we succeeded in finding a possible crossing; more often we were compelled to follow the brink of the ravines for a long way and lead the caravan by an easier road.

In spite of the jungle-choked ravines and bogs, we sometimes incurred the risk of a shortage of water. The ravines were often dry, although they had an inviting appearance of luxuriant growth ; while the bogs were merely formed by the percolating up of brackish water. The dry plain drank up the drainage from the mountains and quickly swallowed all rain that fell, yet at this season chance pools of rain-water might be found, as we were once fortunate enough to discover, when, at the end of a long day's trek, the line of vegetation for which we had aimed was found to be dried up and we were in danger of a waterless camp. On that occasion the dogs drew our attention to a pool of rain-water lying some way off the track, and we camped close by. Water did not necessarily mean grazing, for the following morning we found that all the horses had strayed far and wide in search of grass; we thus found ourselves in the predicament of being seven men and eight horse-loads of baggage dumped in mid-desert, with a small and rapidly drying pool of rain-water to depend upon! All that day and the following night the men scouted the country for the missing animals—no easy matter in a flat plain covered with 10-ft.-high saxaul and tamarisk scrub. Eventually eleven were secured out of sixteen, and, giving up the others as lost, we moved on, just as our now very muddy and much diminished rain-pool was drying up.

After some eight days in the desert, although endeavouring to keep a line towards the north-west, one obstacle after another turned us unwillingly towards the west and south-west, until we actually reached the outer fringe of the cultivation along the Kutun River which waters Shi-Kho. Even then we should have struck northwards along a track which led in that direction had not our guide decamped, tempted by our proximity to the Shi-Kho bazaars; we had therefore to follow suit.

These two weeks spent in wandering over the plain, although trying and disappointing in that we had been thwarted in carrying out our plan, were not wasted. We had learnt much of the complex character of Central Dzungaria, which otherwise would have remained a blank to us.

From Shi-Kho, with a fresh caravan, we journeyed northwards by the main road which leads to Chuguchak, and, by doing so, experienced much we had escaped during the winter's trek along the high-road, namely, the plunging through acres of mud caused by over-flowing canals, the crossing of countless unbridged dykes, and the putting up at night in places which were literally cesspools of filth; all of which had been too hard frozen in the winter to be either a hindrance or an offence. A few marches took us out of the low, hot basin to rising ground; once off the floor of the plain we approached happier and pleasanter lands and at length reached the excellent pastures of the Maili highlands, the first spurs of the northern border-range.

CHAPTER XIX

SPORT IN THE HIGHLANDS OF DZUNGARIA

BY J. H. MILLER

THE middle of June found us once more among the mountains, revelling in the balmy breezes that ruffled the flower-studded grass of the Barlik-Maili Range. Life was again made enjoyable, and we had a further proof of the complex nature of Central Asia, in that, in two short marches we had risen from the enervating, furnace-like heat of the insect-infested plains, to a restful, green land of bubbling brooks and matchless pasture. Wisps of smoke hanging lazily in the air, and the presence of numerous flocks and herds added to the peacefulness of the surroundings, and proclaimed the presence of large Kirei encampments. The Turki words *maili* (fat) and *barlik* (everything) give the best idea of how this region appeals to the nomads, for it is indeed a " fat " land, possessing everything which the heart of a herdsman could desire.

The chance of procuring specimens of that rare sheep —*Ovis sairensis*—lured us to this region, but our quest was tantalizing and unsuccessful. The range of this sheep, which was first discovered by Mr. St. George Littledale in the Sair, or Jair, Mountains at the eastern end of the Tarbagatai, and south-east of Lake Zaisan, extends southwards through the Urkashar and other small ranges as far as the Maili-Barlik group. This is also its eastern limit. How far its range extends westwards along the Tarbagatai seems to be imperfectly known. Wild-sheep exist in the low mountains to the north of Balkash, but whether they are *Ovis sairensis* or *Ovis nigrimontana* is a question which requires investigating.

The head of the river Kosho, which divides the Barlik from the Maili, runs through a broad, grassy upland, thickly dotted with ancient burial-mounds. It is here that the Chief of the Western Kirei had his headquarters.

Early one afternoon, under the guidance of a herdsman, we reached his residence, and lost no time in paying our respects.

Instead of the usual picturesque group of yurts we found ourselves confronted by a high, mud-built enclosure, which had a formidable iron door. Inside the walls was a low building of Russian type, containing the living rooms and a store-room. Most of the remaining space was occupied by two large yurts, used for the kitchen and servants' quarters.

The great man and his family received us at the entrance to his house. It was with the utmost difficulty that we maintained a dignified demeanour, for the greatness of his position had spread to his person in an alarming degree. He must have weighed a clear twenty stone, and his corpulency was accentuated by a voluminous Kirghiz costume. His first wife ran him pretty close, and his sons and daughters showed great promise.

Tea and sweetmeats were placed before us in a room gaudily decorated with carpets,—some of them old and good,—many-hued tin boxes, and trashy goods from the Chuguchak bazaar. Somehow the whitewashed room

did not suit either the occupants or their belongings.
The smoky interior of a yurt would have been much
more appropriate. The old Chief was decidedly sus-
picious of us at first, and laughed at the idea that we
wanted to shoot wild-sheep ; he undoubtedly put us
down as spies. But when we had produced our Chinese
passports, and had proved to him our acquaintance with
the Russian Consuls of both Chuguchak and Kulja, he
began to look at us in a more friendly light.

Like so many of these frontier nomad chiefs, though
a Chinese subject, he was thoroughly in with the Russians, so as to be on the safe side whichever way the
cat jumped.

It was hard to believe that this man had, in spite of
his proportions, made the pilgrimage to Mecca, three
years previously, accompanied by his wife. They had
travelled by horse and boat to Omsk, and from there by
train to Odessa. He dwelt on the overcrowding of the
boats, saying that " they were packed like sheep at a
shearing." While undergoing a lengthy quarantine at
Tebuk, on the Mecca railway, fifteen out of their party
of forty had died, probably from cholera. How foreign
to the heart of the lazy, space-loving Central Asian
nomad must have been the crowding, hurry, and
bustle of train and boat travelling ! But it was all
looked upon as martyrdom for the cause, and submitted
to without a murmur—a striking proof of the hold
Mohammedanism has over its most outlying believers.

Before we left we had quite made friends with our
host, and had the satisfaction of hearing him order men
and horses for our use.

From our camp we looked up to the jagged crest of
the Barlik, only a day's march to the north. It is

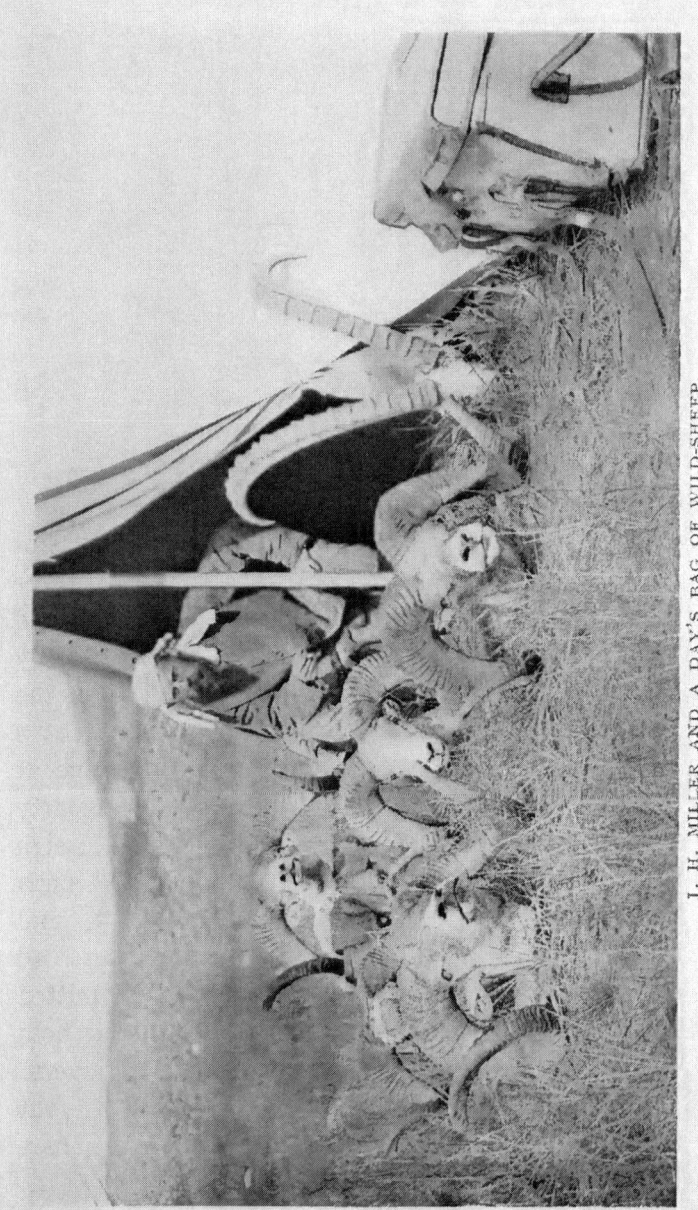

J. H. MILLER AND A DAY'S BAG OF WILD-SHEEP.

550]

the one well-defined ridge in this area of mountains. Both the north and the south slopes are exceedingly steep, especially the former, where precipitous cliffs drop into extensive forests. The grazing is of the best, and large numbers of yurts scattered over the lower slopes account, in no small degree, for the scarcity of game. I shall not weary the reader with an account of the strenuous days spent in searching for those scarce and elusive sheep ; only one small band of ewes and three yearling rams were sighted. A few ibex live a nervous existence among the crags, and wapiti, roe, and bear are said to frequent the forests. In spite of the absence of sport, however, we spent an enjoyable time camping in those emerald valleys of knee-high grass, or scrambling among the higher slopes, carpeted with that short, tufty variety of grass so beloved by mountain game. On the boggy patches below the snow-drifts yellow and purple pansies, gentians, poppies, and other flowers grew in profusion. Marmots and numerous varieties of smaller rodents were almost everywhere in great numbers, enabling Carruthers to add considerably to his collection.

Before moving into the Borotala we spent two days in hunting on the Western Maili plateau, almost over-looking the Dzungarian Gate. This plateau is formed of innumerable small hills and hollows, the latter being of a very uniform height,—something like a sheet of corru-gated iron, except that, instead of being parallel, they were jumbled up in hopeless confusion. There were no commanding positions for spying ; so all we could do was to ride along on the chance of coming upon game.

One morning, while turning a corner in this tantalizing country, I came face to face with the only " respectable " ram we saw the whole time, but he was out of sight before the rifle could be brought to bear. Several more sheep were sighted in this way, but all were ewes or very young rams. We each killed one of the latter for its skin, so as to have something to show for our labour. I cannot recommend any sportsman, desirous of securing a specimen of this sheep, to visit this southern limit of their range ; farther north they may be more plentiful.

A long reach down through waterless, barren gorges, took us to a small spring on the edge of the plain, which was crossed five miles north of Ebi Nor. This huge expanse of water, lying only 700 ft. above sea-level, shimmered like a sheet of silver in the clear atmosphere. We sighted large numbers of gazelle, and three saiga here; but hunting on the march is un-satisfactory, and we did no good with them.

Reaching the Kizil Tagh (red mountains), we once again struck the road which we had trodden nine months before on our way from Chuguchak to Kulja. Now that we were marching by day, our two dogs felt the heat terribly ; being so close to the ground, they received the reflected heat from the parched earth in addition to the direct rays of the sun. It was pitiful to see them rushing to every little bush we passed to dig madly at the ground in search of shade, or walking in the shadow cast by the horses. We often gave them water out of the rims of our felt hats, but that was only effective for a short time. In the cool of the evening they were quite happy again, playing about and hunting desert-rats.

For two days we rested on the banks of the Borotala close to a small Chanto village, which possessed a small bazaar, where we could replenish stores with all necessi-ties. A group of gnarled poplars afforded ample protection from the fierce rays of the sun, and a shady backwater enabled us, by bathing, to rid ourselves of the dust of the desert.

We were now on the threshold of a country which, from the sporting point of view, was completely unexplored, and our hopes ran high as to what might be ahead. Not much could be learnt from the industrious, stay-at-home Chantos, but we hoped to get all the information we wanted as to the sporting possibilities from the Charkhar Mongols, who inhabited the region to the west, so we decided to make for the headquarters of the tribe. On the first day's march up the river we must have passed quite three hundred yurts, with their attendant flocks and herds grazing on the lush grass that grew among the timber that fringed the river. This fringe of trees and scrub, though narrow, is so thick and interlaced as to be almost impenetrable in places ; it is largely composed of a thorny bush, which in winter is covered with golden clusters of small berries, the favourite food of the pheasants which abound in these jungles. When we crossed the Lower Borotala, in November, on our way to Kulja, we shot several, but during the summer they are rarely seen amongst the dense vegetation.

Allowing our caravan to pass the *aoul*[1] of the Amban of the Lower Borotala without halting, we paid a flying visit to his wife, who was in charge, the Amban himself being away in Sweeting on business.

His spouse received us with true nomadic hospitality. In the cool of her gorgeous snow-white yurt we were refreshed with tea and delicious cream made into the shape and consistency of a pancake, which rivalled in excellence the best Devonshire.

[1] Village of yurts.

The costume of a well-to-do Kalmuk [1] woman is very striking. A long blue and red gown, generally ungirded at the waist, reaches almost to her feet, and above this she wears a short, zouave-shaped jacket, of the same colours, heavily embroidered. Ample sleeves cover her hands, and have to be continually hitched back, as they impede her in her household occupations. Long and heavy plaits hang down over each breast, generally encased in cloth covers, to protect the clothing from the mutton-fat with which the hair is covered. Their usual headdress is dark blue, with an upturned brim, very Chinese in appearance. Underneath this is often worn a coral-covered skull-cap. Their ears, fingers, and hair are always decorated with heavy silver and coral rings, and their brooches are often of beautiful workmanship.

On the second night from leaving the village, after a long, gradual ascent from the river, we reached, at dark, the camp of the Amban of the Upper Borotala tucked away under the very foot of the Ala-tau, which loomed mysteriously above us. Much barking heralded our arrival, while flashes of light showed us the men hurrying out to assist us in unpacking the loads and pitching camp.

On the following morning a brightly clad group with the Amban at its head, was drawn up to receive us outside the ceremonial yurt. We were ushered in with much hand-shaking and bowing, and had bowls of that most abominable of drinks; *arak*, placed before us. This spirit, distilled from milk, is, when kept, exceedingly intoxicating. The bowls in which it was served were

---

[1] Used as a general term for all western Mongols.
[2] The Kho-ching section of the Charkhars.

much more pleasing than the drink itself, being carved from knots of walnut-wood, and lined with Chinese "shoe" silver. When darkened with age, they are exceedingly handsome. They were said to have been brought all the way from Lhasa by pilgrims, who presented them to their Chiefs. The Chieftain of the Charkhars was remarkably impressive in appearance, with a hard, strong, imperturbable countenance. He was the sort of man one would picture as one of the generals of Jenghis Khan.

The view from this camp on the slopes of the Ala-tau was one of remarkable extent and impressiveness ; the clearness of the atmosphere was such as is only met with in these dry, elevated regions. At our feet the ground dropped gradually to the Borotala River, which ran like a narrow green band through the khaki-coloured plain, losing itself in a broad belt of scrub and cultivation in the direction of Ebi Nor. Far beyond, filling up the whole of the southern horizon, stretched the great mass of the Tian Shan, from the Talki Pass to the colossal peaks above Manas. At that distance it seemed to rise perpendicularly from the plains, a line of glittering peaks above a dark base. But it was to the west, up Borotala, that we looked with greatest interest, for there lay the unknown.

On leaving this camp we experienced one of those exasperating "starts" that are the curse of caravan-travelling ; there are few things more trying to the temper and patience than the first day with a new caravan. It was not till midday that the horses began to dribble in by ones and twos, and then the saddles and gear were found to be deficient. Lastly, the men who were going with us thought fit to celebrate the occasion with a final carouse, so that, when they did at last turn up, they were mostly incapable.

The replies to our questions as to the sporting possibilities of our venture were, on the whole, satisfactory; but long experience had taught us not to put too much trust in native report. The natives always say what they think will please. " Gayeek tolla " (plenty of game) is the invariable reply, whatever the true facts may be, from Stamboul to the Altai.

Two marches along the foot of the mountains, crossing numerous boulder-strewn water-courses, and dodging protruding buttresses, brought us to the Karaul, which guards one of the few passes over the Ala-tau. In 1908 I had crossed this very pass on my way from the Altai to Kulja, via Lepsinsk. The appearance of the country had then struck me favourably, but a lengthy programme and a short season had prevented investigation.

With the exception of a small post of three men farther up the valley, we had now left the last habitation behind; so we decided to move along slowly, hunting as we went.

Carruthers and I agreed that he should have the monopoly of ibex, since he had never yet secured a specimen, whilst I had shot several good ones in the Tian Shan; and that the sheep were to be my portion, he having shot them on the Aksai plateau.

The southern slopes of the Ala-tau drop very abruptly into the valley; they are steep shale and grassy slopes, with protruding buttresses; there are no foot-hills in the proper sense of the word. The spruce-forest which darkens the northern declivities is entirely absent here, though the torrents that leap down from the snowy

SHEEP-GROUND OF THE UPPER BOROTALA.

crests are fringed by thickets of willow, poplar, and much rich grass.

We called a two days' halt in one of these delightful spots, while we made a thorough exploration of the surroundings. Carruthers ransacked the higher nullahs for ibex, while I scoured the lower slopes in search of rams. A female ibex and a ewe were shot for food, also five wolves. In those two days I must have seen not less than three hundred ewes and young, but not a single ram.

Carruthers saw a few female ibex, and a stag with fine horns, though, of course, still in velvet. Ibex ground without any tree in sight is a curious place to see a stag ; it had probably fled there for protection from the native hunters, who at this season would be busy among the northern forests.

All the wolves in the neighbourhood seemed to have collected in the vicinity of this abundant meat-supply, for I saw no less than fourteen in the two days. On the first evening we surprised an old wolf and six well-grown cubs on the prowl ; after watching them for some time sniffing at marmot-holes, and playing on the hill-side, I shot two of the cubs, whose fur, though short, was in beautiful condition.

On the next morning, having crawled to the top of a ridge quite close to our camp, I saw an enormous wolf coming straight towards us up the opposite slope, evidently hurrying home after a nocturnal foray. He did not see us, so, allowing him to come within forty yards, I bowled him over as he stopped for a moment to look back over his shoulder. Not long after this, while riding high up on the hillside, our attention was directed by loud yaps and snarls to the valley below. It was a pretty sight upon which we looked down. Two old grey wolves were lying on the soft turf, enjoying the sun, while round and over them romped five jolly youngsters, looking just like a lot of large collie pups. It seemed rather heartless to break up this happy family party, but, though wolves are frequently seen while sheep hunting, one generally refrains from firing at them for fear of disturbing nobler game, so that this was a chance not to be missed. To approach them was easy, a friendly ridge covering my descent; but something had frightened them, perhaps the Kalmuk had shown himself on the slope above, for, on reaching a point fifty yards from where they had been lying, I saw the whole family slinking off at a good pace. Three shots, however, accounted for one of the old ones and a youngster.

Our horses showed the greatest fear of these wolf-skins, and commenced to squeal and buck when they were tied on to the saddles. One, which was ridden by my Kalmuk, broke away with a half-tied-on skin flapping round its legs; luckily it kicked the obnoxious thing clear after going a mile or so, or I doubt if we should have seen it again.

We decided to make a long march up the valley without stopping to hunt; by so doing we hoped to get beyond the ladies' quarters into the domain of their lords and masters, for such large numbers of ewes meant fine heads somewhere not far off.

At this time frequent severe thunderstorms swept over us; though unpleasant while they lasted, the cool, clear atmosphere which they produced was an ample compensation.

As we moved up the ever-narrowing valley, a few

gazelle were sighted, but in absolutely unstalkable positions. Here and there bleached sheep-heads lay about; they were very uniform in shape, unlike the mixed types met with on the Yulduz, and in appearance intermediate between *ammon* and *poli*. I shall return to this subject later. Five days after leaving the Kalmuk camp we pitched our tents close to the river, where the valley narrows to such an extent that the mountains rise almost directly from the river-bank. In its western portion the Ala-tau is an imposing mountain-mass, some of the jagged peaks that frowned down upon us being a good 15,000 ft. in height. The view to the south was blocked by the less imposing, round-headed, shale-ridge which divides the Borotala from its large tributary, the Urta Saryk. From each dark crest grassy slopes with out-crops of rock and patches of shale, deeply seamed with numerous small water-courses, dropped towards our camp.

Just as the horses were about to be unloaded, a bear with two cubs was sighted on a terrace across the river; they were only about four hundred yards away, and in full view of the caravan. Thinking that we should be sighted any moment, and forgetting what poor sight a bear possesses, we hurriedly forded the river, and made towards where we thought her to be, without stopping to take our bearings. We were peering about, expecting to come face to face with them every minute, when suddenly a dark head and shoulders appeared for a moment above a rise a hundred yards to our left. We had hopelessly misjudged their position. Even now we should probably have got her if the ground had been favourable, but a hollow hid her from our view, till they appeared again a good five hundred yards away.

I should be ashamed to say how many cartridges were expended in the next minute or two. Even a musketry instructor at Hythe would have marvelled at the rapidity with which our bolts worked ! But, though dust was spurting up all round that hurrying, shaggy figure, the distance was too great, and she showed no signs of being touched ; the last we saw of that trio was the old bear looking defiantly back at us from a hill-top, waiting for those two precious balls of fur which she had outpaced in her flight. I should feel inclined to omit this regrettable incident, were it not an excellent example of what *not* to do under similar conditions. This bear was unusually dark ; most of the skins we have seen in the bazaars are of a browny yellow colour ; but she was nearly black, and of large size.

Large piles of *tezek* and stone kraals proved that herdsmen must visit this region in winter. During the summer not a single Kalmuk dare venture into the upper Borotala or Urta Saryk ; this is owing to their fear of the Russian Kasaks from the north. These freebooters from over the border lose no opportunity of swooping down upon any outlying herds and shooting down with impunity any Kalmuk who interferes. At any rate, this was the tale we were told, and it is doubtless true, though we gathered that the Kalmuks return the compliment whenever a thoroughly safe opportunity presents itself.

In the winter, when the northern passes are closed, Kalmuk herdsmen overrun the upper Borotala and Urta Saryk. In addition, considerable numbers of Chinese Kasaks, who summer on the eastern side of Sairam Nor, move into these more sheltered regions, paying a considerable sum to the Ambans for the right to graze in their domains; these Kasaks are of a very low, degenerate stamp. This intermixing of the races accounts for the fact that nearly all the Kalmuks can talk Turki. On this first day in this new locality, Carruthers took the ground across the river, while I scoured the slopes to the north, and, as luck would have it, he came upon numbers of rams, while I found a large herd of ibex.

Leaving camp when the last of the stars were still struggling against the first streaks of dawn, my hunter and I zig-zagged up to a lofty, commanding position. I dignify my companion with the title of "hunter"; but he and all our other Kalmuk followers were quite useless in this respect, though they were thoroughly willing, and helpful in their knowledge of the country. A herd of a dozen buck-ibex were feeding on a crest some way above us, showing up well against the sky. There seemed to be one or two fair heads among them, so, after ascertaining that they were thoroughly settled in their present position, we left them undisturbed, and continued our search for rams.

A short way farther on we found nine rams. Only one carried respectable horns, and I estimated them to be short of fifty inches, but I determined to try for him, as the meat would be acceptable any way, our hungry crowd having already demolished the two beasts so recently killed. While making this stalk, the rattle of stones drew my attention to another lot of ten rams, all strung out on a narrow sheep-track, crossing a steep shale-slope above us. There was no mistaking the size of one or two of those heads, but it was useless to attempt to follow them up, as they were evidently thoroughly alarmed; led by a grizzled old fellow with fine curling horns, they plunged along over the shale, stopping frequently to gaze down upon us. It was not till the afternoon that we got on terms with the original herd, and then bad shooting necessitated a stern chase before the best ram was brought to bay; it proved to be only a small head of forty-seven inches, but the prospects of soon getting better ones were very bright.

Carruthers had failed to find any ibex, but had come across three bands of rams; so the next day we exchanged ground, he going for my ibex, and I for his sheep.

At the top of an outlying ·bluff, overlooking a likely little valley, we settled down for a thorough "spying." At our feet ran a small stream carrying the melting snow from the drifts far above down to the Borotala; from each side of this short valley rose steep slopes, broken into numerous small arms and hollows. Right at its head, and just below the shale, two herds of rams were to be seen feeding among some ancient grass-covered moraines; there were six in one lot, and eleven in the other. We were too far off to tell their size, but they were certainly worth a close inspection. Leading our horses, we "screed" down to the valley bottom, and were then disgusted to find that the wind (what there was of it) was blowing straight up the hill. However, as there was no other approach, I decided to go boldly on, trusting to local eddies favouring me higher up.

After riding only a short way, while still half a mile from my objective, I left the man and horses, and proceeded on foot. Provided that the sheep were on the right side of the valley, where I had last seen them, there was just a chance that, by ascending the left, I might yet approach unwinded. It was a very slow advance,

FLOWER-STREWN MEADOWS.

WILD-PIG, SHOT IN THE UPPER BOROTALA VALLEY.
Sus scrofa nigripes.

since, as it had been so long out of sight, there was no knowing where the quarry might have moved to. Every little vantage-point had to be crawled up to and cautiously peered over. At last, the farther side of one small knoll was all the dead ground that remained. It seemed impossible that all those sheep could be concealed behind that slight cover; but nothing must be left to chance in this sort of hunting, and I continued to move slowly forward. The wind was gently fanning my right cheek, so all was safe in that direction. Suddenly the top of a horn appeared ahead. Raising myself inch by inch, I gazed down upon the six rams, which were lying down and facing every direction but mine. Alas! though they were only fifty yards off, not one carried a head worth shooting; they were all four or five year olds. There was still just one portion of the slope hidden from view, where the other lot must be, if they had not cleared out; so, wriggling back, I approached this also from above. This time I was not so successful, or perhaps the wind was less friendly, for that well-known alarm-signal, a mixture of a grunt and a sneeze, sounded before a single beast was visible. Hastily swinging round into a sitting position, I saw the twelve rams bunched together, and every head turned in my direction.

Four legs kicking in the air answered the first shot. Another whack, as they bolted, proclaimed that the second bullet had found its billet; luckily, the second ram made straight down-hill, enabling me to finish it off close to the horses, much to the gratification of the voracious old Kalmuk.

One of these heads measured well, being 51¼ in. in length; the other was a massive 49 in., but, one of its horns being very badly broken, it was useless as a trophy. After assisting my companion to skin and cut up one beast, and leaving him to deal with the other, I climbed up to a spur which overlooked a fresh stretch of country. This district was alive with game, a large herd of female ibex and their young, and some small rams being visible to the naked eye.

As we left the scene of our success, with the heads slung over the Kalmuk's saddle, the vultures began to assemble, for no meat is ever left to rot in a country possessing such keen-eyed scavengers as these.

This was to prove one of those red-letter days when everything goes right, and big-game hunting seems to be the easiest thing in the world. After such a day one is apt to push into the background and forget the days of fruitless search or unsuccessful endeavour, when, sometimes through faults of one's own, and sometimes owing to sheer bad luck, one returns to camp, night after night, with fatigue accentuated by failure.

It was still early in the afternoon, when, while riding carelessly down a stony water-course, with thoughts of camp and one of Pereira's savoury stews foremost in my mind, a guttural "Tocta" from my companion banished all such thoughts from me. The old fellow had already dismounted and was pointing over the back of his horse up a side-nullah we were passing at the time. " Tash, gulja, bilmaida " (Rocks or rams, I don't know), was his next remark. Spotting the grey smudges which had caught his eye, soon seventeen rams were focussed in the field of the telescope. They had evidently just risen from their siesta, and were standing aimlessly about while their leader decided in which direction they should start grazing ; when he had made up his mind, he led them at a trot down-hill till they were lost in a fold of the ground. The commencement of the evening meal is quite one of the best times to approach sheep, as they are then so engrossed with the early courses that their usual precautions for safety are somewhat relaxed.

I will not weary the reader with details of this stalk, for to any one but a participator the account of one is very much like the account of another. Suffice it to say that, half an hour later, I was doing an uncomfortable caterpillar-like slither on my back down a steep hill-side towards a V-shaped hollow, into which the sheep had disappeared.

Descending a smooth slope in this manner is an unsatisfactory way of approaching game, because its slightly convex formation alone conceals the hunter, and, when the quarry does at last come into view, the recognition is liable to be mutual. So it was in this case. A mass of grey backs and curling horns suddenly appeared almost straight below. At the same moment a head was turned in my direction, and at the next the opposite hillside seemed to be alive with flying sheep. There was no time to waste deciding which was the best head, though none of them were very small; so, following that sound hunter's motto, "When in doubt, shoot the leader," I had the satisfaction of seeing him pitch forward on to his head, to the shot. A very similar reply answered the next, and, as they stood for a second on the crest, yet another received his death-blow, and came galloping straight down the hill, falling dead on the very spot which they had just left. The two best of these heads measured 53 and 48½ in. respectively—very fair heads for *karelini*, which I fancy do not average so big as the *littledalei* of the Tian Shan, though they occasionally reach 60 in., as proved by a head picked up later.

While we were busy with our knives a terrific thunderstorm, which had been brewing for hours, burst over us ; the rain came down in torrents, and the thunder crashed right over our heads.

With two heads slung over each of our saddles, and the fifth held by my companion in front of him, not to mention several dangling legs of mutton, we slowly made our way towards camp.

The Borotala is never an easy river to cross late in the day, being very rapid and full of boulders. Weighed down as our horses were, we nearly came to grief several times ; but these mountain-bred ponies never lose their heads, and have a wonderful aptitude for recovering themselves from a stumble, so they brought us through safely. We were a tired and sodden, but contented couple as we came in sight of the camp-fire gleaming in the dusk.

I was very disappointed to find that Carruthers, though he had killed what he considered the best, had only secured a 43-in. head out of the herd of ibex, because I had estimated several to be decidedly better than that. If only they had been really big bucks, what a day it would have been !

Our highest camp was at the juncture of the two heads of the river, and only a few miles from the frontier. A few roe-deer find shelter here among the patches of low juniper on the hillsides and the dwarf willows that fringe the stream-beds. Carruthers shot a very pretty head with long, thin horns, while I secured two wild boars, a few of which had also taken up their quarters among the willows.

We had hopes of this wild boar proving to be undescribed, since no specimen has ever found its way to the South Kensington Museum, although several have been shot by sportsmen in the Tian Shan. On consulting Mr. Oldfield Thomas on the subject, however, I learnt that it had been described by Blandford from two specimens procured during the Second Yarkand Mission. He named it as a variety of the European wild boar, calling it *Sus scrofa nigripes*, on account of its black legs and feet.

While in this camp we received a visit from a Russian Cossack of the frontier guard, accompanied by six rascally-looking Kasaks, all armed with " Berdan " rifles and belts of cartridges. There is little doubt that he had received orders from his superiors, who were sure to have heard about us, to look us up, and see what we were doing so close to the frontier.

Our Kalmuks told us afterwards that, if they had been by themselves, they would have been robbed, and probably severely beaten. There is no doubt that these frontier police do nothing to check the border raiding, and in many cases are hand in glove with the Kasaks. While refreshing our unbidden guests with tea, we did our best to pump them as to the sporting possibilities of the northern slopes of the Ala-tau. The Russian informed us that big ibex and rams, besides large numbers of wapiti and bear, could all be obtained round his hut, only a day's march over the divide, and extended to us a cordial invitation, dwelling, as an extra inducement, upon the excellent "Fransuski khleba " (French bread) which his wife would bake for us. We thanked him profusely, though we had not the slightest intention of risking arrest by moving a yard over the frontier.

As the Borotala had proved most unproductive of big ibex, Carruthers decided to move on ahead into the Urta Saryk, where they were said to be much more plentiful, while I retraced my steps and hunted the ground below the spot where the five rams had been killed.

I spent a restful day in riding down-stream with the caravan, through country already well hunted over, little thinking what disheartening days lay ahead of me. Leaving orders with Pereira to move along the foot of the hills and to camp in the first large, lateral valley, I started off with the same trusty old Kalmuk to hunt my way thither by a higher route. The first little valley we entered was full of rams. Three were lying down high up to my right, eight more were feeding low down to the left of the stream, while a large herd of some fifteen small rams, were to be seen far up under the shale. Among the eight was one that stood out from all the others. It took much careful manœuvring to dodge those three pairs of watchful eyes on the right, but, after a wet scramble up the stream-bed, a spur hid them. Only three hundred yards of easy ground now lay between me and that " head of heads," which I already looked upon as mine, when, happening to glance back in the direction of the man and the horses, I was horrified to see hundreds of cattle driven by several horsemen streaming out from a side-nullah, and this in a country which I had considered to be absolutely free from such disturbances.

Of course, the rams had seen them before I had, for, when they next appeared, they were a good four hundred yards off, and going strong. Two impossible shots only hastened their flight, those 60-in. horns looking larger the farther they retreated from me, and making

ROE-DEER AND KALMUK HUNTER.

OVIS AMMON KARELINI.
In winter coat.

me inclined to empty the remainder of the magazine in the direction of the cause of all the trouble. I learnt later that these cattle had been purchased by a Russian merchant in Ili Valley, and that he was driving them by this short cut to some place on the northern side of the Ala-tau.

Great numbers of derelict horns were seen that day. They were all of a very uniform type, quite as much so, in fact, as are the ammon horns one sees in the Altai. This is a great contrast to the various twists and thicknesses that are so noticeable in the Central Tian Shan, particularly on the Yulduz plateau. The finest pair of horns measured in the Borotala—and I taped a great many—were: length 60½ in., girth 16½ in., and spread 38 in. My three best (shot) heads measured, in inches:

Length.	Girth.	Spread.
53	16½	33¼
51¼	15½	29
49	16¾	—

The distribution of *Ovis ammon karelini* [1] stretches from the north-east end of the Ala-tau Mountains, which is their northern limit, westwards along the range to the head of the Borotala, and from there eastwards along the whole length of the northern declivities of the Tian Shan, from Sairam Nor to the Karlik Tagh, which forms the most easterly extremity of the range. They are found throughout the Central and South-western Tian Shan from the Eastern Yulduz as far as the Aksay and Atbashi plateaux, for in the latter locality they were observed by Carruthers during his visit to that region in 1908. Throughout the whole of their northern and eastern

[1] I am adhering to the nomenclature adopted by Mr. Lydekker. See *Field*, January 16th, 1909.

distribution, which includes the Ala-tau, Borotala, Northern and Eastern Tian Shan, only *karelini* are met with. For instance, the horns seen in the Karlik Tagh, right on the edge of the Gobi, were in every respect similar to those of the Borotala. It is in the region of the Manas-Yulduz divide that the puzzle commences, for on the Yulduz *littledalei* are to be found on the same ground with *karelini* and in almost equal numbers. I have been informed by an observant sportsman, Colonel H. M. Biddulph, who recently visited that region, that in all probability a third, unnamed variety, will be proved to exist. I will briefly describe these three varieties in the hope that it may be of assistance to sportsmen who contemplate visiting the Tian Shan, besides being of interest to naturalists.

The first and most common variety is *karelini*, in which the horns are more rounded in section than is the case with *poli*, but only slightly more massive. The twist of the horn is intermediate between *typica* and the open type of *poli*, there being rarely any sign of the great nip-in of the former and never any of the openness of the latter. The average horn measurements of a fully adult *karelini* are: length, 52 to 55 in.; girth, 15 to 16 in.; and spread, 32 to 36 in. Colonel Biddulph picked up a colossal *karelini* head close to the Narat Pass on the Yulduz, in 1911. It measures: length, 70$\frac{3}{4}$; girth, 16$\frac{1}{4}$; and spread, 46$\frac{1}{2}$ in. Judging by the appearance of this remarkable head, which rivals the largest recorded head of *poli*, the sheep that carried it cannot have died more than three years previously.

As a rule, sportsmen who visit the Tian Shan can only spare a very limited time for going after sheep, owing to the other species of game that claim their attention, and so visit only the most accessible localities. I am convinced, however, that a systematic search among the more inaccessible regions would reveal small lofty valleys, tucked away among the peaks and glaciers, which no native ever visits. Here would be found rams carrying considerably larger heads than those recorded in Rowland Ward's *Records of Big Game* (sixth edition) under the heading of "*littledalei.*" The jumble of mountains round about the head-waters of the Manas River I consider one of the most likely localities in this respect.

The other variety, *littledalei*, resembles the open *poli* type in the twist of the horn, but is considerably shorter in length, although exceeding it in girth. Average length of fully adult ram 50 to 54 in., girth 16 to 17 in., and spread 44 to 48 in.

The third variety, which is as yet imperfectly known, is apparently considerably rarer than the other two. It approximates to the *O. a. hodgsoni*, its chief characteristics being great massiveness, short length, and narrow spread. There is practically no second twist to the horn. Colonel Biddulph, to whom I am indebted for information respecting this third variety, measured several heads in the Western Yulduz and found them to average, length 40 to 50 in., girth 16 to 18 in., and spread 17 to 20 in. As this type of horn appears to differ just as much from the other two as they do from one another, it has every right to be considered a distinct variety; however, adult heads will have to be brought to England for examination, before a definite decision can be arrived at.

As to the question of body-measurements and colour-variation, I am of the opinion that the *karelini* and *littledalei* do not differ in any important respect, but that any slight variations are merely due to age and seasonal changes.

I venture to suggest that if, at the next big-game trophy exhibition that is held in England, every one who possesses sheep-heads from the Tian Shan and adjacent ranges, would make an effort to lend them, they could be grouped together and their respective characteristics clearly shown.

I cannot, here, go as deeply as I should like into the interesting but complex question of the wild-sheep of Central Asia, but, having just touched upon the subject, I must now return to the narrative.

While riding along disconsolately, early in the afternoon, still smarting under our defeat of the morning, we came upon a pair of sixty-inch horns lying in a sheltered hollow which was a perfect " Golgotha," where the remains of dozens of mighty rams strewed the ground. As this pair of horns was in almost perfect condition, I decided to keep it. Soon afterwards, while continuing our careless way towards camp, our attention was directed simultaneously to a movement far up on the shale of the divide.

There was no mistaking those graceful, sweeping horns, which looked many sizes too big for their owner. It was our old friend of the morning, with his companions. Though knowing full well that they were in an unapproachable position, the temptation to make one more effort to secure that coveted trophy was irresistible. Telling my companion to throw away the picked-up head, so as to quicken our progress, we made a rapid detour, in the hope of getting round and above them.

When our panting, steaming ponies had carried us as far as it was advisable to take them, I dismounted

IN THE URTA SARYK VALLEY.

and continued on foot up that most heart-breaking of obstacles, a steep shale-slope. I was plodding along very much in the same condition as the ponies when a shout from my man made me look back. Following the direction of his outstretched arm, I realized what a fool I had been to attempt to approach a herd of sheep already thoroughly alarmed, for there on the snowdrift, silhouetted against the sky, at the very top of the divide, were those mobile *gulja*.

I had had enough of sheep-hunting for that day.

Without bothering to recover the discarded horns, which had no interest for me now that the equally fine pair on a living specimen had for the second time given me the slip, we hurried down to the camp. A good meal, followed by a pipe, and warm blankets, soon put a very different complexion on affairs, and I regretted not having at least a photograph to show of that fine pair of horns.

As before, my trusty follower and the caravan *bashi*, who alone knew the country thoroughly, arranged between themselves the ground to which the camp should be moved. As we started off once more in the crisp early morning, the despondency of the previous evening had given place to that thoroughly optimistic frame of mind which is one of the chief requirements of a big-game hunter, and alone enables the hardships and disappointments of this most fascinating of pursuits to be cheerfully surmounted. Five herds of rams were seen that day; numbering something like seventy beasts, but they had all been thoroughly disturbed by the slowly moving herd of cattle and noisy herdsmen, who had passed through the very middle of this narrow strip of sheep ground, causing them to retreat to their stronghold in the shale.

Many hours were wasted in attempting to approach a herd with some good heads in it, for when, after much patient restraint, I had got them into a suitable position, three insignificant beasts which had been lying hidden gave the alarm and stampeded their betters.

As evening advanced, my old guide led the way down to where he expected to find the camp; but, though we scoured the surrounding country and hunted for tracks, not a trace could be found. Returning to the high ground, two small tarns were visited, but with the same result. It was by that time nearly dark, so, discovering several large piles of *tezek* stacked like peat, we decided to spend the night where we were. Judge of our disgust when, after congratulating ourselves on the prospect of a large fire, my match-box was found to be empty, and my companion to be without the usual flint and steel! I am afraid that on this occasion I was far from carrying out the theory of always being prepared for a night out; a lump of doughy bread, the remains of lunch, alone constituted our food-supply. The old Kalmuk, to whom such little inconveniencies as this were of frequent occurrence, was quite content with his morsel of bread, augmented with copious pinches of *nahs*.[1] I made myself as comfortable as I could on the lee side of a pile of *tezek*, and, lying on a saddle-cloth with a thick coat over me, I slept soundly till wakened by the frost in the small hours of the morning.

I shall never forget the commencement of that day, perched up as I was in those lonely surroundings without a sound breaking the stillness; even the munching of

[1] *Nahs* is a form of snuff, made from a mixture of powdered tobacco and the ash collected after burning a certain plant. It is not administered through the nose, but scooped up on to the tongue from the palm of the hand, and allowed to rest there while it slowly dissolves.

the horses had ceased, and they stood with hanging heads, satiated with a night's grazing on the short, rich grass. A faint grey light began to creep into the east ; the stars disappeared slowly before its ever-increasing strength ; the snowy summits turned from grey to a delicate pink, and then hardened as that longed-for sun-line crept down towards us ; and then, with a leap, the great fiery ball rose clear of the hills and bathed us in its welcome rays. Snow-cock began to chuckle round us, and chats and snow-finches to flit from rock to rock. Black specks far away on a skyline indicated a hungry herd of sheep. Of all this wild life, the lazy, over-eaten marmot alone remained curled up at the bottom of his snug burrow, waiting for the sun to gain in power before he ventured out. But the beauties of nature do not compensate for the absence of breakfast, and we lost no time in searching the surrounding country from a neigh-bouring eminence. As no human being was within sight, we decided to make straight for the Urta Saryk, since, even if Carruthers' camp were difficult to find, there was a small Kalmuk post at which we could get food. Four hours' riding took us off the plateau, down the well-timbered valley to the main stream.

Here we fell in with some herdsmen, one of whom we " pressed " as a guide. At four in the afternoon, after fording the river, we came upon that welcome green tent pitched among some pines, and lost no time in putting ourselves outside a kettle of tea and pounds of bread and meat.

A man was at once despatched to find our caravan : it turned up next day with a very anxious Pereira at its head. We were never able to find out exactly who was to blame in this matter, since each of the Kalmuks noisily maintained that the other was at fault. However, Pereira was not going to risk the culprit escaping, so he gave both a mild beating.

We now moved slowly up the Urta Saryk in search of ibex. In its central portion, this valley is a rough, precipitous gorge, with a roaring torrent, full of boulders and deep holes, rushing down it. On the south side a heavy forest and on the north bare cliffs rise from the very edge of the water. Here and there on the left bank, between the foot of the cliffs and the river, are narrow flats, covered with timber and grass, which make ideal camping-grounds. Leaving Carruthers encamped in one of these places, with several likely ibex-nullahs round it, I proceeded up-stream with two men and a pack-horse to explore the valley to its head. Sometimes we were scrambling along the hillside, and at others pushing our way through the tangled growth by the river. We " jumped " several roe-deer, and crossed some bear and wapiti tracks. After we had passed a delightful little waterfall, which hurled itself from the cliffs 200 ft. above, straight into the river beneath, we found the timber thinning, till only juniper and a club-shaped, cactus-like plant covered the slopes.

Towards its head the valley widened considerably, and formed a grassy flat. Here we spent a night at a native winter camping-ground ; which must be a cold, bleak spot at that season ; and for this very reason the snow would not lie deep, thus enabling the flocks to get at the abundant grass.

The actual head of the valley is composed of small glaciers and moraines. Among this wilderness we came upon five ibex, none with horns of great size. To keep the men in good cheer I killed one for its meat. During

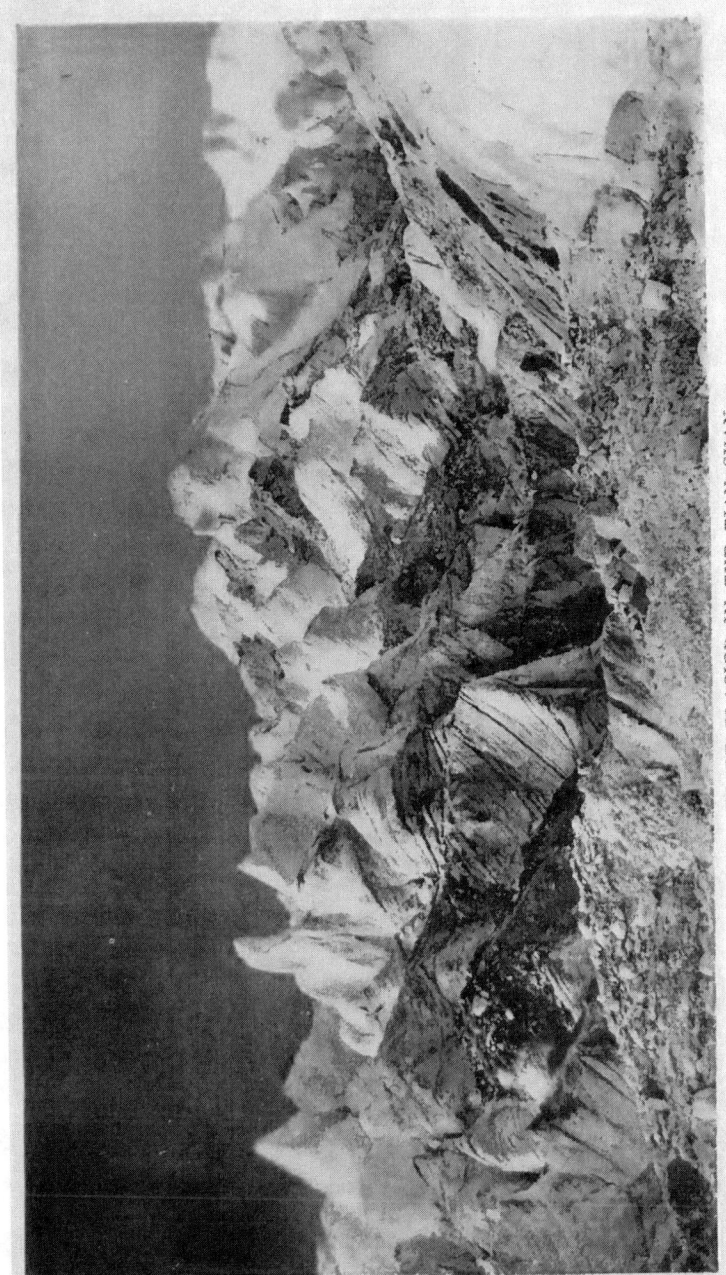

THE MUZART GLACIER IN THE TIAN SHAN.

the late summer buck-ibex carry great quantities of fat, which is highly prized by all the natives. All through this hunting-trip our followers dried and salted great slabs of both ibex and sheep meat to take home withthem.

Our return journey was made on the north side of the valley, along a broad, grassy shelf below the main ridge and above the cliffs that drop to the river. Several herds of ibex were seen here, some of females and others of bucks, feeding on the smooth, grassy ledge above the cliffs, like rabbits outside a cover at home. One of these herds was among the largest I have ever seen ; it was composed of over a hundred bucks. Most of them were small, but several carried horns which appeared to me to measure not less than 50 in., though I got only a hurried glance at them. A rough descent brought us down to the river and camp. The welcome sight of several pairs of ibex-horns in front of the tents proved that Carruthers' spell of bad luck had at last broken ; the best of them was a heavy, symmetrical head of 49 in.

The question now arose whether we should remain in this region—Carruthers to continue his search for big ibex, and I to recross the ridge and continue my inter-rupted sheep-hunt ; or should march at once for Kulja, and from thence hurry up into Kok-su for a few weeks' hunting before we started on our long journey to India.

The expedition to the Kok-su was at last decided on, but we bitterly regretted our decision later, when, owing to a lengthy delay in Kulja waiting for our heavy baggage to arrive from Urumchi, it had to be abandoned.

A long march brought us to the north end of Sairam Nor, where several families of Kalmuks had pitched their summer camps. What a different aspect the lake pre-

sented now to when we last saw it in January ! Bordering
its dark blue waters were slopes of waving grass which
ran up to patches of dark pine-forest on the surrounding
hills.

The courteous old Amban had sent one of his men
all the way to the lake to inquire after us and bid us
good-bye. Having paid off our men, who had really
worked very well, though they were annoying at times,
we continued on our way to Kulja with a scratch
caravan collected from the surrounding yurts.

The Upper Borotala is undoubtedly one of the finest
sheep countries in Central Asia ; nowhere have I
seen sheep so numerous as there. But the locality frequented by the rams during summer is comparatively
small, and can be hunted out by one gun in about six
days, so that it is important to hunt very slowly, and
not to disturb large areas every day. As to the ibex,
they are certainly fairly numerous in the Urta Saryk, and
good heads are to be obtained ; but whether their horns
reach the enormous dimensions of those which inhabit
the tributaries of the Tekes River, remains to be proved
by future hunters.

Any one intending to visit this new hunting-ground,
which can be reached in four days from Kulja, should
employ a Chanto caravan, so as to be as independent as
possible of the Kalmuks. It is, however, essential to have
two or three of these people with the party to act as
guides and messengers, and to accompany one out
hunting. For this reason it is advisable to call on the
"Tzian Tziun" at Sweeting, who will authorize the
Kalmuks to comply with one's wishes. He has entire
control over the nomads, and the very mention of his
name strikes terror into their hearts.

CROSSING THE KARAKORUM PLATEAU.
Altitude 17,000 ft.

I should advise any one who does not fancy doing all the hunting himself, to engage one of the well-known *shikaris* from the Tekes, the Kalmuks of the Borotala being quite useless in this respect.

With the return to Kulja, although we were still many thousands of miles from home, we considered our programme of work accomplished. This narrative was intended to deal with the undescribed regions of Upper Asia, and, although we had yet to traverse a wide area of country before reaching the coast, our route led us across well-known and much-visited lands. From Kulja we crossed the Central Tian Shan, and, travelling by way of the great oases of Chinese Turkestan, such as Aksu, Kashgar, and Yarkand, we passed through a region whose physical features, history, social and economic conditions, have all been exhaustively dealt with by such illustrious explorers as Hedin, Stein, and Huntington. Even the great Karakorum, the highest and perhaps the most awe-inspiring trade-route in the world, is now a hackneyed journey, granting, no doubt, an experience not to be missed, and offering unique lessons to the student of Central Asian geography, but to which we could make no addition by a narration of our experiences. From the breathless summit of the Karakorum we bade farewell to Inner Asia, and our route led on to Ladakh, Kashmir, and Hindustan.

CHAPTER XX

THE GAME OF THE PLAINS

By J. H. MILLER

IN these days, when neither distance, nor time, nor hardship deters the true big-game hunter from penetrating to the most remote quarters of the globe in pursuit of his hobby, and when new and untrodden hunting-grounds are becoming scarcer year by year, it is of interest to recount all the kinds of wild-game that roam the plains of Dzungaria, which we crossed and recrossed during our wanderings, and which, until we penetrated its fastnesses, no white hunter had seriously exploited.

In the spring of 1900 Messrs. Church and Phelps travelled from Kulja to Urumchi, by the road which runs along the southern borders of Dzungaria. The former, in his interesting book, *Chinese Turkestan*, mentions what he and his companions saw and heard of game on their line of march, but with this exception, I am not aware of any one having gone into the matter. Though ever-increasing numbers of hunters yearly visit the Tekes district of the Central Tian Shan, on the south, and, in a less degree, the Little Altai on the north, this intervening region has remained practically a *terra incognita*. The few travellers who, from time to time, have crossed portions of this country have merely hurried through, preferring to trust to the well-known sporting localities

THE GAME OF THE PLAINS 581

rather than chance the uncertainties of pioneering new ground.

As long as "sixty-inch" Ammon can be secured in the Altai, and the district drained by the right affluents of the Tekes can produce such magnificent heads of sheep, wapiti, ibex, and roe as are yearly secured, what need is there to look for a new country ? But the toll of the native hunters, and that of the less destructive, but yearly increasing Europeans, will tell in time, and drive them to seek for fresh fields of sport. To many travellers also, the knowledge that several other sportsmen are hunting within a comparatively small radius, and the feeling that they themselves at any time may be poaching in another's "nullah," does away with that sense of freedom which is half the joy of big-game hunting. The fascination of treading new ground, where there is no likelihood of coming across empty jam-tins and match-boxes, and where the lure of the next skyline is ever calling, is to some an essential adjunct to the actual hunting.

These sketches of days spent in the chase, and in studying the habits of big game, I submit to the public, in the hope that they may prove of interest to naturalists and sportsmen ; both to the few who contemplate visiting the regions mentioned, and to the majority who, though continually hearing it, are compelled to turn a deaf ear to the call of the "red gods."

There is probably no region in Central Asia where one finds such a decided and sudden change in altitude, and therefore in flora and fauna, as in Dzungaria. From the low, sandy, and jungle-covered plains lying to the north of Manas, which, although they lie at a distance of 1,600 miles from the ocean, are lifted only 700 ft. above it, one can look up to peaks that lift their snow-capped summits 20,000 ft. into the heavens. Every intermediate zone possesses its own fauna. On the boggy plateaux, which lie tucked away among the jagged sommits, roam the great wild-sheep, as elusive to the hunter as they are to the naturalist. The wolf, their constant persecutor, also inhabits these upland solitudes. Slightly lower down, the steep slopes and crags above the timber protect vast herds of ibex, whose greatest enemy is that most beautiful of cats, the snow-leopard. The dark forests of spruce and scrub conceal wapiti—of all beasts in this land the most persecuted by man—roe-deer, bear, and wild-pig. These are the chief large game of the mountains. The stony foot-hills which merge almost imperceptibly into the plains are a favourite locality for gazelle and the wild-ass, though both are also found far out on the steppes. The dense jungles which cover so large a portion of the lowlands, and through which sluggish, mosquito-ridden rivers wind their way, are the haunts of the tiger, roe-deer, wild boar, and a variety of wapiti never yet identified, but probably similar to the Yarkand stag. The last on the list, and in some ways the most interesting, is the ungainly *Saiga tartarica*, a lover, for the most part, of the lowest and most saline depressions.

It must not be hastily concluded, by those unfamiliar with Central Asian conditions, that, because of this tempting list of game, inhabiting a comparatively small area, a large and varied bag is easy to obtain. In the first place, it is a far-distant land, to reach the western portion of which necessitates either three weary months of steady marching from India, or from five to six weeks if one employ the quicker, though in some ways more tantalizing, Russian routes. Even when the

PART OF OUR BAG AT TAKIANZI.

582]

happy hunting-ground is at last reached, several months of strenuous hunting are necessary, often without the assistance of any one who can be dignified by the title of *shikari*, before a few good heads of, perhaps, four or five varieties are obtained. I am taking it for granted that, to any one keen enough to face the vicissitudes of such an undertaking, trophies of only the first quality are acceptable.

It was in January, while on our way from Kulja to Urumchi, along the road with the misleading title of " The Imperial Highway," or, as it is better known to the Chinese, " Pei-lu " (North Road), that we first came properly in touch with the Dzungarian gazelle (*Gazella subgutturosa*). To the Chinese it is known as " hwang yang " (yellow sheep), to the nomads as " kara karuk " (black tail), and to the Chantos as " jeran." Near Sairam Nor we passed several camels laden with frozen carcasses of these gazelle, and wild boar, which were being sent by the Kalmuk chiefs to the Tzian Tziun resident at Sweeting. This exalted personage has entire control over all the nomads of these parts ; hence these diplomatic gifts.

After leaving the exposed Sairam Nor basin, which lies at an altitude of 5,600 ft., and possesses a very just reputation for excessive cold in winter, we rambled—in our carts—down over a stony steppe to the little village of Takianzi, situated among small scrub and tall reed beds. We reached the seria in the early morning, after a terribly cold night in the carts. Several herds of gazelle had been passed on the road, so that a broken wheel formed a welcome excuse for devoting a day to hunting in the vicinity. The news of our decision having been flashed through the small bazaar, we were besieged by half the male population, each man being, according to himself, a mighty hunter, and the only one who really knew where the game was to be found. Having selected the two least noisy and pushing—who chanced to be Kalmuks—we sallied forth.

As we rode towards the foot-hills, which rose like a white sheet beyond the dark scrub, the vegetation began to grow thinner. It was composed of patches of thorn about 5 ft. high, tall, coarse grass, and a few stunted poplars, intersected by open glades. Our guides informed us that any moment we might expect to see " kara karuk " ; but, as there were yurts scattered around, and Kalmuk boys were noisily herding cattle, it hardly seemed a likely place for such shy animals as gazelle. However, we noticed almost immediately, some yellow forms which were moving about among the bushes. They were only does and quite small bucks; but, as we wished to make certain of getting a few specimens, and found them absurdly easy to approach, we shot three between us.

Then, leaving the men and horses behind, we soon found some good bucks. Three of the best, all carrying good horns of between 12 and 14 in. in length, were added to the bag. There is no doubt that, if light had permitted, several more could have been shot, since, in addition to their numbers, the ground was ideal for stalking, and they showed little fear of man. Like ostriches, as long as they could not see us, they seemed to consider themselves safe. When a shot was fired, they would quickly trot away, and start feeding again within a few hundred yards. The only accountable reason for this stupidity is that, when in their summer haunts, on the smooth, bare plains, they know well that, as long as no human being is in sight, they are perfectly safe, and so they consider the same to hold good when they are among the scrub. Any one who has attempted to approach gazelle in the former type of country will hardly be able to believe that they are ever easy to get up to. It was a complete revelation to us.

We were not able to skin all the beasts that evening, and we had the greatest difficulty in getting the skins off on the following morning. The carcasses had been frozen solid during the night, though lying inside our room in the serai. Before they could be skinned they had to be hung over a fire and thawed out—a slow and messy job. Though we met with gazelle here and there through the scrub-belt as far as Urumchi, we never again saw them in their winter quarters in such numbers as at Takianzi, and regretted not having spent another day there.[1]

In the zone of Piedmont Gravel on the south side of the Karlik Tagh gazelle-drives were organized for our benefit, but, as is usual with this mode of hunting, beloved by all natives, they proved most unsuccessful, one buck, which fell to Carruthers' rifle, constituting our only success. The method the Chantos adopt is for a large party of ten to twenty horsemen to ride out to a likely locality. On finding a herd, they ride rapidly forward on whichever side the ground is most favourable for concealment and for taking advantage of. This

[1] The winter coat of this gazelle is very dense and from 2 to 3 in. in length. The upper part of the body is dark fawn; legs, belly, and rump white; tail black (6 in. in length); neck and head very pale fawn, but, in some cases, almost white, and frequently there is a dark streak under the eyes and black hairs round the base of the horns. The characteristic of this gazelle, as compared with the other Central Asian species, is that the horns are considerably more divergent and less closely and boldly ringed.

move is generally carried out in full view of the game, but, though they bunch together and display their white rumps, curiosity holds them back from moving away. As the hunters ride along, every two hundred yards or so a man slips from his saddle and conceals himself behind some slight cover, or, if none exist, as is generally the case, he will build a slight breastwork of stones, resting his antique muzzle-loader over the top. When half the number have been left behind in this fashion, the remainder, leading the riderless horses, make a wide detour, and spread out on the opposite side of the herd. With flanks well advanced, they then move in open order towards the guns. Occasionally large numbers are killed in this manner, for the terrified gazelle lose their heads and run down the whole line of guns. More often, however, they break away at the sides, or back through the drivers.

The Kirghiz, and occasionally the Chantos, have a much more sporting way of hunting gazelle, by means of trained golden eagles, called in Turki "*bouragut.*" This method is only attempted in winter, when the game is easy to approach, and the sportsmen have plenty of time on their hands. Often we saw a man riding along with a hooded eagle on his well-gauntleted right hand. The great weight of the bird is supported by means of a forked stick for the wrist, which fits into a socket in the front of the saddle. We were never fortunate enough to see a flight ; but Major Cumberland, in *Sport on the Pamirs and Turkestan Steppes*, gives such a good account of a kill he witnessed on the Tarim east of Aksu, that I cannot do better than quote his description.

" I was anxious to see the eagle work, and, as I could

DZUNGARIAN GAZELLE (*Gazella subgutturosa*) IN WINTER COAT.

586

see nothing of a stag, went off with the Yuzbeggie in the afternoon to try for another jeran. I was mooning along thinking of something else, when all of a sudden the Yuzbeggie started off as hard as he could gallop across the *maidan* (plain). I followed suit, and soon made out a doe-jeran in the distance. It stood and looked at us in amazement, and then cantered off, not very fast, while we still continued our headlong career, every now and then floundering on to our noses over a tussock of grass or into a hole hidden by the snow, until we got to about a hundred yards from our game, which only then realized the situation, and extended its stride. The *shikari* now hurled the eagle, which he had unhooded and held clasped to his breast during the run, at the jeran. The eagle, instead of rising like a falcon and sweeping on its prey, flapped along with its great wings quite close to the ground ; and, although it seemed to fly very slowly, gradually caught up the jeran, which was impeded in its course by the high grass, and at last grabbed it by the rump with its strong talons. It regularly dragged the deer down, and held on for some time, the little gazelle kicking out like mad. We still galloped on, and I wondered what the finish would be. The *shikari*, when he got up to them, without drawing rein threw himself off his pony, and grabbed the deer by the hind-leg, just as it had kicked itself free, and, pulling out his knife, cut its throat."

In addition to gazelle, hares, foxes, and even wolves are killed by means of the golden eagle ; but, in the case of wolves, dogs are generally used to assist the bird.

Towards the end of April, with the exploration of the Karlik Tagh completed, and the rigours of the winter well behind us, we were able to devote the remainder of our time in Dzungaria almost entirely to natural history and hunting.

Between that town of stagnation, Barkul, and the small wayside station of Ta-shih-tu, a plateau-like mass of hills, with an average altitude of between 5,000 ft. and 7,000 ft., projects northwards from the main range into the plains of Eastern Dzungaria. The bulk of this uplift is of a very open nature, composed of low, rounded hills with flats between. Water is scarce, only represented by small springs at long intervals, and these are generally decidedly brackish. For this reason the nomads visit the region only in winter, their place being taken during the summer by large herds of gazelle and kulon.

When we marched through, westwards, the short, tufty grass, which possesses such marvellous feeding properties, was in its prime, having been well watered by the recently departed snow. Thousands of gazelle and a few wild-asses, straight from their winter quarters on the lowlands to the north, were busy making up for their scanty winter fare. Almost all day game was in sight, though rarely within shot.

One delightful picture remains indelibly fixed in my memory. It was on one of those invigorating spring mornings with a hot sun, but clear, cool atmosphere, which make the highlands of Central Asia such an ideal summer resort. Carruthers and I were riding ahead of the caravan, as was our custom, for to ride behind camels requires the patience of a Job and an Oriental's indifference to time. On reaching the crest of a rise, we looked down on a miniature plain, perhaps a mile long by half a mile broad, and surrounded by quite low hills. The bright green grass shooting from the earth and gravel formed a delightful setting to the picture. In the very centre, away from any dangerous irregularities of the ground, lazed a large herd of gazelle and ten wild-asses. Most of the former were busy feeding, but the latter had finished their breakfast, and were about to indulge in a siesta. Some were already lying down, others were enjoying a sand-bath, sending clouds of dust floating away to leeward, while two by mutual consent were nibbling shoulders. What a picture Mr. J. G. Millais could have made out of that scene, with all its atmosphere and movement!

They were all in an unstalkable position, but shortly afterwards a slice of luck enabled me to shoot a gazelle with a very fine pair of long, open-spread horns. He was among a small herd of six, all males, and in what they might justly have considered a perfectly safe position. There was, however, just one large mound between me and them.

Having reached it in safety, I lay there watching them and trying to imagine that they were nearer than they looked; the most optimistic estimation would not make them less than four hundred yards off; much too far to make at all sure of hitting a small, indistinct beast like a gazelle. But, as I lay and watched, they played into my hands, for, strung out in single file, they began to advance slowly almost straight towards my position. By that time Carruthers had joined me, and, as they approached, we criticized their horns, and decided that the third in the line carried the best pair. Waiting till he stopped for a moment to scratch his face with a hind-foot, I fired at his shoulders. It was a bad shot, for the bullet merely grazed a horn and inflicted a slight flesh-wound on his back. He was, however, completely stunned by the shock, and a well-placed second bullet finished the business.

I will now relate our experience with another denizen of the plains, one that has rarely been seen by Europeans in its native haunts. Of all the beasts in nature, few exceed the saiga (*Saiga tartarica*) for grotesqueness of form or gait. He seems to be altogether a mistake, to have been made after all other beasts, when the ingenuity of the Creator had already been exhausted. He is not closely related to any other animal, and is a puzzle to naturalists, who class him with the antelope, though he is a disgrace to that graceful family. His horns resemble the gazelle's in shape, though not in colour, while the skull is like that of no other beast. The shape of his body, the texture of his coat, and his bleating, all remind one of a sheep, while the slinking, stooping gait is more akin to that of some of the smaller jungle-living deer. His chief characteristic is, of course, the great soft " Roman " nose, which is out of all proportion to the body.

In the Pleistocene period the saiga ranged over Western Europe, even as far as Great Britain, but at the present day the southern steppes of Russia between the Don and Volga form its western limit. From there its range stretches eastwards, throughout the more desert portions of Russian Turkestan, with the Siberian Railway for its northern limit, and the Trans-Caspian Railway and Tashkent-Kulja post-road for its southern.

In the vicinity of the low depressions of Lakes Balkash and Ala Kul it is said to be numerous. It has for many years been supposed that the saiga extended over the Russian-Chinese frontier eastwards to Dzungaria, but I am not aware of any one having actually seen, much less shot one, with the exception of that distinguished Russian explorer, Colonel Kozloff, who mentions having come across saiga in the Gobi east of Barkul.

We had frequently heard about it both from the nomads and the Chinese. To the former it is known as " burkark " (stooper), and to the latter as " ling yang " (white sheep), names which depict two of its chief characteristics.

It was not till we reached Guchen, that busy western terminus of the great North Gobi caravan-route, that we first obtained absolute proof of its existence in Eastern Dzungaria. Considerable numbers of its curious amber-coloured horns were hanging up in the Chinese shops there for sale. The Chinese consider them to possess valuable medicinal properties, and give as much as fifteen " sairs " for a pair. Every year consignments are sent to Pekin, where they are made into medicine, though we were unable to ascertain for what ailment it is a remedy. The high price put on the head of a saiga induces a small army of hunters, mostly Chantos, to spend the summer months in their pursuit.

During our journey eastwards in February we could not devote much time to hunting, our object being to reach Kumul as quickly as possible. We were, however, fortunate in coming across a local hunter, who was to prove invaluable on our return journey in the spring.

Owing to the impossible nature of the road, caused by the melting snow, we were delayed for two days at the small wayside post of Ta-shih-tu, situated on the main road, where it commences to cross to the south side of the mountains.

There can surely be no more abominable form of hostelry in the world than the average Chinese caravan-

II—18

serai, especially if it is in charge of that scum of Western China, the crafty Dungan. In winter the traveller has to put up with either intense cold—and how that icy wind can howl through those ill-fitting doors and paper-less windows, or a room full of pungent smoke! In summer there is no alternative ; it is always a case of " dust and stench and staleness " plus unremitting attention from a variety of insect-pests.

Hearing from the man in charge of the serai that during the winter months numbers of wild-sheep, or, as he called them in Chinese, Ta lăo yang (large-headed sheep), descend from the main ridge to the low hills round Ta-shih-tu, we spent the first evening spying with a telescope from a commanding position. A few wild-sheep had been found, and we were splashing our way through the slush and mud back to supper, forming plans for a hunt on the morrow, when we fell in with a wild-looking figure making for the same direction. He proved to be one of those curious, semi-nomadic, and semi-sedentary Mohammedans one finds in this eastern end of the Tian Shan. His wild-looking, unkempt appearance at once appealed to us ; over his shoulders was slung the most antique muzzle-loader I have ever seen, with a long, forked rest, and its barrel and stock held together with bindings of raw hide. It was one of those weapons better to have fired at one than to have to fire. His clothing consisted of a ragged old sheep-skin coat, almost black with the blood of many a beast, bound round the middle with a greasy cloth from which hung his powder-horn, flint and steel, and a serviceable-looking knife. Below this he wore short sheep-skin trousers, and round his legs were wound puttees of felt. Moccasins, made from the breast-skin of ibex, covered his feet : excellent footgear for dry ground, but the very worst for the country in its then damp state. A tight-fitting, black skull-cap was all that protected his head, which matched so closely the colour of his hairless face, tanned black by constant exposure, that, at a few yards off, it was impossible to see where one ended and the other began. A glance was sufficient to tell that he was a hunter, without the evidence of a bundle of freshly killed sheep meat, tied up in the skin of the animal. He was just the man we had been looking for, and we lost no time in questioning him as to the game of the region. Nears—for that was his name—was one of those children of the wilderness who, having spent their lives, from boyhood, in hunting, have an unsurpassed knowledge of the habits of the various species of game which roam their mountains and plains. The way he could distinguish game, read spoor, and forecast the movements of the animals was almost uncanny. Yet in other respects he was nervous and childish in the extreme.

The two days at Ta-shih-tu were spent in hunting for sheep. There were a good many of them about, but I saw only one with a good head, and he, with the wariness of his kind, eluded me at the last moment. Two rams which I had killed carried only small horns, but their skins were of interest, being in full winter coat, with a pure white neck-ruff over three inches in length.

As I have already pointed out, the sheep of the Karlik Tagh are *karelini*, being in every respect similar to those of the Borotala. They inhabit the whole of this eastern extremity of the Tian Shan wherever they can find seclusion from the natives. Though their horns do, undoubtedly, occasionally reach a great size there, the percentage is much smaller than farther west in the

Tian Shan and Ala-tau. This I attribute to the inferiority of the feed in the Karlik Tagh. Owing to the dry influence of the neighbouring deserts, the growth, for the most part, is of a decidedly steppe-like nature, there being but little of that boggy grass-land which is met with in the plateaux farther west. During the early part of the summer the sheep are independent of water, finding ample moisture in the wild onions that grow nearly everywhere. Later on, when these get dried up, they visit the springs and streamlets. It is then that the native hunter lies in wait for them, skilfully concealed within shot of the water; but it is very rarely that this method of hunting wild-sheep is adopted by natives of Central Asia, water, as a rule, being abundant over all the country inhabited by the great wild-sheep.

In these two days I was able to form a very favourable opinion of Nears as a hunter. Besides knowing all about the business, he was silent, keen, and persevering, in fact, as nearly ideal a *shikari*, as it would be possible to find anywhere. We did not wish to take him with us on our way eastwards, but we engaged him to guide us to the haunts of the saiga on our return in the spring. He informed us that, to reach the best place he knew of, would take two marches northwards to the very edge of the hills where they merge into the steppes.

As we rode northwards, it was hard to believe that the country was the same which we had passed over only two months before. The snow had all gone, and, in its place, the earth was covered with short tufts of bright green grass and small desert plants of various kinds. In the hollows, where the snow had lain deep, and left behind abundant moisture, patches of dwarf yellow tulips and blue anemones flashed in the sun. The icy blasts of winter had been replaced by balmy breezes, and already the midday sun was beginning to get uncomfortably powerful.

Animal life had also awakened after its winter's sleep. The various kinds of small desert mammals were busy repairing their burrows, which honeycombed the ground in many places. Smart brown-and-white chats bobbed fussily in and out of their breeding-holes. Small lizards darted away at almost every step. These my dog, Wung, considered to be his own particular perquisite, and was never tired of chasing them. They were generally much too quick for him, but occasionally he made a lucky shot with his clumsy puppy paws, and then he would march proudly along with the lizard's tail hanging out of one side of his mouth, till another caught his eye, and the game started all over again. Small groups of gazelle were frequently within view, and the tracks of wild-asses crossed ours, but our thoughts were now directed to the saiga, and a sharp look-out was kept for it. A meagre spring of none too clean water befriended us the first night.

A desert hare was shot at this place. No native of Central Asia, unless he is hard put to it, will eat a hare, for they are said to be unclean beasts. In the summer, when there is ample grass for them, this accusation is, I think, unjust, but during the rigours of winter they do undoubtedly live on offal round about the native encampments.

At the end of the second day's march we reached another spring, from which Nears had hopes that we should see a few saiga. It was this very place that he had visited on many occasions. He gave us glowing accounts of his hunting exploits, the number of saiga he had killed, and how at certain seasons they collect into vast herds of as many as a thousand. He did not, however, hold forth much hope of our seeing large numbers at this season (early May), as there was still ample feed and moisture further out on the plains. It is not till the end of May, when the open steppes begin to get burnt up, that they move in towards the fringe of the foot-hills, where there are scattered springs, and where abundance of grass is to be found throughout the summer.

Leaving Pereira to make the camp snug, and Carruthers busy setting his traps, Nears and I rode off to an out-lying bluff that protruded into the limitless plains, like a headland into a tranquil sea.

With the horses concealed below the crest, we lay on the top, scanning the flats beyond, Nears with his eyes, and I with the only slightly more powerful Zeiss glasses. For some time the antics of a fox, busily in search of his evening meal, in the shape of desert rats, riveted my attention. He was not a hundred yards away, and his method of making the rats bolt was inter-esting and amusing in the extreme. Having found an occupied hole, he would start digging furiously, first at one entrance and then at another, and in between he jumped up and down on the top of the burrow. He was not always successful in his endeavours, but bolted two while I watched, one of which he seized with a lightning-like spring. I was contemplating trying to shoot him for his skin, when Nears, whose eyes had been busy farther afield, touched me on the shoulder, and pointed out over the plain, saying " Iky burkark " (Two saiga). Two white spots were plainly visible with the naked eye. Directly one of them was focussed within

THE SAIGA ANTELOPE.
Saiga tartarica.

1905

the field of the telescope I knew that I was at last looking at one of those rarely seen beasts. They were quite unapproachable where they were, so I contented myself with watching them, till the fading light drove us back to camp. I had, at any rate, the satisfaction of knowing that there were some saiga in the neighbourhood.

Even in sheep-hunting one should be on the move before sunrise, but, to be successful with the saiga, camp must be left behind while the stars are yet in the sky. The reason of this is that this wary beast is essentially a lover of the open plains, where he is used to an uninterrupted view for several miles in every direction. But, as the merciless summer sun scorches the moisture out of the lower levels, he is driven irresistibly in towards the edge of the hills, where fresh green grass flourishes late into the summer, and where he can slake his thirst at occasional springs. So unsafe, however, does he feel, among even the lowest hills, that he only comes in to feed and drink at dusk, and soon after sunrise is far out on the plains once more, where he passes the day, lying down in the shelter of some small desert shrub.

It was still dark on the following morning when we mounted and made once more for the bluff. Just at break of day we left the horses tied head to tail in a hollow ; this bluff rose only about 100 ft. above the surrounding plain. Making our way along its crest, we almost walked on to the top of a " burkark " feeding in a hollow. It was a female with no horns, so I did not fire, though I doubt if I should have hit it if I had, as the light was still very bad, and it only presented a stern shot. This was the first time I had ever seen one of these beasts on the move. Not only in structure does the burkark differ from all other animals, but also in its movements. Even when thoroughly alarmed, it never raises its head above the line of its shoulders. Its movements resemble those of a clockwork animal more than anything else. On being disturbed it gets into its full pace immediately, and during the first hundred yards gives two or three curious leaps, with the fore part of its body only ; it exhibits none of the graceful movements of the gazelle, but moves its legs rapidly, without disturbing the steadiness of its body, the motion resembling that of a pacing horse.

We now moved very slowly along, carefully spying the slopes of the bluff which faced the plains. All along the crest was a line of low stone sangars, which, Nears informed me, were used by him and other hunters later on in the summer. He told me that he had frequently seen several herds of burkark, numbering hundreds, from this very position during the month of July.

Soon after this we spied a solitary buck feeding at the foot of the slopes. He was in a very favourable position for a stalk, and we had no difficulty in getting within fifty yards. I then made one of the worst shots imaginable, missing him clean, though he offered an easy broadside shot. His escape, however, was shortlived, for after a rapid spurt of a hundred yards he stopped for a moment to look back ; there was no mistake about the accuracy of the second shot, for it caught him fairly in the shoulder. He proved to be only a young buck with immature horns. Being in the middle of changing from his winter to his summer coat, he had a very untidy appearance. This animal stood 27½ in. at the shoulder, and weighed, when cleaned, 40 lb. Besides being only a young beast, he was in very poor condition, and I should estimate the weight of an adult male in good condition at from 50 lb. to 60 lb.

We saw three more saiga, and numbers of gazelle, but all well out on the flat, and away from any cover. As we ate our breakfast on the very point of the little promontory, with no sound to break the stillness of the desert except the chuckling cry of the sand-grouse as they winged their way in towards some spring, I could not help marvelling at the immensity of the view that lay spread before us in the clear early morning atmosphere. Westwards stretched the "illimitable plains," without the vestige of a hillock to break the endless monotony ; to the north a wavy line indicated the sand-dune area, which we had visited from Guchen, while far beyond was hazily visible the blue outline of the southern spurs of the Altai. Looking comparatively near on the south and south-west, rose the snow-capped summits of the Tian Shan, culminating in the glittering crests of the Bogdo peaks. It is largely the recollection of such scenes as these which fires the nomadic blood in our veins, and compels some of us to flee, for a time, from the hurry and bustle of civilization to seek the solitary regions of the earth.

That evening one of those terrific dry winds which seem to come from nowhere and end as suddenly as they start, sprang up and raged throughout the night ; everything, including our mouths, was filled with grit ; and it was only by constant attention to ropes and pegs that the tents were kept standing.

Next day we left the hills and travelled westwards towards Guchen. While our camp was being struck we amused ourselves with shooting sand-grouse. For an hour or more, flocks of these birds flew round the spring, offering many sporting shots. After circling round a few times they realized that there was no chance of their getting to the water, so headed off towards some quieter spring. That evening we joined the caravan-route, a broad, well-trodden track, and rested for the night at a small serai. There were two Chanto saiga-hunters also spending the night there, from whom we were able to learn more about their quarry. During the winter the burkark collect into vast herds, number-ing frequently from eight hundred to a thousand, and retire to the lowest and most sandy and saline portions of the plains, at an altitude of only from 700 ft. to 900 ft. above sea-level, relying on the snow and desert shrubs for their food and water. In April they split up into small parties of from two to six and spread over the steppes, finding abundance of food in the desert flora which shoots up as the snow melts.

They drop their young (generally two) about the middle or end of May, and later in the summer again collect into herds of several hundreds. From June to August is the season during which they are principally pursued, though a few hardy hunters brave the rigours of the winter in their pursuit. It is at daybreak that the hunters catch them in country sufficiently undulating for a stalk, or lie concealed behind a low breastwork of stones commanding a spring. In July heavy storms occasionally sweep over the steppes, leaving large pools standing in the hollows. At these casual drinking-places the hunters dig skilfully concealed pits, and one old veteran told us that at such a place on one occasion he allowed a herd of several hundred to come within twenty yards of him before firing. During the breeding season the females utter a sheep-like bleat to call their young to them ; a wounded animal will sometimes utter the same cry.

The summer programme of these two hunters was to hunt the burkark till the beginning of June, and then hurry up into the forested mountains to the south for a month's " bogo " (stag) hunting, and then back to the burkark again. When it is remembered that the Chinese merchants will readily give as much as from a hundred to two hundred roubles for a good pair of wapiti horns in the velvet it can be understood that a hunter who secures even a moderate pair, and ten or twelve pairs of saiga-horns, has made more than enough to support himself and family for a year. Often several hunters combine and divide the spoils equally.

The natives have a method of hunting the saiga which is often successful in the flattest and barest country ; on one occasion we saw them employ this method. On finding some burkark, some eight men ride slowly towards them in pairs with an interval of about eighty yards between each pair, the two flank pairs being well advanced ; as soon as the game becomes alarmed, and begins to move away from them, the horsemen quicken their pace till they are tearing along at full gallop. In this first rush the horsemen gain slightly on their quarry, who, thinking that they are going to be surrounded, break back. As soon as the horsemen see them about to do this, one of every pair slips from his horse and lies flat on the ground with his gun ready. The others continue to advance, leading the riderless horses. The saiga then break back between the horsemen, often giving the prostrate men an easy chance.

I have not yet dealt with the wild-ass, or "kulon,"

which is the name by which it is known among the natives of Dzungaria. To do so I must retrace our steps to the time when, in January, we were travelling eastwards along the snow-covered surface of the Pei-lu. Though, in answer to our frequent questions, we were continually being vaguely assured of their existence, it was not till we reached Shi-Kho that any definite information was forthcoming. A blacksmith there informed us that not only were kulon constantly seen from the road between Shi-Kho and the village of Yandzhikhai, but that two Chantos actually possessed a tame one not far from the latter place.

Two stages over rising treeless ground, with an unbroken expanse of snow in every direction, and a cutting wind which froze the breath to our beards and moustaches till we could hardly open our mouths to speak, brought us to the small village with the un-pronounceable name. On hearing from the head-man that the Chantos owning the tame kulon lived ten miles to the south, on the edge of the foot-hills, I decided to pay them a visit, the opportunity of seeing one of these animals in captivity being too good to lose.

Early in the morning after our arrival, Pereira and I, with one man as a guide, started off, making a detour in search of a herd of kulon which had been recently seen in the vicinity. We did find their tracks, but soon had to give up looking for them, owing to a blinding snowstorm, which made it impossible to see more than fifty yards in any direction. It was a mystery to me how our guide found his way, for any track that there might have been was completely covered by the snow. However, with almost uncanny native instinct, he led us unerringly to our destination, a large mud-hut by a

CENTRAL DZUNGARIA IN WINTER.

A DOMESTICATED KULON AND ITS CHANTO OWNER.

frozen stream. We were soon all sipping tea in front of a blazing fire, which made our faces tingle and the water drip from our snow-covered garments. The kulon was with us inside the house in company with several calves. It was perfectly docile, but had stubbornly resisted every effort on the part of its captors to break it to the saddle. Two years previously these two Chantos had surprised a herd of mares and young among some low hills. Galloping down upon them, they had captured one of the foals, then only a day or two old, and had brought it up on goats'-milk. Though I offered the men a considerable sum for it, they would not part. I should have liked to have taken it home to England, and to have given it to the Zoological Society, where this variety of wild-ass is unrepresented, though I doubt if it would have survived the long journey to India.

On the following morning I took several photographs of it. From the roof of the house I spotted a large herd of kulon, but they were on such flat country that it was not worth while attempting to approach them, and I contented myself with a long look through the telescope. I decided, on the suggestion of our hosts, to return to Yandzhikhai through some low hills, where there were said to be sheep at this season. To my great surprise we did see several sheep, one or two carrying quite good heads, but, though the formation of the ground was very suitable for stalking, I failed to shoot one, the reason being that, thinking we should not be likely to see anything worth a shot, I had donned a pair of Russian felt boots, to keep my feet warm while riding. Though they are about the best footgear for that purpose, they are quite the worst in which to climb steep, snow-covered slopes. Judging by the shape of their horns, these sheep were *O. karelini*, which had been driven down from the high plateaux to the south by the rigours of the winter. On the following day, while driving along the main road, we saw a herd right down on the plain at the foot of the hills, and certainly not more than 1,000 ft. above sea-level. I should imagine that there must be some magnificent sheep-ground somewhere among the confused mass of mountains at the head of the Manas River, close to the Yulduz divide.

It was in Guchen that we next came in touch with the kulon. A wild-looking, bow-legged Kirghiz was seen hobbling through the bazaar with the skin of a freshly killed kulon over his shoulder. He informed us that he came from the *kum* (sand), to the north, and that kulon were very numerous there. As we were anxious to visit this sand-dune area, we seized the opportunity of killing two birds with one stone, and on the following morning started off in a north-easterly direction, with this Kirghiz as our guide. Two long days in the saddle brought us to his aoul situated on the edge of the sand, among tall saxaul scrub. So easy is it to lose one's way in the maze of sand-dunes that even the nomads, who are past masters in the art, or, more correctly, instinct, of finding their way, have to build cairns of brushwood to mark the position of their camps.

There certainly were fair numbers of kulon about, but, as they stuck to the flat, hard country, away from the sand, a near approach was quite out of the question. I have vivid recollections of wriggling along serpent-wise, with my sleeves and pockets full of snow, trying to keep concealed behind a bush held in front. Five hundred yards was as near as I ever got, but it was only thanks to their curiosity ; they saw through my feeble attempt at concealment long before that. Just when I was considering the chances of a long shot they would wheel round and gallop off, a muddle of tails and hoofs amid a cloud of flying snow. We were told that, during severe storms, they come in among the sand-dunes for shelter, and it is then that they are shot.

No doubt the reader is wondering why I took all this trouble to try and shoot a beast which is of little or no value as a hunting trophy, and which, at any rate in Tibet, is looked upon by hunters as nothing less than a pest, owing to the irritating habit it has of approaching the hunter out of curiosity, and so warning nobler game of his presence, though in this respect the "kiang" of Tibet must be very different from his near relative, the kulon of Dzungaria. I was anxious to secure a specimen of the wild-ass, so as to be able to prove to which variety it belongs, no specimen having been previously brought to England from this region.

It was not till July, when crossing the Dzungarian Gate north of Ebi Nor, on our way from the Barlik-Maili Mountains to the Borotala, that I at length secured two specimens at the very last opportunity which presented itself. I can remember that day well, as being one of the hottest I have ever experienced. While the caravan started off on its day's march across the depression to a spring in the Kizil Tagh on the western side, my hunter and I struck off in a southerly direction to visit a spring situated at the edge of the hills on the eastern side. He informed me that this spring, being the only one for many miles, was much frequented by kulon.

Although, when we reached the spring, a maze of fresh tracks in the loose, dry earth made by both kulon and gazelle proved his statement to be true, a careful search in the vicinity revealed no signs of their presence. We had started off at a sharp trot westwards, intent on catching up with the caravan, and had left the hills behind us, when some moving, mirage-distorted objects caught our eyes. The glasses showed them to be kulon, moving slowly, almost straight towards us. Hastily dismounting, we led the horses into a slight hollow which effectively hid us all from view. After moving forward a short way all together, I left my man with the horses, and continued to advance by myself, making for a clump of sandstone mounds. On reaching their welcome shelter I at once saw that I was in a very favourable position, for the kulon, now only some 500 yards away, were taking a line that would bring them within 100 yards of my position. They were moving slowly along, occasionally nibbling at the low saxaul bushes, which covered the ground in places, evidently making for some shady spot among the hills, there to indulge in their midday siesta. As soon as they were fairly opposite my position, I fired at the leader, killing him dead in his tracks, and then made two disgraceful shots as they galloped away. After going 100 yards or so they stood a moment to look back, and I dropped another. They were both four or five-year-old males, and measured respectively 50 in. and 53 in. at the shoulder; they looked very smart and well-groomed in their short, glossy summer coats.

With the exception of the belly and rump-patch, which are white, the body is sandy fawn, the whole of the legs being of the same colour, though of a slightly lighter shade ; from the short, dark-brown mane to the tail-tuft runs a chocolate-coloured dorsal stripe, with a

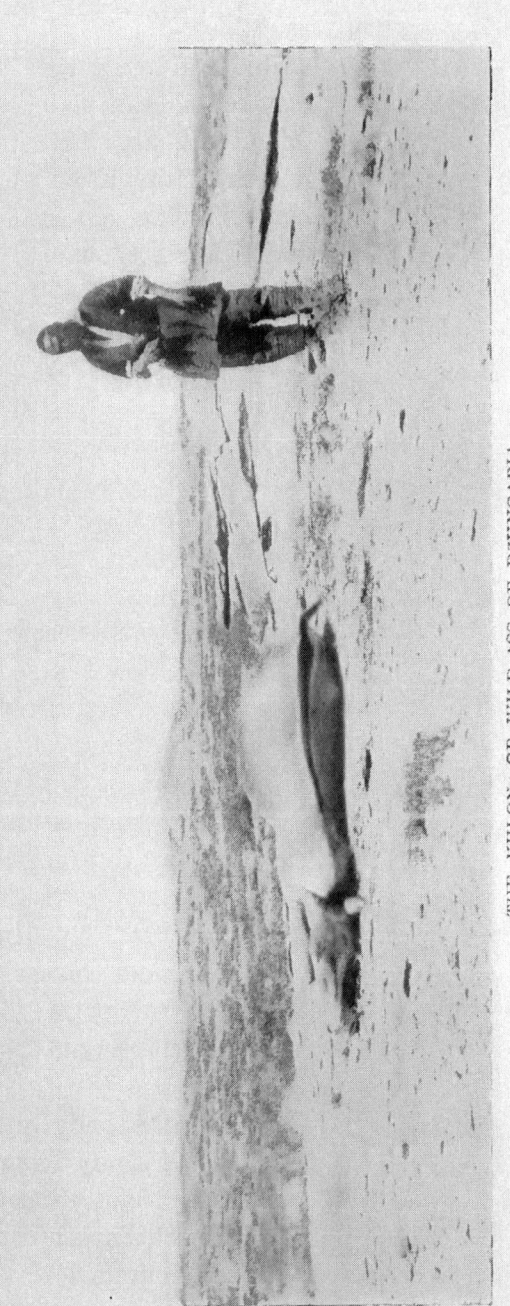

THE KULON, OR WILD-ASS OF DZUNGARIA.
Equus hemionus.

625]

narrow, dirty white, or very light fawn, margin. The
tail, with its black end-tassel, is very mule-like ; in fact,
in its whole appearance the animal resembles a mule
more than a donkey. The ears are short and horse-like,
with dark-brown tips and thickly-haired edges ; the
upper portion of the face is of a dark, sandy fawn,
merging into an almost white nose ; the throat and
chest are " isabelline." The nose of the kulon is only
very slightly rounded in profile.

On comparing one of my specimens with an adult
Tibetan kiang (*Equus hemionus kiang*), in summer
coat, in the possession of the British Museum, I found
several marked differences, as might be expected from
the different environment of the two animals. The
kiang is never found below an altitude of 15,000 ft.,
while the kulon of Mongolia rarely reaches an altitude
of 3,000 ft., and, at any rate in Dzungaria and portions
of Russian Turkestan, is found at an altitude of only
700 ft. above sea-level. This accounts for the former
carrying a much rougher and more wavy coat than the
latter. The general body-colour of a kiang is " rufus "
chestnut instead of the pale fawn of the more desert-
loving kulon ; its dorsal stripe is also less pronounced
and without any light margin. But the greatest difference of all is that, in the kiang, the whole of the legs are
white, while in the kulon they are light sandy fawn,
right down to the hoof.

My specimens are undoubtedly *Equus hemionus
typicus*, called by Mongols " Chigetai " and by Turki
people "kulon." Its extreme eastern distribution is
at present imperfectly known ; Sir Francis Younghusband, in his journey across the Northern Gobi, mentions seeing kulon in the Gobi at the extreme eastern

II—19

end of the Altai. They are found north of the Altai
Range on the plains, round the large lakes in the Kobdo
region ; we met with them near Barkul, and in several
other places throughout Southern Dzungaria. Westwards they extend throughout Northern Russian Turkestan, being exceedingly numerous in the neighbourhood
of Lake Balkash. During the summer they frequent
foot-hills, where the grass does not get so burnt up as on
the plains ; during the winter they roam all over the
steppes, eating snow in place of water. The natives hunt
them occasionally for their skins and meat, which they
consider more palatable than the best mutton. The
heat was so great at the time these two specimens were
killed that within ten hours the hair showed signs of
" slipping " in places, and it was only with the greatest
difficulty that one complete skin was saved.

The wild-ass is not the only species of *equus* that
exists in Dzungaria, for there is no doubt that the wild-
horse (*Equus caballus prjevalskii*) also inhabits the
northern portions of that region. We were never lucky
enough to see any, but the natives, both Kalmuk and
Kazak, all told the same tale, often volunteering the
information that, in addition to the kulon, there were
wild-horses. They described them as being very like the
kulon, but having longer and blacker manes and tails ;
also, they said, the meat was not so good. They told
us that there were large herds of them in the vicinity
of Lake Ulungur, and eastwards along the southern foot
of the Altai ; also north of that range.

I have now only to mention what I might call the
" low country " wapiti, and the tiger. As we were
never fortunate enough to see either of these in the flesh,
there is not much that I can write in connexion with

them.   The habitat of the stag points to its being identical with *Cervus cashmirianus yarkandensis* of the Tarim basin, on the south of the Tian Shan.   The altitude, the dense reed-beds, and the poplar forests are identical. To the best of my knowledge, no specimen of this Dzungarian stag has ever been brought to Europe for identification.   They are not much hunted by the natives, owing to the density and mosquito-scourged nature of their country,   the mountain wapiti (*Cervus canadensis asiaticus*) being   more   numerous   and   much   easier   to secure.   Their habitat is the whole of the jungle-covered country from just east of the Manas River to the south-east of Ebi Nor.

The tiger inhabits the same country as the wapiti, though, perhaps, keeping rather more to the dense reed-jungle.   It is, however, not entirely restricted to the plains, for in the Kash, Kunguz, and Jingalong valleys, on the Upper Ili River, it is found at an altitude of from 4,000 ft. to 5,000 ft. among the thick scrub on the edge of the spruce forest.   Every year a few tiger-skins find their way into the Urumchi, Manas, or Shi-Kho bazaars. They are, in nearly every case, secured in winter, by the farmers and herdsmen living on the edge of the jungle, by means of poisoned carcasses of sheep or goats.   Very few of the natives would dare to fire at a tiger, with their generally inaccurate firearms.   We met several men who had seen them, but they all admitted that they had an absolute dread of them.   Wild-pig, which abound throughout all the country, are undoubtedly the tigers' staple food, but during the winter they occasionally raid a farmer's flocks, and it is then that poisoned car-casses are laid out for them.

During the summer, mosquitoes, the density of the

jungle, and the boggy nature of large areas of the country, make hunting impossible. In winter, when the whole land is frozen, and covered with snow, and much of the vegetation is knocked down by the frost, a hardy sportsman would stand a good chance of getting a shot at a tiger, though I doubt if they are anywhere numerous. Having found out where a beast had recently been seen, the best plan would be to take up one's quarters in a yurt in the vicinity. Messengers would then be despatched far and wide, informing every one that a substantial reward awaited whoever brought in reliable information as to the whereabouts of a tiger. The sportsman would probably have to put up with a long, cold wait, but the triumph of securing such a rare trophy would be ample recompense. At the same time, there would always be the chance of a stag, about which nothing is known definitely at present.

It must be remembered that the tiger which inhabits Dzungaria and the Tarim basin, also the Ala Kul, Balkash, Syr Darya, and other portions of Russian Turkestan, is a very different animal to the Manchurian variety. It is not so long-haired, and it is considerably smaller and less finely marked.

APPENDIX

APPENDIX A

In the brief sketch, given in Chapter XIII, of the inhabitants of Dzungaria only slight mention was made of the Dungans, or Tungans, as the Mohammedan Chinese of the north-western parts of the Empire are called.

These people, however, claim much attention, and a more detailed description of them is required, not only on account of the peculiar position they hold in the Chinese Empire, but on account of the disturbances they caused in past times and the danger they threaten to become in the future. Moreover, in a book dealing with countries forming the frontiers of Islam and Buddhism, the fact of a considerable and increasing population of Mohammedan Chinese calls for further information on the subject.

The Dungans of Dzungaria are located on the outskirts both of the Chinese Empire and of the Islamic world. They are in an entirely different position to the Mohammedan Chinese of the central provinces, for, instead of being isolated, they are in close proximity to the great Mohammedan centres of Central Asia, and the vicinity of this great Mohammedan population —both in Chinese and in Russian Turkestan—grants them an increased prestige.

It is not surprising to find a strong Mohammedan element in China when we realize the fact that, not only had the power of Islam spread from the Atlantic to Central Asia within a century of the death of Mohammed, but that the Arabs themselves had been in communication with China for nearly two centuries before the birth of Islam. We have to remember that, when the first waves of the Arab conquest spread across Central Asia, China was in closer communication with, and more influenced by, Western Asia than it is even in these days. Early in the seventeenth century China was in actual danger of experiencing the savage onslaught of Kutaiba, the Arab conqueror of Central Asia; for, after bringing the lands bordering on the Chinese Empire under his subjection, the Arab general seriously considered the question of demanding the submission of the Celestial Empire. On one occasion they even came to blows, the Chinese army of 200,000 men being defeated; but the flow of Islam into Western China was finally arrested by the death of Kutaiba and the overthrow of the Omeyide dynasty. The spread of Islam is one of the marvels of history, and it is not strange that an Empire with a number of Mohammedan protectorates, as China has, should produce a "half-caste" element professing this faith.

In the days following the introduction of Islam into Central Asia, China had dominion over many tribes of Turkish descent who were the earliest to embrace the new religion. These people came of a fighting race, and on several occasions were able to aid China when troubles at home found her in a difficult position. For example, we are told, that in the middle of the eighth century some 4,000 "Arabs" (probably Uigur, Tadjik, or Usbeg Mohammedans from the present-day Chinese and Russian Turkestan) came to the assistance of the Emperor of China and helped to quell a rebellion. These troops, we are expressly told, never returned to their original home, but settled in the home provinces of China and married Chinese wives. It has been suggested that these people were one of the sources from which sprang the five *or more* millions of Mohammedans who now thrive within the Empire. On other occasions, also, people of Mohammedan faith settled in China. Records exist which tend to show that, at the end of the eighth century, there were as many as 4,000 families residing in Sianfu, who had originally come from Central Asia. These people had entered China for various reasons, and, owing to the difficulty of returning home,—caused by the unsettled state of Central Asia at that date,—they had asked permission to remain as settlers. The Chinese granted them their desire, and used them as mercenaries, paying them a monthly allowance.

Another proof of the theory that the Chinese Mohammedans are
of Turki origin, is found in the derivation of the title "Hui-hui,"
by which they are known throughout the Empire. This term,
according to Dr. Bretschneider, was given formerly to the Uigurs
of Northern Mongolia, a people of pure Turki origin who were
afterwards driven out of Mongolia, and formed a kingdom in
Southern Dzungaria and Chinese Turkestan. These people embraced Islam, and were no doubt the main source from which
emanated the Turki Moslem communities in China Proper.
It is easy to understand how, in time, the name came to be
applied to all Moslems.

The next great movement which brought China into close
communication with Western Asia and Islam was that resulting
from the conquests of Jenghis Khan. This great Mongol conqueror destroyed the capitals of the Islamic civilization, and
the seats of Mohammedan learning, and, by virtue of this, China,
under the Mongol Emperors, became almost the sole protector
of Islam in Central Asia. Vast numbers of Mohammedans now
began to flock into China. Jenghis Khan himself spared the lives
of all those who could be of use to him, and transported Arab
and Persian skilled artisans, and men of learning into Cathay.
This resulted in the establishment of a strong Mussulman community in China, which increased rapidly in power and in
wealth, which kept its religious independence, although it lost
its individuality as a nation, and which rapidly assimilated
its neighbours and surroundings, until the entire community
became Chinese in all but name.

The Chinese Moslem can generally be distinguished from
other Celestials by his physiognomy, his build, and some small
details in his habits. So closely, however, do they sometimes
approach each other in type, that they are almost indistinguish-
able except for certain differences discovered only after much
observation. On the whole, it was the manner and bearing
of the Dungan that most impressed me and proved him as
different to his fellow-subjects. Energy and keenness, even if
mixed with some insolence, make him preferable to deal with.
Usually of a fine build, with a bridged nose and a modified
almond-shaped eye, the Moslem always shows some trace of his

Turki origin, and his habit of following the Mussulman custom of shaving the lower portion of the upper lip enables one to identify him in far Western China. I am unaware if this habit is adopted by all followers of the Prophet throughout China Proper.

It is said that the Mohammedan can be detected by his manner of speech, and that many speak dialects of corrupt Mongolian or Turki origin; but this detail could only be distinguished by scholars who are well acquainted with the various and confusing dialects of the Chinese language.

It will be noted, therefore, that the Mohammedan Chinese were originally "half-breeds," and, consequently, through increased virility, they have had an advantage which has enabled them to become an important and numerous element of the Chinese Empire. Islam does not appear to have been propagated in China either by the sword or by the making of converts, but solely by the rapid increase of an originally small community of foreigners, who married Chinese wives and naturally brought up their families in their own faith. The most significant remarks on this subject were made by the writer Du Halde in 1735, which I will quote from Mr. Broomhall's *Islam in China*. He speaks of the "Mohammedan sect, settled above six hundred years ago in divers provinces, where they live in quiet, because they take no great pains to extend their doctrine and make proselytes. In ancient times they increased their numbers solely by the alliances and marriages they contracted; but for some years past they have made a considerableprogress by help of their money. They everywhere buy up children whose parents, unable to educate them, make no scruple to sell them. During a famine which wasted the province of Shantung they purchased above ten thousand. They marry them, and either buy or build a considerable share of a city, and even whole country towns, to settle them in. Hence, by little and little, they are grown to such a head in many places as not to suffer any to live among them who goes not to the mosque; by which means they have multiplied exceedingly within three hundred years."

The exact number of Mussulmans within the Chinese Empire cannot be estimated with any degree of certainty. The Moslems themselves, who alone have any idea of their numbers, exaggerate the total to such an extent, in their endeavour to increase their prestige, that the figures cannot be relied upon. The estimates vary in a bewildering way from 3,000,000 to 70,000,000 ; but it seems that some reliance is to be placed in Mr. Broomhall's carefully collected data and general summary of the maximum and minimum Mussulman population of the different provinces. The conclusion he comes to, is that the total number of Mohammedans within the Empire is somewhere between 5,000,000 and 10,000,000. This, of course, includes the Turki-Moslem population of Sin-Kiang,—which probably amounts to between 1,000,000 and 2,700,000 of the total,—as well as the true Chinese Moslem, the Hui-hui, or Dungan.

In spite of recent persecution the Moslems retain a strong hold on what they possess, and, owing to their greater virility, increase more rapidly than the Chinamen, and are therefore able to keep up their numbers and make good the check caused by recent insurrections, and the massacres which followed. It is, however, probable that the Moslems have, on the whole, lost and *not* gained ground during the last fifty years.

Whether the pan-Islamic movement will cause a religious revival or not, remains to be seen. Closer relations may spring up between the Chinese and the Central Asian Moslem communities, owing to the definite advance of the Moslem nomadic tribes from Russian Central Asia into China, and to the rapid increase of the resident population of Dungans in Dzungaria. In fact, the chain of Islam across Asia is now complete.

There is small likelihood, however, of a complete understanding taking place between China and her Moslem subjects. The feeling between the two sections is more bitter to-day than before the insurrection of 1862-77. The Moslem in China is also probably more fanatical than his far western co-religionist, who is slowly becoming accustomed to European ideas and to the advance of science and increased facilities of communication. Travellers in China state that only amongst the Moslems do they meet with studied insolence and undisguised dislike. The rebellions of 1862-77 tended to prove that the fanatical feeling existing between the Moslems and Chinese had in no sense abated

The mention of the Chinese Moslems of Sin-Kiang, or the New Dominion, called for these further details on the subject of Islam in China. With regard to this region, the Dungans —the general term for the Chinese Moslems of the far western province—are concentrated in Southern Dzungaria, whereas the remainder of Sin-Kiang is almost entirely peopled by Turki Moslems, who were doubtless the progenitors of the half-bred Turki-Chinese Dungans, with whom, however, they now possess nothing in common beyond the religious point of view.

It appears that the Dungans are mostly colonists from the Moslem populations of Kansu and Shensi. The name has a doubtful origin ; Vambéry suggests that it means "convert," and that the Dungans of Dzungaria represent the Chinese who were converted to Islam in the fifteenth century by an Arab taken by Timor, or Tamerlane, from Damascus to Central Asia. The colonists, transported thither by the Emperor Kien-lung in the eighteenth century, also embraced Islam and added to the number of Dungans.

Vambéry's theory of the *conversion* of the pure Chinese to the Mohammedan faith remains, however, without confirmation, although several writers agree with his explanation of the term Dungan. Amongst these is Abd-ul-Aziz, a Mullah of Kulja, who wrote on the Moslems of China. The name Dungan, or Tungan, according to him, is derived from the verb *tunmek*— " to turn "—in the Turki language, as used in Central Asia. The word has become familiar to Europe through the Russians who have adopted it from their Turki subjects in Turkestan Abd-ul-Aziz does not believe that the Arabs had anything to do with the origin of the Dungans, as their physiognomy and customs are Mongolian ; but he does not mention to what extent he considers that the Turki people of Central Asia mingled with, and married, Chinese women in the past.

Other writers, again, affirm that all attempts to discover the exact meaning of the word Dungan have proved unsatisfactory. In China Proper the Moslems are always called " Hui-hui " ; the most accepted translation of the word signified by the character " Hui " is the phrase " to return," which may be the equivalent of the Arabic " Islam "—" to return and to submit."

APPENDIX B

THE ANCIENT STRANDS AND BARRIERS OF SAIRAM NOR

SAIRAM NOR is a lake-basin situated in the mountains to the north of Kulja, at an altitude of 5,900 ft. above sea-level. The mountain-wall surrounding the basin is complete, except at a narrow opening on the east, between the Kanjik ridge on the north and the Kuz-imchik on the south, through which, it appears, that the basin once drained to the Ebi Nor basin on the Dzungarian plains below. At the eastern end of the Sairam Nor basin, there

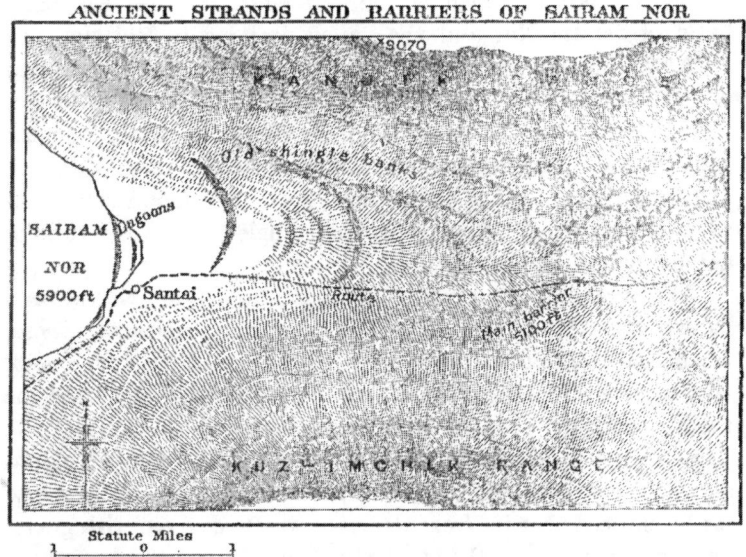

are signs that the level of the lake was once much higher than it is at the present day, and that in all probability the area was transformed into a lake-basin, at no very distant date, by the formation of skrees from the Kanjik and Kuz-imchik ridges, which raised a barrier and enclosed the drainage. The distance between the eastern edge of the lake and the barrier is about five miles; the whole of this area was once occupied by the lake, as proved by the succession of shingle-banks which remain, showing where once the strong west winds heaped up those barriers, in the same way as they are doing on a minor scale at the present day.

Along the eastern edge of the lake these barriers are in actual process of formation. As will be seen by the diagram, there are two completely formed shingle-banks enclosing lagoons and a third one not so completely formed. In the course of time the lagoons will dry up and more shingle-banks will be left high and dry on the shore. An almost imperceptible rise leads to another very large, crescent-shaped bank; beyond this are two small banks, and then another large one; farther still, at a longer interval, is the last bank before arriving at the actual barrier of skrees, which is the watershed between the lake-basin of Sairam Nor and the valley draining to Ebi Nor.

All the banks conform to the shape which the eastern end of the lake must have had when the water-level stood at that of a given bank; this is especially noticeable at the oldest or most easterly one. The banks are, of course, now covered with soil and support the scanty steppe-flora such as is found round the edge of the basin. No lagoons or shingle-banks were seen in any other part of the lake.

The prevailing wind is from the west, the Sairam Nor plateau having a reputation for winds of extraordinary violence. These, when concentrated in the narrow neck formed by the Kanjik and Kuz-imchik ridges, have their strength intensified, and the gradual heaping up of shingle-banks takes no great time. A proof of the strength of the winds was given us when we passed along the southern edge of the lake in the month of January, for we noticed that its frozen surface was so covered with gravel and grit blown on to the ice that it was brown instead of white. All this was gradually being swept up towards the eastern end, and no doubt eventually went to add to the accumulation of material which is being slowly banked up there.

The precipitation of rain in summer and snow in winter is considerable, and the area which drains into the lake would be sufficient to cause an overflow, were it not for the fact that the drainage seems to be exhausted by the surrounding country, before it reaches the lake. It is noteworthy that there are no streams entering the lake above ground, neither did there appear to be any water-courses which might carry the surplus of water, during especially heavy rainfalls. Sairam Nor is probably formed entirely by spring-water, which is counteracted by evaporation. Although the natives would not use the water, we found that its salinity was scarcely noticeable. The native story that ruins are to be seen below the water, may be another proof of the comparative recent formation of Sairam Nor.

APPENDIX C

THE SUMMITS OF KARLIK TAGH

As a guide to future travellers, and for any one who may be urged by a desire to climb the unconquered peaks of Karlik Tagh, I add this note and the accompanying diagrams, to show the position and comparative altitude of the highest points of the range. Further exploration—of an alpine nature—will alone show to what extent my deductions are correct; the adjoining sketch may, however, stand as a groundwork, and the numbered peaks as a standard, on which to base further work.

Fig. I shows the view from Hami, or Kumul, at a distance of fifty miles from Peak No. II. It is only from such a distance

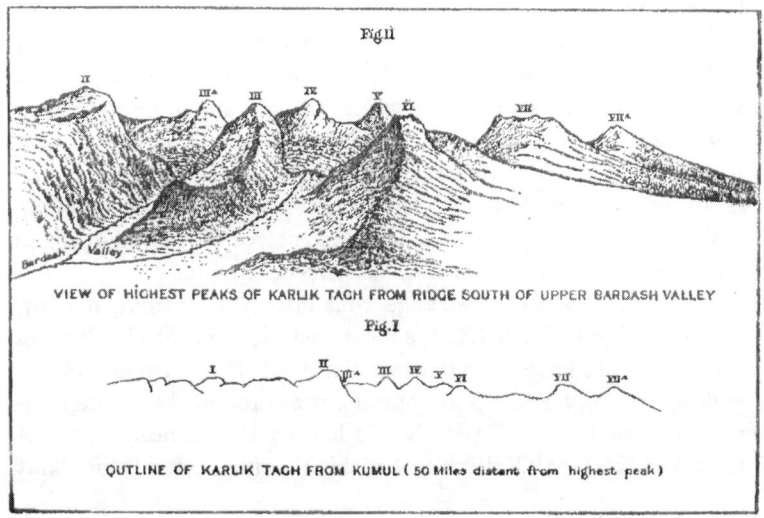

VIEW OF HIGHEST PEAKS OF KARLIK TAGH FROM RIDGE SOUTH OF UPPER BARDASH VALLEY

OUTLINE OF KARLIK TAGH FROM KUMUL (50 Miles distant from highest peak)

that a general view of the highest points can be obtained ; on approaching closer the outlying foot-hills hide all the peaks west of No. VII, and add to the difficulty of taking reliable clinometrical readings. From a point a few miles to the south of Peak No. VI, and in a direct line between it and Hami—where the first sketch was made—I obtained another clear view of the same peaks. These two sketches prove to be almost duplicates of each other.

From the first, I placed Peak II, as the highest point visible on the south side of the range, although I had doubts as to Peak I, for it seemed to lie so far back that it might have even equalled No. II ; but a chance view of Nos. I, II, IV, and VI from the Khamar Pass between the Edira and Bardash valleys, proved to me that No. I was of considerably lower altitude. Peak I lies at the head-waters of the Edira Valley, and from its two small glaciers spring the two sources of the Edira River.

Peaks II, III*, III, IV, V and VI are all reached by the Bardash Valley, and all, with the exception of No. V, lie in a semicircle around the head-waters of the Bardash River, and drain into it. The exact position of No. V remains undecided ; it either stands on the watershed between Nos. IV and VII and drains into an unexplored right affluent of the Karchamak, or it is a high peak which lies entirely over the watershed (*i.e.* on the north side).

The next group of peaks eastwards is composed of Nos. VII and VII*, which, with VII* lying in between the two (but invisible from the positions at which the accompanying sketches were made), form a semicircle around the head of the Khotun-tam valley. The summit of Peak VII would be accessible from the ridge which lies between the Khotun-tam and Karchamak valleys, and a very extensive and instructive view of the alpine region would be obtained if an ascent were made.

East of Peak VII* the range runs out in a straight, narrow, serrated ridge to Peak IX, the most easterly summit visible from the south. It keeps a very even altitude ; there are no cols or passes, and only a few peaks stand out as landmarks distinguishable at a distance. Peak IX lies behind the highest source of the Little Koshmak Valley; east of this the ridge extends for about

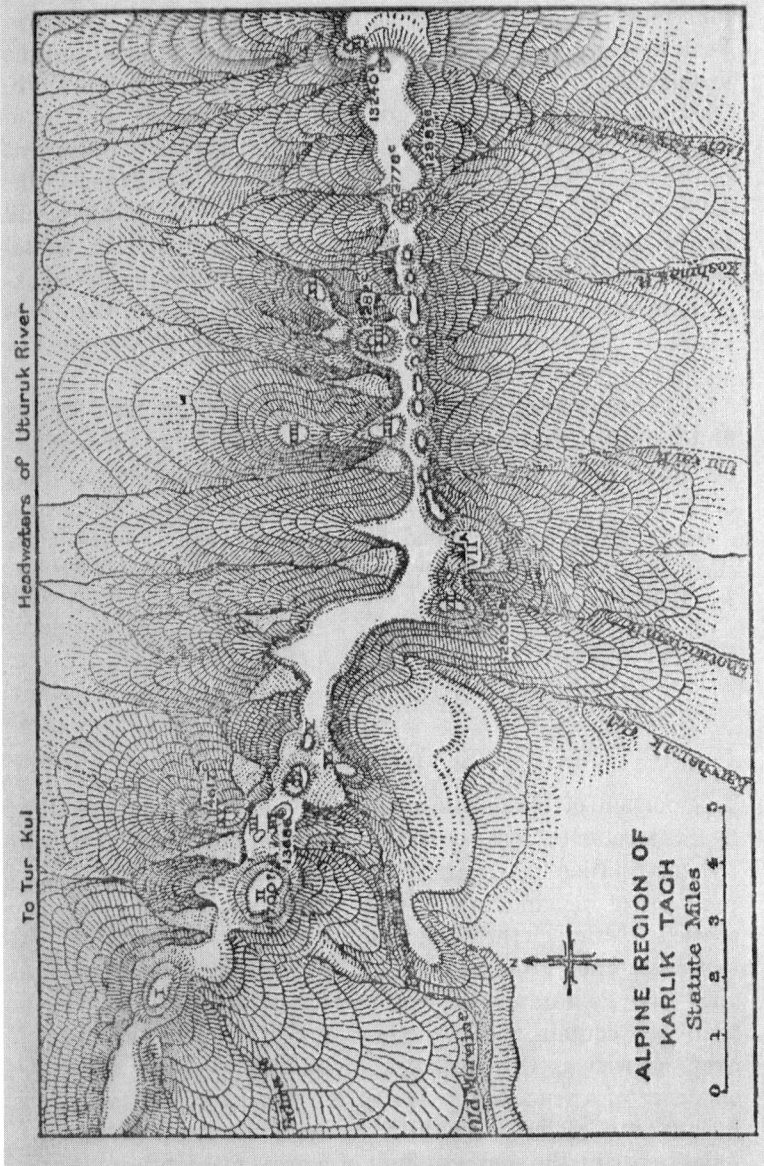

ALPINE REGION OF
KARLIK TAGH
Statute Miles

To Tur Kul

Headwaters of Uburuk River

four miles at an altitude just below that of perpetual snow. Peak X, which we ascended to a height of 13,240 ft., lies over the watershed on the north side, and is not visible from the south. On the northern side there are many outlying peaks,—spurs of the main ridge and equal to it in height. The most prominent of these are Nos. XI, XII, XIII, XIV, and XV. Between Peaks XIV and XV is an alpine region, which I was unable to fill in in detail; the configuration of this part of the actual watershed remains doubtful. I think that there is a wide expanse of snow-field, and that the range is deeper here than elsewhere, which hindered me from recognizing—from the north—my old points such as Peaks II to VII.

The culminating point of Karlik Tagh was estimated by the first explorers at 12,000 ft. Kozloff, in 1895, put the altitude of the highest peak at 15,000 ft. A later estimate was that obtained by Stein's surveyor, who marked two principal peaks, —which seem to correspond to my Nos. I and II,—and puts their height, by clinometer, at 12,930 ft. and 13,070 ft. respectively.

APPENDIX D

THE LIFE-ZONES OF NORTH-WESTERN MONGOLIA AND DZUNGARIA

THE portion of Inner Asia comprising the countries described in these volumes, forms a somewhat remarkable area as regards the distribution of Asiatic flora and fauna ; it also contains the lines of demarcation between the ranges of many different species. Although the whole of the Yenisei basin, North-western Mongolia, and Dzungaria are situated within one zoographical area—the Palæarctic, yet the variety of altitude and climate that they contain and the extent of latitude that they stretch over, as well as the variety of flora they produce, allow the existence of a remarkable variety of animal life. These regions include the easterly range of many European and Western Asiatic species, the southern limit of a great many Siberian varieties, the northern range of some Chinese and Indian, as well as the entire range of a few species peculiar to this part of Asia. As

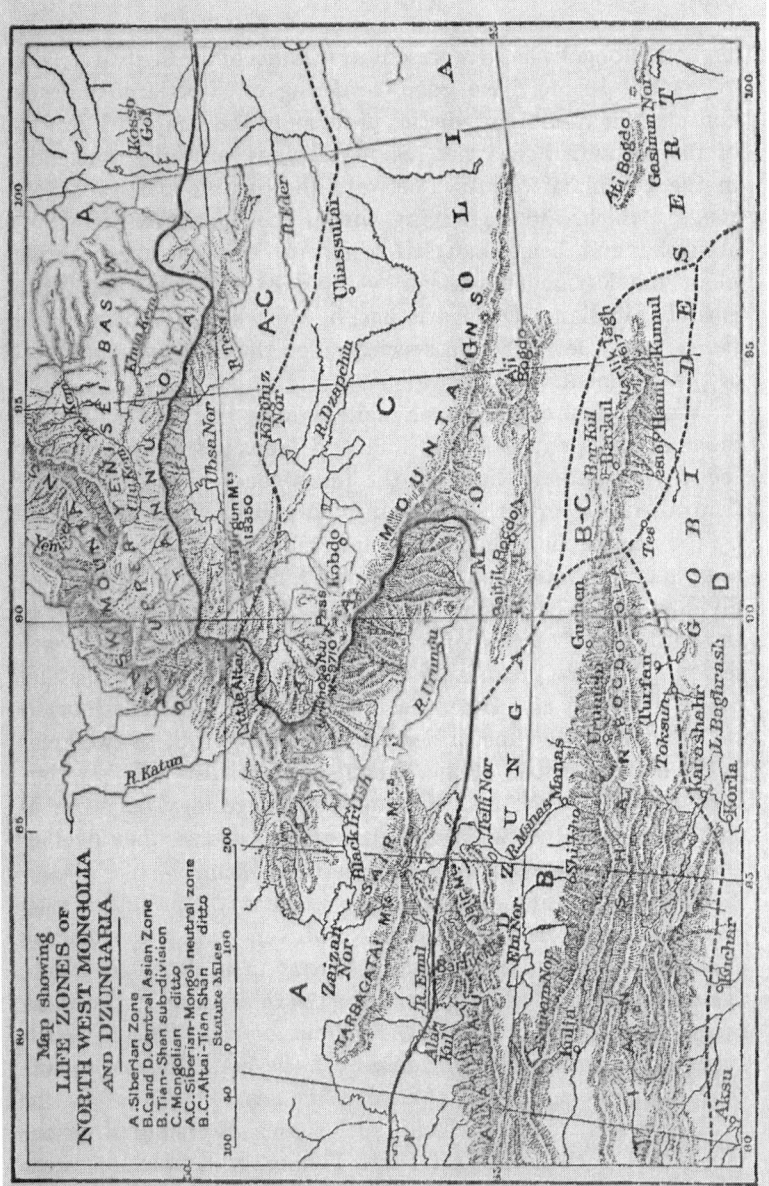

Map showing
LIFE ZONES OF
NORTH WEST MONGOLIA
AND DZUNGARIA

A .Siberian Zone
B.C. and D.Central Asian Zone
B. Tien-Shan sub-division
C. Mongolian ditto
A.C.-Siberian-Mongol neutral zone
B.C. Altai-Tien Shan ditto

a whole, Mongolia has a representative fauna of the Central Asiatic type; but its northern edge, bordering on Siberia, includes a considerable number of species peculiar to the temperate forests of the northern Palæarctic region. This is especially noticeable in the Uriankhai country, between the Syansk and Tannu-ola ranges, which, although lying within the boundaries of Outer Mongolia and being in itself a terrace between the Siberian plain and Mongolian plateau, yet possesses a fauna and flora entirely Siberian. Dzungaria has, on the whole, a Central Asian fauna, but a few Siberian species range thus far into the heart of the continent.

We can, first of all, draw a main dividing-line between typical Siberian and Central Asian flora and fauna ; this will roughly follow the southern limit of the forest-zone. The southern or Central Asian portion of this division will again be subdivided by the insular Tian Shan mountain-group, which forms in itself a peculiar and isolated faunistic and floristic zone. Another dividing-line is necessary between the Tian Shan and Altai, to show the exact limits of the special types peculiar to each region. The first great faunistic division to be delimitated is that between Siberia and Inner Asia. In the course of our journey we first passed the line of demarcation between these two areas in the neighbourhood of the Tannu-ola Mountains. This watershed between Arctic and Mongolian drainage may be taken as the junction of the two zones, although, of course, they overlap and there is a broad neutral zone between them.

Broadly speaking, the Tannu-ola is the *southern* limit of such species as the reindeer, moose, beaver, many fur-bearing animals, squirrels, black-game (*Tetrao tetrix*), hazel-grouse (*Tetrastis bonasia*), and capercailzie (*Tetrao urogallus*); the same range forms roughly the *northern* limit of such Central Asian types as the wild-sheep (*Ovis ammon*), wild-horse (*Equus prjevalskii*), marmots, and a host of small mammals.

The neutral zone, of which I spoke, consists mainly of mountain-groups such as the Altai and Turgun, or Kundelun, which extend southwards into Mongolia across the watershed of Arctic drainage ; these by their altitude compensate for the more southern latitude. On these mountains we find that the ranges of many Siberian and Mongolian species overlap. The Turgun Range, for instance, is more truly Mongolian than the Tannu-ola. This forms the northern limit of the yak; it is here we first meet with the *ovis ammon*,—although it formerly ranged on to the southern slopes of the Tannu-ola; here, too, begin the snow-leopard, the marmot, and the snow-cock. Siberian types are represented by the ptarmigan (*Lagopus rupestris*), which ranges thus far over the Tannu-ola.

The Altai Range is difficult to define as belonging exclusively to either faunistic zone; but I should continue the line of de-marcation, which runs the length of the Tannu-ola, along the Little Altai and thence in a south-easterly direction along the crest of the Great, or Mongolian Altai to the head-waters of the Black Irtish. In other words, all that part of the Altai which drains into the Arctic should belong to the Siberian, whilst the remainder should represent a portion of the Mongolian zone. The Urungu basin should probably be included in the former. Beyond the Altai, in a south-westerly direction, lies the lowland of Dzun-garia, which connects the plains of Siberia with the plateau of Mongolia, and across which continues the line of demarcation between the two main life-zones, as well as another secondary line to show the subdivision between Altai—whether Mongolian or Siberian—and Tian Shan fauna.

The first and most important line, which we have so far traced to a point on the crest of the Altai somewhere between the sources of the Black Irtish and the Urungu rivers, now continues across the central plains of Dzungaria, cuts in between the mountain groups of Barlik and Urkashar on the south and the Sair and Tarbagatai on the north; and runs westwards into Northern Turkestan. This line forms the southern limit of the Siberian larch tree (*Larix sibirica*) and the northern limit of the Chukar partridge (*Caccabis chukar*) and the Tian Shan spruce (*Abies schrenkiana*). But most forms peculiar to the Tian Shan area stop at the Ala-tau, and do not extend their range across the Dzungarian depression, or Gate, to the Barlik Mountains.

Practically the whole of Dzungaria belongs to the Central Asian zone, which includes the subdivisions of the Tian Shan and Mongolia. The plains form a neutral ground for some widely distributed species, whose ranges here meet and overlap. The saiga antelope (*Saiga tartarica*) of the Russian and Siberian steppes, for instance, extends across Dzungaria as far as Long. 92° East, but no farther; the wild-ass (*Equus hemionus*) also ranges as far eastwards, its place being taken farther east by Prjevalsky's wild-horse. On the 90° meridium of Longitude, Prjevalsky found that the ranges of these two overlapped.

The southern border-range—the Tian Shan, together with the Ala-tau and Barlik groups, constitute an isolated area in the midst of the Central Asian zone, while in the east the Altai Mongolian forms another subdivision which needs careful demarcation.

A certain amount has been written and much conjectured, as to the probability of the "overlapping" of the Altai and Tian Shan fauna and flora in the ranges of Barkul and Karlik Tagh. The traveller Grum-Grjimailo considered that he had established a sure proof that the Barkul and Karlik Tagh Mountains should be distinguished from the Tian Shan and included in the Altai system (see *Geog. Journ.*, vol. xiii, 1891); but I think that his evidence goes to prove that these ranges form a *neutral* ground between the two main mountain-systems. Orographically they belong to the Tian Shan group, but, from the point of view of their flora and fauna, they show affinities relating to both systems.

The Altai and Tian Shan mountain systems approach each other to within a hundred miles, the intervening space being occupied by high steppe, which forms the first rise from the Dzungarian lowlands to the Mongolian plateau. This eastern extension of the Tian Shan chain, which approaches so closely to the Altai Range and which extends far into Mongolia before disappearing in the Gobi Desert, is composed of the ranges called the Bogdo-ola, Barkul, and Karlik Tagh, and, still farther east, the Ati Bogdo. It is somewhere amongst these mountains that the true dividing-line exists between the two subdivisions.

The western portion of this line has been already determined as lying between the Barlik-Urkashar and the Tarbagatai groups; thence it runs across the plains towards the south-east; on reaching the Baitik Bogdo the line divides into two, which enclose a neutral zone before meeting again in the Western Gobi.

The southern of these two branch-lines cuts across the Tian Shan system at the Tou-shui plateau between the Bogdo-ola and Barkul ranges, and thence passes along the south of the Karlik Tagh. The northern line runs south of the Baitik Mountains—the almost isolated range between the Urungu River and Bogdo-ola Mountains, and thence continues towards the east, either *embracing* the Ati Bogdo in the neutral zone or leaving it to the Altai-Mongolian subdivision. All to the north of these lines is Altai and Mongolian, to the west and south is Tian Shan and Chinese Turkestan fauna; but the neutral zone, thus enclosed, has a strange mixture of both fauna and flora. This area is composed chiefly of the Barkul and Karlik Tagh ranges; the most easterly portion—the Ati Bogdo—must remain in an indefinite position, for I have not been able to find sufficient details regarding its fauna to place it definitely within either.

Of the fauna of the Karlik Tagh, the wild-sheep is of a species peculiar to the Tian Shan (*Ovis ammon karelini*), and it is the same with the wapiti, ibex, and roe-deer; the snow-cock and rock-partridge are also Central Asian varieties. The forests of the Karlik Tagh are chiefly composed of the Tian Shan spruce (*Abies schrenkiana*). But, on the other hand, the presence of larch (*Larix sibirica*) gives the Karlik Tagh the aspect of Altai scenery; and the existence of certain mammals,—such as picas, or tailless hares (*Ochotona*), and mole-rats (*Ellobius*) of species closely allied to those of the Altai system—show the affinity that the fauna of this region has to that of the Altai. The brown partridge of this region is the Mongolian variety (*Perdix daurica*).

The Ati Bogdo Range, which lies about 180 miles to the east of Karlik Tagh,—but is only connected with it by a succession of very low desert-hills,—probably belongs to the neutral zone. Kozloff, the Russian explorer, reports finding larch forests, wild-sheep, and roe-deer in this range; and in all probability these would prove to be of the same varieties as found on Karlik Tagh. Altai fauna extends even farther to the east, for it follows the long, low extension of spurs which run out in an east-south-easterly direction from the main Altai to the neighbourhood of Lat. 44° and Long. 401.° All these ranges contain the wild-sheep and the snow-cock peculiar to the Altai and North-

west Mongolia. There is a westerly delimitation to the neutral
zone in a hard-and-fast line drawn across the Tou-shui (or Chi-
ku-ching) plateau between the Barkul and Bogdo-ola ranges,
which defines the beginning of true Tian Shan flora and fauna.

If we take the principal varieties of animal-life separately,
and show their distribution, it will be seen how these zones conform or overlap, as the case may be. The wild-sheep, for instance,
which are so typical of the large fauna of Asia, range, in suitable
localities, over the whole of the area described, with the exception
of the Upper Yenisei basin. The Mongolian zone holds the
Ovis ammon typica, the Tian Shan has only the *Ovis ammon
karelini*, while a small variety, *Ovis ammon sairensis*, exists on
the isolated ranges mid-way between the habitats of the other
two, namely, the Barlik, Urkashar, and Sair Mountains, which lie
on either side of the main divisional line between Siberian and
Central Asian fauna, in Northern Dzungaria. Of the goat tribe,
ibex (*var. Capra sibirica typica*) are found over the whole area
from Siberia to the Tian Shan, those belonging to the central
part of the latter region being distinguished as a variety—
C. sibirica almasyi.

The deer are well represented throughout the entire region,
but the peculiarly local distribution of forests in Inner Asia causes
their habitats to be unevenly scattered and spasmodic. Wapiti
(*Cervus canadensis asiaticus*) and roe-deer (*Capreolus pygargus*)
exist all over the Upper Yenisei basin and in the forested
Altai ; while closely allied varieties (*Cervus canadensis songarica*,
or *eustephanus*, and *Capreolus pygargus tianshanicus*) range over
the northern forested slopes of the Tian Shan, Ala-tau, and
Barlik ranges, and extend eastwards as far as does the forest.
The large wapiti probably stop at the Karlik Tagh, but the
roe-deer range to the Ati Bogdo. Another species (*Cervus
cashmirianus yarkandensis*), whose main habitat is Chinese
Turkestan, ranges into Dzungaria, being found in the jungles
of the Manas River. Musk-deer are found only in the mountains
of the Upper Yenisei basin ; the range of the reindeer, as described
in Chapter VIII, does not extend southwards beyond the walls
of this basin. Another northern form, the beaver, still exists
in the uppermost sources of the Yenisei, and, it is said, in the

highest tributaries of the Black Irtish in the Mongolian Altai. Many other fur-bearing animals range as far south as the main dividing-line between Siberian and Central Asian fauna, but no farther; although in some cases they turn up again, in slightly modified forms, in the Tian Shan.

The gazelle are typical of an arid climate,—such as Inner Asia possesses,—and they are generally to be met with in the open plains south of the main dividing-line. In Mongolia, however, a mountain—or rather a plateau—variety exists, and this gazelle (*Gazella gutturosa*) extends its range northwards on to the high steppes such as exist in Siberia at the head-waters of the Ob River. The common gazelle of the region is the Goitred Gazelle (*Gazella subgutturosa*) and its allies, which have a wide range from Western Asia to Mongolia. Bear are found wherever there is sufficient forest-area, and wild-pig range over the entire region both on plain and plateau; of both these forms, however, the Tian Shan zone produces slightly different varieties. Tiger are met with only in the most southerly portion of the region, and are of the small, thin-haired Central Asian type. The long-haired Manchurian tiger does not range into the neighbourhood of the Yenisei basin, which is the only portion of our region which might be expected to hold it. Snow-leopards are to be found on all mountain ranges as far north as the Turgun and Altai.

Of bird-life, there is not much to record, except regarding the ranges of resident, non-migratory species, such as the game-birds. From a collection of about 256 species, I scarcely found a variety that I had not already collected in Russian Turkestan, this alone showing how truly Central Asian is the fauna of Dzungaria. The distribution of the game-birds shows, however, certain distinctive areas. The northern forests hold the capercailzie, the black-cock, the hazel-grouse, and on the hill-tops the ptarmigan. Of these only the black-game extend to the Tian Shan, the ptarmigan reach to the northern part of the Mongolian Altai, the capercailzie and hazel-grouse go no farther southwards than the Upper Yenisei basin.

The dividing-line between the Tian Shan and Altai fauna demarcates the northern limit of the Chukar partridge, but the

Brown partridge (*Perdix perdix*) extends its range from Siberia into the Central Asian zone, being found as far as the Bogdo-ola Range. The Bearded, or Daurian Partridge (*Perdix daurica*), ranges from its true habitat—Mongolia, northwards into the Siberian zone and southwards into the Altai-Tian Shan neutral zone. Pheasants are, of course, found in all suitable localities throughout the entire area. The Mongolian pheasant inhabits the Ili Valley and all the Dzungarian river-valleys, such as the Borotala, Manas, and Irtish ; while a rare variety (*Phasianus hagenbecki*) is found on the lower Kobdo River in North-west Mongolia. Two varieties of snow-cock are found within the region, one—*Tetraogallus altaicus*, is peculiar to the Mongolian-Altai zone, and the other—*Tetraogallus himalayensis*, ranges into the Tian Shan and Altai-Tian Shan neutral zone, from its true habitat, the Himalayas.

APPENDIX E

TERMS OF THE RUSSO-MONGOLIAN PROTOCOL [1]

THE following is a careful précis of the agreement, signed on November 3rd, 1911, between Russia and the Mongolian Princes, with regard to the rights and privileges of Russians in Mongolia and Mongols in Russia.

(1) Russian subjects shall, as in the past, have the right freely to live and travel in all parts of Mongolia, to conduct business, establish factories, and arrange affairs with all individuals or companies, official or private, whether of Russian, Mongol, Chinese, or other nationality.

(2) Russian subjects shall, as in the past, have the right to import and export at all times all products and manufactures of Russia, Mongolia, China, and other countries duty free, and to conduct free trade exempt from all duties and taxes.

(3) Russian banks shall have the right to establish branch banks throughout Mongolia, and conduct banking business with all individuals and companies.

[1] As published in the *Morning Post* of December 20th, 1912, and inserted here by kind permission of the editor.

(4) Trade can be conducted for ready money or on credit, but in the case of credit transactions the Mongol Princes or the Treasury cannot be held responsible for the credit of private individuals.

(5) No monopoly can be established either in commerce or manufacture. The Mongolian authorities shall not prevent Mongols or Chinese from doing business with Russian subjects, nor prevent their employment in Russian commercial industrial enterprises.

(6) Russian subjects shall have the right to lease or buy land in all towns and cities throughout Mongolia and establish commercial enterprises and manufactures, build houses, stores, and go-downs, and lease vacant land for agricultural purposes. Pasture-lands and places set apart for religious purposes are not included.

(7) Russian subjects are free to arrange with the Mongolian Government concessions regarding mining, forestry, fishing, and other business enterprises.

(8) The Russian Government shall have the right to establish Consulates in Mongolia wherever it is deemed necessary after consultation with the Mongolian Government. The latter shall have a corresponding right to appoint Mongolian representatives along the Russian frontier.

(9) Wherever Russian Consulates are established or Russian business is conducted, Russian trade settlements can be established, which will be under the administration of Russian Consuls, or, where there are no Consuls, under the administration of the senior Russian merchant.

(10) Russian post offices can be established throughout Mongolia, with postal services to the Russian frontier, at the cost of the Russian Government.

(11) Russian Consuls shall have the right to use Mongolian post-stations without charge provided that the number of horses to be furnished by the Mongols shall not exceed one hundred monthly nor the number of camels thirty.

(12) All Mongolian rivers flowing into Russian territory and the branches thereof are open to navigation by Russian subjects with Russian vessels. The Russian Government will assist the

Mongolian Government in the conservation of these rivers and the improvement of navigation by buoying and lighting, and Russian subjects shall, in accordance with Article 6, be granted areas on river frontages as stopping-places for Russian vessels, and can there build wharves and go-downs.

(13) Russian subjects desiring to transport goods and live stock shall have the right to use rivers and roads in Mongolia, and with their own money can build bridges, and establish ferries, and collect fees from the people using these bridges and ferries.

(14) Grazing-lands in Mongolia shall be reserved for the use of flocks belonging to Russian subjects when migrating, and such lands can be used for three months without payment, after which period charges can be made.

(15) All rights and privileges enjoyed hitherto by Russian subjects along the frontier for hunting, fishing, and the cutting of grass in Mongolia are confirmed.

(16) In regard to the procedure to be followed in connexion with business and other agreements between Russian subjects and Mongols and Chinese, it is provided that property transfers must be written and that the contracts must be submitted to Mongolian officials and the Russian Consuls for approval. If a dispute arises in a case it must be submitted to arbitration. If it is still unsettled, the case must be sent before a mixed tribunal, which shall be permanent where a Russian Consul is stationed. In other places a temporary tribunal shall be organized by a Russian Consul and the Mongolian Prince in whose territory the defendants reside, each side engaging to execute the findings of the Court, the Russian Consul on Russian subjects, and the Mongol Prince on the Mongols or Chinese.

(17) The protocol takes effect from the date of signature.

The protocol is drawn up in Russian and Mongolian in duplicate, and the copies were signed, sealed, and exchanged at Urga on the 24th day of the last month of autumn of the second year of the Mongolian Sovereign, or November 3rd, 1911.

BIBLIOGRAPHY

ADRIANOFF, A. B. : Travels in Altai and Trans-Syansk. St. Petersburg. 1896. (Russian.)

ATKINSON, T. W. : Travels in the Regions of the Upper and Lower Amoor, London, 1860.

—— Oriental and Western Siberia. London, 1858.

BELL, M. S. : The Great Central Asian Trade Route from Pekin to Kashgar (*Proc. R.G.S.*, Vol. XII. (1890), pp. 57–93).

BONIN, CHARLES ENDES : Voyage de Pekin au Turkestan Russe par le Mongolie, le Koukou-nor, le Lop-nor et la Dzoungarie (*La Géographie, B.S.G.*, Paris, Vol. III. (1901), pp. 115–122, 169–180, *map*).

BORRODAILE, A. A. : Notes of a Journey in Northern Mongolia in 1893 (*Geographical Journal*, Vol. V. (1895), pp. 562–574).

BROOMHALL. M. : Islam in China. London, 1910.

CAMPBELL, C. W. : North-east Mongolia and Karakorum (*Geog. Journ.*, Nov. 1903, Vol. XXII., and Blue Book).

CHALON, P. F. : En Mongolie : le pays des Saiotes (*Revue de Géographie*, Vol. LIV. (1904), *passim, map and illust.*).

CHURCH, P. W. : Chinese Turkestan with Caravan and Rifle. London, 1901.

CURTIN, J. : The Mongols : A History. London, 1908.

DELMAR MORGAN, E. : Prjevalsky's Journeys and Discoveries in Central Asia (*Proc. R.G.S.*, April 1887).

DEMIDOFF, E. : After Wild Sheep in the Altai and Mongolia. London, 1900.

DENIKER, J. : Les explorations russes en Asie Centrale, 1871–1895. (*Annales de Geographie*, Vol. VI. (1897), pp. 408–430, *map*).

DENNIKER : The Races of Man. London, 1900.

DONNER, OTTO : Voyage en Turkestan, et en Dzoungarie en 1898 (*Fennia*, Vol. XVIII. (1901), No. 4, pp. 53, *map*).

EDEN, RICHARD : The History of Travayle in the West and East Indies and other Countries lying to either way. 1st Edition. 1555.

ELIAS, NEY : Narrative of a Journey through West Mongolia (*Geog. Jour.*, Vol. XLIII., 1873).

ELIAS AND ROSS : Tarikh i Rashidi. London, 1895.

ERMAN, A. : Travels in Siberia. London, 1848.

ETHERTON, P. T. : Across the Roof of the World. London, 1911.

FRONTIERS OF DZUNGARIA : Vol. I., Part I. Tomsk, 1912. (Russian.)

FUTTERER, DR. K. : Durch Asien. 2 vols., *maps and illust.* Berlin, 1901–1909.

636   BIBLIOGRAPHY

GIBBON, EDW. : Decline and Fall of the Roman Empire. London, 1825.

GILMOUR, J. : Among the Mongols.

—— More about the Mongols. London, 1893.

GOWAN, W. E. : Mongolia, with an Introduction on " The Partition of China " (*Imp. and Asiatic Quarterly Rev.*, Vol. V. (1898), pp. 387-400).

GRANÖ, J. G. : Archæologische Beobachtungen von meiner Reisen in den nördlichen Grenzgegenden Chinas, 1906, 1907. *Map and illust..* Helsingfors, 1909.

—— Archæologische Beobachtungen von meiner Reisen in Sudsibirien und der Nordwest-Mongolei, 1909. *Maps and illust.* Helsingfors, 1910.

GRUM-GRJIMAILO, G. E. : Description of Travels in Western China. 3 vols. (Russian), *maps and illust.* St. Petersburg, 1896, 1907.

—— Summary of Journey. Trans. by E. Delmar Morgan (*Proc. R.G.S.,* Vol. XIII., 1891).

HADLEY, J. : Tramp in Dark Mongolia. London, 1910.

HAKLUYT : The Journey of Friar William of Rubruck (*Hakluyt Soc. Publication.* Second Series. No. IV., 1900).

—— Notes on Russia. *Hakluyt Soc. Pub.* (Vol. XI., 1851-2).

—— Cathay and the Way Thither. *Hak. Soc. Pub.* (Vol. XXXVI., XXXVII., 1866).

HANNAH : A brief History of Eastern Asia. London, 1900.

HOWORTH, H. H. : The History of the Mongols. London, 1880.

HUC, E. R. : Travels in Tartary and Tibet. 1852.

—— Christianity in China and Tartary and Tibet. 1857.

—— The Chinese Empire. 1855.

HUNTINGTON, ELLSWORTH : The Pulse of Asia. London, 1910.

—— Problems in Exploration. Central Asia (*Geog. Journ.,* Vol. XXXV. 1910).

JEFFERSON, R. L. : Roughing it in Siberia, etc. London, 1897.

KEANE, A. M. : Asia. Vol. I. London, 1906.

KLEMENTZ, D. : Voyages de Dmitri Klementz en Mongolie occidentale, 1888-1897 (in *Bull. de la Société de Géographie.* Paris, Vol. XX. 1899, pp. 308-329, *map*).

KOZLOFF, P. K. : Mongolia and Kam. Works of the Imperial Russian Geographical Society's Expedition, 1899-1901. Several vols. (Russian), *maps and illust.* St. Petersburg, 1905-1911. Summaries in *La Géographie*, Vol. III. (1901), pp. 41-46, and V. (1902), pp. 273-278, *with maps.*

KRILOFF, R. N. : Journey to the Uriankhai Region, 1892 (*Bulletin of the Imperial Russian Geographical Society,* Vol. XXIX. (1893), pp. 274-291, *map.* (Russian).

—— Description of the Uriankhai Region (*Memoirs of the Imperial Russian Geographical Society,* Vol. XXXIV. (1893), No. 2, *maps and illust.* (Russian.)

KROPOTKIN, PRINCE P. : The Orography of Asia (*Geog. Journ.,* Vol. XXIII., 1904).

KROPOTKIN, PRINCE P.: The Desiccation of Asia (*Geog. Journ.*, Vol. XXIII., 1904).

LACOSTI, COMMDT.: Exploration en Mongolie septentrionale (*La Géographie B.S.G.*, Paris, Vol. XXI. (1910), 375–374, *map*).

——Au pays sacré des anciens Turcs et des Mongols. Paris, 1911.

LANSDELL, H.: Chinese Central Asia. London, 1893.

LEDES, HANS: Eine Sommerreise in der nördlichen Mongolei, 1892. (*Mitt. d. K.K. Geog. Ges. in Wien*, Vol. XXXVIII. (1895), pp. 26–57, pp. 85–118).

LITTLE, ARCHIBALD: The Far East. Oxford, 1905.

MARKOFF, A.: Towns of Northern Mongolia (*The Scottish Geog. Mag.*, Feb. 1896).

MERZBACHER, G.: Exploration in the Tian Shan Mountains (*Geog. Journ.*, Vol. XXXIII., 1909).

MÜLLER, F.: Unter Tungusen und Jakuten. Leipzig, 1882.

MURRAY, H.: Discoveries and Travels in Asia. 3 vols. Edinburgh, 1820.

OBRUCHEFF, V. A.: Expedition to the Barlik and Tarbagatai in 1905 (*Preliminary Report*). Tomsk, 1907. (Russian.) (Also *Petermann's Mitt.* (1910), Pt. I, 21–22).

—— Expedition to Djair, Semisstai, and Urkashar, W. Zungaria, in 1906. Tomsk, 1907. (Russian.) (Also *Petermann's Mitt.*, 1908, 24–39, *map*).

—— Geographical Investigations in Barlik Maili and Djair during 1909. Tomsk, 1910. (Russian.)

—— Geographical Sketch of the Auriferous Deposits of Siberia. Part II.

—— Central Siberia. First section: Sayansk Region. *Map*. St. Petersburg, 1911. (Russian.)

OSTROVSKY, P. E.: The Importance of the Uriankhai Region to Southern Siberia (*Bulletin of the Imperial Russian Geographical Society*, Vol. XXXV. (1899), pp. 321–353). (Russian.)

PAIKOFF: The Upper Yenisei. (*B. of Imp. Russian Geographical Society*, Vol. XXXIV. (1898), pp. 433, 462).

PAQUET, DR. A.: Subsibirien und die Nordwestmongolei (*Mitteilungen der Geog. Ges. in Jena*, Vol. XXVII. (1909), pp. 1–127, *maps*).

PELLIOT, PAUL: La mission Pelliot en Asie centrale (*Ann. de la Soc. de Géog. Commerciale*. See *Indo-chinoise*). Hanoi, 1909. *Map*.

PIASSETSKY, P.: Russian Travellers in Mongolia and China. Translated by J. Gordon-Cumming. London, 1884.

POTANIN, G. N.: Potanin's Travels, 1884–86. St. Petersburg, 1893.

—— Sketches of North-west Mongolia. 4 vols, *maps and illust.* St. Petersburg, 1881–83. (Russian.)

—— Survey of G. N. Potanin's Journey in North-west Mongolia, 1876–77, and *map* (*Petermann's Mitt.*, Vol. XXVII., Pt. V., 1881).

POTANIN, M.: Travels in Eastern Siberia and Mongolia, Tibet, and China. Moscow, 1895. (Russian.)

POTT, H.: A Sketch of Chinese History.

POZDNYEFF, A. : Mongolia and the Mongols : Results of the Expedition to Mongolia in 1892–93. 2 vols., *illust.* St. Petersburg, 1896–98.

PRICE, M. P. : Siberia. London, 1912.

PRJEVALSKY, N. M. : Third Journey in Central Asia. St. Petersburg, 1883. *Map and illust.* (Russian.) Reisen in Tibet. 1879–1880. *Map and illust.* Jena, 1884.

RADDE, G. : Reisen im Süden von Ost-Siberien in den Jahren, 1855–59. 2 vols. St. Petersburg, 1862–63.

RADLOFF, D. W. : Works of the Orkhon Expedition ; Atlas of Mongolian Tombs. *Map and illust.* St. Petersburg, 1892. (Russian and German.)

—— Vorlaufiger Bericht über die Resultate der Expedition (*Bull. Acad. Imp. Sciences*, St. Petersburg, Vol. XXXV. (1896), pp. 353–398).

RECORDS OF THE PAST : Vol. V., Feb. 1906. Part II.

RICHARDS, I. : Comprehensive Geography of the Chinese Empire. Shanghai, 1908.

RICKMERS, W. R. : The Duab of Turkestan. Cambridge, 1913.

RITTER, K. : Eastern or Chinese Turkestan. St. Petersburg, 1869.

ROBOROVSKY, V. I. : Works of the Imperial Russian Geographical Society's Expedition to Central Asia, 1893–95. 3 vols. St. Petersburg, 1899. (Russian.) (Summary in *Geographical Journal*, August 1896. *Map.*)

—— Conclusion of Roborovsky's Expedition (Note in *Geo. Journ.*, Vol. IX., 1897).

SAPOZNIKOFF, V. V. : The Mongolian Altai, and the Sources of the Irtysch and Kobdo. Tomsk, 1911. (Russian.) (See also *Petermann's Mitt.*, Vol. LV. (1909), p. 372.)

SCHUYLER, E. : Turkestan. London, 1876.

SEEBOHM, H. : Siberia in Asia. London, 1882.

SEMENOF, P. P. : Dzungaria and the Celestial Mountains (*Journ. of R.G.S.*, Vol. XXXV., 1865).

SKRINE AND ROSS : The Heart of Asia.

SOSNOVSKI, MIROSHNISHENKO, MATUSSOVSKI, AND MOROZOF : Recent Russian Explorations in Western Mongolia (*Geographical Magazine*, Vol. II. (1875), pp. 196–200, *map*. *Proc. R.G.S.*, Vol. XX., 1875–6, p. 421).

STEIN, M. A. : Ruins of Desert Cathay. London, 1912.

—— Sand-buried Ruins of Khotan. London, 1903.

SWAYNE, H. G. C. : Through the Highlands of Siberia.

TAYLOR, I. : The Origin of the Aryans. London, 1892.

TCHIHATCHEFF, P. DE : A Scientific Journey in the Eastern Altai and the Adjacent Regions on the frontiers of China. 1845. (French.)

THOMSEN,: Early Turkish Inscriptions. (German.)

TYLOR, E. B. : Early History of Mankind. London, 1878.

VAMBÉRY, A. : An Approach between Moslems and Buddhists (*The Nineteenth Century*. April 1912).

VLADIMIRTSOFF, B. V. : A Visit to the Derbets of Kobdo (*Iz. Russ. Geo. Soc.*, 1910, 46). (Russian.)

WRIGHT, G. F. : Asiatic Russia. New York, 1903.

YOUNGHUSBAND, COL. F. E. : The Heart of a Continent : A Narrative of Travels in Manchuria, across the Gobi Desert, through the Himalayas,. the Pamirs, and Hunza, 1884–1894. *Map.* London, 1896.

——— Lamaism in Tibet (*Sociological Review*, Vol. IV., No. 2, April 1911).

YULE, COL. SIR HENRY : Travels of Marco Polo. Edited by Cordier.. London, 1903.

ERRATA FOR "MAP OF THE KARLIK TAGH AND
BARKUL MOUNTAINS"

1. For Bagdash read Bardash.
2. Barkul Dawan or Koshete Dawan, 8,700 ft.
3. Cart-track leads from Kumul via this track to Barkul.
4. Marsh-land at eastern end of Tur Kul as at western end.
5. Ara-Tam should be close below contour-line representing 4,000 ft.
6. Altitudes, 13,686 and 13,282 should be denoted 13,686ᶜ, and 13,282°
   (clinometer reckoning).
7. Peak, Alt. 13,240 ft. was ascended.
8. Glaciers exist at the other two main sources of the Bardash River.
9. The names of Narin, Koral, Edira, Bardash, and Khotun-tam give
   their names to the rivers on which they are situated.
10. The river to the west of the Shopoli Valley is the Narin.
11. For Bogdo-olo read Bogdo-ola.

INDEX

Abakan, 41, 43, 45; steppe, 108; route from, to Kemelik, 113; early inhabitants of, 198, 200; tribes of, 205; cattle of, 238
— Tartars, 45, 240; affinities of with Uriankhai, 200, 201; dwellings of, 208, 209
— district, as early home of Kirei, 352
Abd-ul-Aziz, 618
Abies schrenkiana, 418, 516 n., 625; on Karlik Tagh, 629
" Accordion " folding boat, 87
Achinsk, 32; we leave, 35; country south of, 35, 36
Achit Nor, 22, 273, 277, 278, 286, 287, 289, 321–3; wild-fowl of, 321, 322
Adak, 486; visited by Potanin, etc., 496; astronomical position of, 496; visited by Kozloff, 498, 521, 522
Adrianoff, A. B., 6, 21, 65, 72, 164, 170, 201, 207, 221; publication, 635
Æolian action, 468–9
Agriculture, 70; in Minnusinsk district, 41; in Upper Yenisei basin, 161, 173, 183–4, 275; at Ulankom, 275; in Emil Valley, 407; in Dzungaria, 458; at Kumul, 482; in Karlik Tagh, 500–502, 503–504, 506–507, 508, 511, 512, 525; in Barkul basin, 527, 528; on Manas River, 542, 543
Aimak, territorial division, 202, 207
Ainar River, 122
Aji Bogdo, 452, 519
Aksai, plateau, 556; wild-sheep of, 569
Aksu, 579
Ala Kul, 411–12, 413, 416, 417, 418; saiga near, 590
Ala Shan, 23
Ala-su Valley, 125, 126, 137, 140, 213, 216

Ala-tau Mts. as portion of northern border-range of Dzungaria, 379, 411, 415, 418, 554; routes across, 556; southern slopes of, 556–7; western position of, 559; wild-sheep of, 569; game of, 630
Ala-tyube, island in Ala Kul, 413
Algiak Pass, 92, 105, 113, 167
Altai, 4, 22, 23; explorations of Sapoznikoff in, 24; Russian, or Little, 24; Mongolian, or Great, 24, 326; eastern extremities of, 346–7; altitude of, 371; first impression of Mongolia, 371–2; as great natural boundary, 372; ease of passes across, 372; precipitation on, 372, 380; length of, 378; importance of to Dzungaria, 378; Kran Valley of, 397–9; passes across between Kobdo and Guchen, 451; flora and fauna of, 625
Altai-Tian Shan divide, 347, 462–3, 497, 626; as birthplace of Kirghiz race, 352; as Kirei territory, 357; beauty of, 361–2; climate of, 329; Uriankhai of, 325, 326–7
Altai-Tian Shan region, 4
Altan Khan, 205
Altitudes of Minnusinsk Steppe, 41; of Aradansk, 85; of Syansk passes, 92, 113; average of Upper Yenisei basin, 99; of mountains sorrounding, 101, 102; of Tannu-ola, 101, 190, 195, 264; peaks, 134; tree-limit on, 138; of Saklia Valley, and range, 263, 264; of Turgun Mts., 281, 283, 284, 286
Amazon River, 39
Amil River, 43, 45, 46; rise and fall, 79, 167; width of, at Petro-pavlovsk, 91; route from, to Sisti-Kem, 113
Amursana, leader of Dzungars, 386
Ancestor-worship, 61, 243

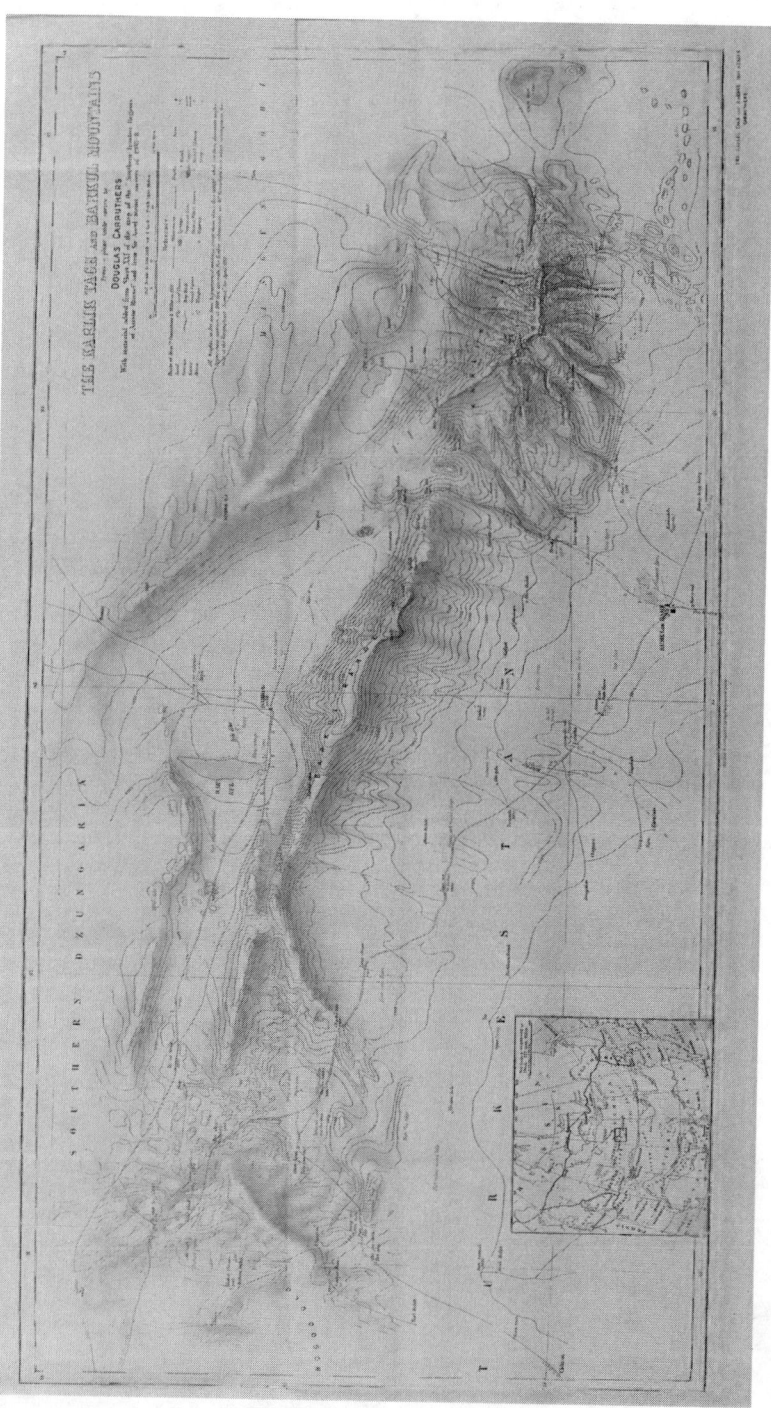

THE KARLIK TAGH and BARKUL MOUNTAINS

From a plane table survey by

DOUGLAS CARRUTHERS